Lecture Notes
in Business Information Processing   304

Series Editors

Wil M.P. van der Aalst
  Eindhoven Technical University, Eindhoven, The Netherlands
John Mylopoulos
  University of Trento, Trento, Italy
Michael Rosemann
  Queensland University of Technology, Brisbane, QLD, Australia
Michael J. Shaw
  University of Illinois, Urbana-Champaign, IL, USA
Clemens Szyperski
  Microsoft Research, Redmond, WA, USA

More information about this series at http://www.springer.com/series/7911

Arto Ojala · Helena Holmström Olsson
Karl Werder (Eds.)

Software Business

8th International Conference, ICSOB 2017
Essen, Germany, June 12–13, 2017
Proceedings

 Springer

Editors
Arto Ojala
University of Jyväskylä
Jyväskylä
Finland

Karl Werder
University of Duisburg-Essen
Essen
Germany

Helena Holmström Olsson
Malmö University
Malmö
Sweden

ISSN 1865-1348   ISSN 1865-1356 (electronic)
Lecture Notes in Business Information Processing
ISBN 978-3-319-69190-9   ISBN 978-3-319-69191-6 (eBook)
https://doi.org/10.1007/978-3-319-69191-6

Library of Congress Control Number: 2017956718

Printed on acid-free paper

This Springer imprint is published by Springer Nature
The registered company is Springer International Publishing AG
The registered company address is: Gewerbestrasse 11, 6330 Cham, Switzerland

Preface

Software plays an ever-increasing role in today's society. People's lives are affected by software on a daily basis, as used, for example, in the smartphone plus its mobile applications, the e-mail client at work, or online shopping conducted from home. The pervasive nature of software increases its potential to change business models and value propositions, within the phenomenon summarized as "digitalization." In fact, software works as a key enabler of digitalization, providing opportunities to create innovative business models that would have been impossible even a decade ago. AirBnB and Uber are good examples of such new software-based firms, highlighting how software businesses can disrupt entire industries. A more recent example can be observed in *G-cluster* – a small software business that started to market a digitalized game console in Japan. The game console can be embedded in various devices, including set-top boxes, TVs, tablets, and mobile phones. These three examples illustrate how software facilitates the digitization of products in such a way as to compete with large and well-established firms.

For the 8th International Conference on Software Business (June 2017) we received 30 submissions. The papers went through a competitive review process, with two or three experts in the field reviewing each paper. On the basis of the reviewers' evaluations, and consideration by the track chairs, 11 full papers and five short papers were selected for the proceedings. Here, we have organized the papers according to the following themes: Software Startups and Platform Governance, Software Business Development, and Software Ecosystems and App Stores.

The contributions address three research areas, investigating different phases in the lifecycle of a software business. The phases of a software business start with its *inception* as a software startup, continuing with the *development* of the software business, leading thereafter to a thriving software *ecosystem*. Overall, three challenges can be seen as meriting particular attention. The first challenge relates to software startups and platform governance. The contributions here provide data on the acquisition and growth of software startups as influenced by venture capital. Another paper provides guidance on the process of moving toward validated product ideas within software startups. A third paper explains how we can govern software ecosystems in such a way as to implement an *Internet of Things*. The second challenge relates to software business development. Two papers discuss the pricing of data products, and explore business models for software-defined networks. In addition, we learn about firm performance within the Finnish software industry, and the modeling of competitive relationships. The third research challenge relates to software ecosystems and app stores. The papers presented explain how software ecosystems co-evolve, and shed light on competition in software firms. In addition, one paper addresses mobile security threats in software ecosystems, while another paper focuses on the health measurement of data-scarce software ecosystems. The contributions make it clear that the scope of software businesses is expanding from traditional software firms toward firms that develop software specifically to advance their business in the form of digital services.

As Program Committee chairs, we would like to thank the members of the Program Committee and the additional reviewers for their efforts in evaluating the submissions and ensuring the high quality of the conference. The efforts of the Steering Committee and all the chairs were of enormous value in building a successful ICSOB 2017 conference. Finally, special thanks are due to all the scholars who submitted papers to the conference, all the authors who presented papers, and to the audience, who participated in very interesting discussions during the conference.

August 2017   Arto Ojala
                                              Helena Holmström Olsson
                                                           Karl Werder

Organization

General Chair

Arto Ojala   University of Jyväskylä, Finland

Program Chairs

Helena Holmström Olsson   Malmö University, Sweden
Xiaofeng Wang   Free University of Bozen-Bolzano, Italy

Steering Committee

Jan Bosch   Chalmers University of Technology, Sweden
Sjaak Brinkkemper   Utrecht University, The Netherlands
João M. Fernandes   University of Minho, Portugal
Georg Herzwurm   University of Stuttgart, Germany
Slinger Jansen   Utrecht University, The Netherlands (Chair)
Christopher Jud   University of Stuttgart, Germany
Thomas Kude   ESSEC Business School, France
Casper Lassenius   Aalto University, Finland
Eetu Luoma   University of Jyväskylä, Finland
Konstantinos Manikas   University of Copenhagen, Denmark
Tiziana Margaria   University of Limerick and Lero, Ireland
Arto Ojala   University of Jyväskylä, Finland
Helena Holmström Olsson   Malmö University, Sweden
Björn Regnell   Lund University, Sweden
Kari Smolander   Lappeenranta University of Technology, Finland
Pasi Tyrväinen   University of Jyväskylä, Finland
Krzysztof Wnuk   Blekinge Institute of Technology, Sweden
Anna Lena Lamprecht   Utrecht University, The Netherlands
Andrey Maglyas   Lappeenranta University of Technology, Finland
Xiaofeng Wang   Free University of Bozen-Bolzano, Italy

Program Committee

Carina Alves   UFPE, Brazil
Siamak Farshidi   Utrecht University, The Netherlands
Farnaz Fotrousi   Blekinge Institute of Technology, Sweden
Samuel Fricker   Blekinge Institute of Technology, Sweden
Sami Hyrynsalmi   Tampere University of Technology, Finland
Slinger Jansen   Utrecht University, The Netherlands
Christopher Jud   University of Stuttgart, Germany

Contents

Short Papers

Software Startups and Platform Governance

How Are Product Ideas Validated?

The Process from Innovation to Requirements Engineering in Software Startups

Pertti Seppänen[✉], Nirnaya Tripathi, Markku Oivo,
and Kari Liukkunen

M3S/M Group, University of Oulu, 90015 Oulu, Finland
{pertti.seppanen,nirnaya.tripathi,markku.oivo,
kari.liukkunen}@oulu.fi

Abstract. Although software startups are considered important for economic development due to their ability to quickly create cutting-edge technologies and their potential to scale to a wide market, contextual knowledge about the product idea development process of startups is poorly understood in the literature. This study explores the idea validation process of software startups in an attempt to understand the practices used for idea validation, discover how the process is affected by the founder's prior competencies, and determine the effect of those practices on requirement gathering. We conducted an exploratory multiple case study in nine software startups to determine the kind of practices they used for idea validation. We identified ten practices used as elements of the idea validation process. Our results show that idea validation is a highly non-linear process in which several validation practices are used in varying combinations and timing. The most frequently used practices included copying existing products, prototyping, utilizing expert support, and cooperating closely with customers. The founder's prior competencies also influenced the selected practices. Copying and prototyping were common practices when the founders had prior competencies in the application area, while utilizing expert support was a widespread practice to compensate for the founder's missing competencies. We also observed that the idea validation practices identified in the study serve requirement gathering at different levels of abstraction, varying from business-related requirements down to design-level requirements.

Keywords: Software startup · Initial team · Idea validation · Competency needs · Requirement gathering · Lean startup · Product development · Product development process

1 Introduction

The number of software startups and their role in technical and economic development have increased globally. Many recent success stories, such as Facebook, Spotify, and LinkedIn, originated from startup companies [1]. Studies have explored software startups from different viewpoints, such as challenges, success factors, startup processes, and models [2–9]. In recent years, the lean startup approach [5] has gained

© Springer International Publishing AG 2017
A. Ojala et al. (Eds.): ICSOB 2017, LNBIP 304, pp. 3–17, 2017.
https://doi.org/10.1007/978-3-319-69191-6_1

popularity among researchers, presenting principles for developing a business model built on a relevant problem/solution and product/market fit. Some derivatives of lean startup have been created [7, 10], fine-tuning the original ideas. Steinert et al. [6] proposed a similar concept focusing on seeking the great idea.

In software startups, self-destruction is a bigger cause of failure than the competition [4, 11]. Broad and reliable validation of a product idea from innovation to prototype and creating the first product is a crucial period in a software startup's evolution, independent of the model or process that the work is following [4]. The importance is further increased due to the challenges a startup faces, such as limited resources, inexperienced teams, and dependency on a single product [1]. Studies on suitable practices for validating ideas are, however, missing, as shown in a thorough mapping study of software startups [1].

In this paper, we study the practices used in a sample of European software startups for idea validation, the effect of available competencies on the idea validation process, and the role of the practices during requirement gathering. We broaden the principles of the build-measure-learn process defined in [5] from the validation of a business case to cover also the technical aspects of the idea. While validating the idea a startup gathers requirements for the product. To highlight that we map our findings to a requirement gathering model presented in [12].

We define the key concepts of our paper as follows: Idea validation refers to all the actions and steps that are directly targeted to improve the idea and validate its technical and commercial feasibility. An idea validation practice refers to the elements of the idea validation process. Competencies refer to the skills and knowledge needed to conduct the process successfully [13].

The research was conducted as a multiple case study [14]. We interviewed a sample of software startups in four European locations and analyzed the collected research data via thematic analysis following the guidelines of [15].

The rest of the paper is structured as follows: Sect. 2 describes the background of and motivation for the study; Sect. 3 presents the research method and data analysis technique used; and Sect. 4 presents the empirical results. Section 5 discusses the answers to the research questions. Section 6 concludes the paper, briefly describing the limitations of the study and directions for future research.

2 Background and Motivation

Innovative startups play an important role in the economy because of their potential to grow through rapid expansion even in highly competitive markets. However, internal problems are a bigger cause of startup failure than the competition [3, 4].

2.1 Startup Models and Processes

Increasing interest in startups has led to the development of models describing the evolution of a startup. Crowne [9] introduced a startup model with four phases: startup, growth, stabilization, and maturity. Paternoster et al. broadly studied software startups in [16] and introduced a greenfield model of software startups. The lean startup approach [5] and the hunter-gatherer model [6] deal with business model creation by focusing on finding a winning innovation.

The lean startup model proposes practices for managing the uncertainty that characterizes startups' business prospects by defining the minimal viable product (MVP) and the build-test-learn loop for finding a problem/solution fit and a product/market fit for a product idea. Bosch et al. in [7] used lean startup as a basis and proposed an early stage software startup development model (ESSDM) while exploring the distinctive challenges of a startup in searching for a product idea worth scaling. Wang et al. [17] identified a set of challenges perceived during the idea conceptualization stage, such as building the product, creating a business model, and building an MVP.

Two recent mapping studies by Paternoster et al. [1] and Klotins et al. [18] on software engineering in startups conclude that startups typically don't follow strictly defined processes.

Coleman et al. [8] concluded in their grounded theory study that the key persons' earlier experiences act as the basis of the process development in startups. The same phenomenon was identified in our prior research on the initial team of a software startup [13].

In a startup, the early development steps, during which the idea is validated, build the basis for the next process steps, requirement engineering and product specification. According to [12], a typical product development project in an established company is organized so that the marketing department of the company acts as the customer whereas the development department acts as a supplier. In the context of a startup, there are seldom separate departments and strictly specified roles, but the initial team takes care of all aspects of the product development, including the steps that validate the idea and bring it forward [13].

The current literature in the context of software startups demonstrates only limited knowledge of the actual work done to validate the idea, for instance the lean startup [5] describes building an MVP and measuring its value in fairly abstract terms. That leaves a research gap, how the companies conduct the work and how they acquire the knowledge needed in validating the idea.

3   Research Design

This study aims to address the research gap identified in the previous section: the process run in software startups to validate the innovation's technical and commercial feasibility. We also study how the competencies of the founder affect that idea validation. To fulfill the research objective, we propose the following exploratory research questions [19].

3.1   Research Questions

RQ1: What practices are utilized when validating an idea in software startups?
The objective of the first research question is to find what practices are used as elements of the idea validation process.

RQ2: In what ways do the prior competencies of the innovator/founder affect the idea validation practices? The aim of the second research question is to understand how the prior competencies of the innovator/founder affect the idea validation process.

To answer the research questions, we carried out a multiple case study on a sample of software startups following the guidelines set out in [14].

3.2   Case and Subject Selection

We collected the research data by interviewing a sample of software startups in May and June 2015. We opted to collect a sample of companies with different backgrounds, products, business cases, and evolution phases. We used local startup incubators to help finding candidates on random basis. The sample included nine startup companies in four European locations: Bolzano, Italy; Trondheim, Norway; Oulu, Finland; and Helsinki, Finland. Out of the sample, four case companies had embedded products while five were developing pure software products. We included embedded cases because validating the idea of an embedded product may be different from a pure software product due to needed electronics and mechanics. The case companies, their product types, business cases, and current statuses are summarized in Table 1.

Table 1. Descriptions of the case startups.

Case	Location	Product type	Customers	Interviewee(s)	Status
A	Italy	Pure software	B2C	Founder	Dissolved
B	Norway	Pure software	B2C, B2B	Founder, expert	Product on market
C	Norway	Pure software	B2C, B2B	Founder, expert	Product on market
D	Finland	Embedded	B2C	Founder	Dissolved
E	Finland	Embedded	B2C	COO	Prototype series
F	Finland	Embedded	B2B	CTO	Prototype series
G	Finland	Pure software	B2B	Founder	Established business
H	Finland	Pure software	B2B	Founder	Prototype series
I	Finland	Embedded	B2B	CTO	Established business

Eight case companies were ordinary startups and one was an internal startup. We opted to include an internal startup in our sample to find out possible differences to ordinary startups. The size of the case companies ranged between four and twelve employees, in most cases between five and seven. The operational age was between 12 and 60 months. In some cases, the original idea was refined and tested several years before the company was founded.

3.3   Data Collection Procedure

We selected interviewees via the key informant technique in order to collect rich qualitative data [20]. The interviews involved the founders, chief operating officers (COOs), and chief technology officers (CTOs) of the case companies. We used direct techniques in the form of semi-structured face-to-face interviews [21] and created a thematic interview guide before we conducted the interviews. The interview guide contained questions that broadly covered the early phases of the startups from the original idea to the present situation.

In case companies B and C, we interviewed two persons from the same company, and in one case, the same interviewee covered case companies D and E. Thus, the total number of interviewees was ten. All the interviews were conducted in English. They were recorded and later transcribed by a professional transcription company.

3.4 Data Analysis Procedure

We opted to analyze the empirical data by using thematic synthesis as defined in [15]. We followed the recommendations of [15] to utilize the integrated approach by combining inductive and deductive coding, a method that determines an initial set of codes and defines new ones during the coding process when new topics emerge from the research data.

As the first step, the interview recordings were transcribed to MSWord documents. The documents were read thoroughly by the first author, and a decision was made to include all interview data for coding in order to utilize the benefits of the inductive-deductive approach.

In the thematic synthesis, the interview data was analyzed sentence by sentence by using NVivo11, and the data related to innovation validation were identified and coded. The codes were then collected into ten themes summarizing the idea validation practices. The themes were further incorporated into three categories, engineering-related, business-related, and combined, as shown in Table 2. The classification was based on our research data, for example, on the context and purpose in which each practice was used in our sample companies. Several practices were deployed in both engineering-related and business-related domains.

Though creating prototypes may be a part of creating MVPs, we classified the former as engineering-related practices and the latter as business-related ones. The reason was that in our sample prototyping was done mostly for validating engineering solutions, while an MPVs is meant for measuring the business value, as defined in [5]. Similarly, we do not classify changing the technical solution identified in some case companies as pivoting, as defined in [5]. Changing the technology solution doesn't necessarily mean a change to the business case, as pivoting by definition does.

Three practices—expert support, host company support, and educational support—deal in our sample only with broadening the knowledge and skills available in a startup. They were handled separately from each other because the sources of the support and the contexts when utilizing them were different.

To find answers to RQ2, we identified codes related to the founder's product creation competencies. The founder's perspective was selected based on the findings of [8, 13], which indicate that the founder is the key person in conducting innovation-related work in startups and that the key person's previous experiences strongly affect the process development. The codes identified in the research data were incorporated into three competency-related themes as shown in Table 3.

Table 2. Identified practices for idea validation.

Identified practice	Description	Category
Copying existing products	Utilizing the idea, functionality, business model, customer segment, engineering solution, or other relevant information of an existing product	Engineering, business
Technology feasibility study	Studying the engineering solution(s) to discover engineering challenges and their solutions	Engineering
Market study	Conducting a market study addressing a broad customer segment and focusing on the business value	Business
Prototyping	Creating prototype(s) to discover and test engineering solutions	Engineering
Minimum viable product (MVP)	Creating MVPs as defined in lean startup [5] to test customer acceptance	Engineering, business
Expert support	Acquiring support from individuals with senior expertise	Engineering
Host company support	Experts of the home company provide the startup with experience and knowledge for the idea validation	Engineering, business
Educational support	Teachers/instructors provide the startup with experience and knowledge for the idea validation	Engineering, business
Pivoting	Pivoting as defined in lean startup [5]	Business
Close customer cooperation	Working closely with the first customer(s) on both technology and business	Engineering, business

Because this study focused on software startups, the key areas arising from the research data were competencies in software development and in the application domain. The theme software development covered competencies in all software development areas, such as analysis, design, implementation, testing, requirement engineering, and related process development. Similarly, all competencies related to the application area of the planned product were gathered under the theme application area competencies.

Because four out of nine case companies were developing embedded products, we included competencies in disciplines other than software. In that theme, we ranked other technology areas needed for product development, such as hardware and mechanics development.

We compared the competency themes and the idea validation themes for each company in order to identify the relationships between the competency and the idea validation themes and to find answers to the research questions.

4   Results

In this section, we discuss the startup cases and describe the identified idea validation practices and the effect of the competencies on the idea validation practices.

Table 3. Themes for competencies.

Founder's experience
Software-related disciplines
Disciplines other than software
Application area

4.1 Case Description

Case company A developed a web-based service for multimedia sharing in a university environment. The product was a pure software product developed by a team of students. The founder was a professor with very strong competencies in software development, software engineering, and innovation but no prior experience in the application domain.

Case company B developed a web-based ticketing service. The product was a pure software product. The founders had just graduated from the university with degrees in non-software-related topics. The founders did not have prior competencies in any competency areas of interest.

Case company C developed a smart emergency call service that provides the emergency call center with access to the caller's relevant health information in addition to automatically providing the location of the caller. The idea emerged from an existing similar system in the US and from the founder's own experiences after an accident.

Case company D tried to develop an embedded device that measures online the human body's fat burning rate during physical exercise. The measurement was based on analysis of certain marker substances in the user's exhaled breath. The development of the sensor technology failed, and the company was dissolved. The founder had prior competencies in software, hardware, and mechanical development but no competencies in the application domain.

Case company E was developing an embedded device that measures the work and effort of a human muscle in physical exercise. The founders had a background in health care and medicine and thus had prior competencies in the application domain. However, they did not have any competencies in the technology areas needed to create a product. The product idea emerged from the founders' daily work and the solution principles were copied from existing electromyography (EMG) devices.

Case company F was an internal startup within a bigger company with a focus on software services. The product was an embedded Internet of Things (IoT) device that integrated a multitude of sensors and communication solutions. The host company had almost a hundred very experienced developers and managers with strong prior competencies in the application area and all technology areas needed to create the product.

Case company G was developing a software tool for improving aircraft maintenance at a big aviation company. The product was a pure software product. The founder had just graduated from the university but had strong prior competencies in software development. He had also worked on a temporary contract in the maintenance department of the customer company.

Case company H was creating a graphical user interface platform for smart devices, especially focusing on smart watches. The idea was much older than the company and had emerged from the founder's earlier work. The founder had done two prototyping rounds with two different implementation approaches before finding the final one and founding the company. The founder had strong competencies in the application area and in software development.

Case company I developed an embedded ultrasound device with complex software, hardware, and mechanics. The idea emerged from a similar device the founder had learned about. The founder was a seasoned entrepreneur who had strong competencies in software development, reasonable competencies in hardware development, and some competencies in the application domain.

4.2   Idea Validation Practices

We summarized the results of the thematic analysis in a multidimensional chart combining the idea validation practices and the founder's prior competencies per company, as shown in Fig. 1. In the chart, a small square at the intersection between a company and an identified theme shows (a) on the left-hand side what idea validation practices were used in the case company and (b) on the right-hand side what the founder's prior competencies were. The vertical light yellow bars highlight the most frequently used idea validation practices, and the horizontal light blue bars indicate the effect of the founder's prior competencies on the utilized practices.

The chart in Fig. 1 shows that use of the idea validation practices varied considerably between the case companies. Most of the companies utilized several practices to validate the product idea. Copying existing products, prototyping, and utilizing expert support, together with customer cooperation were the most frequently used practices. The business-related practices for idea validation, utilizing a market study, utilizing an

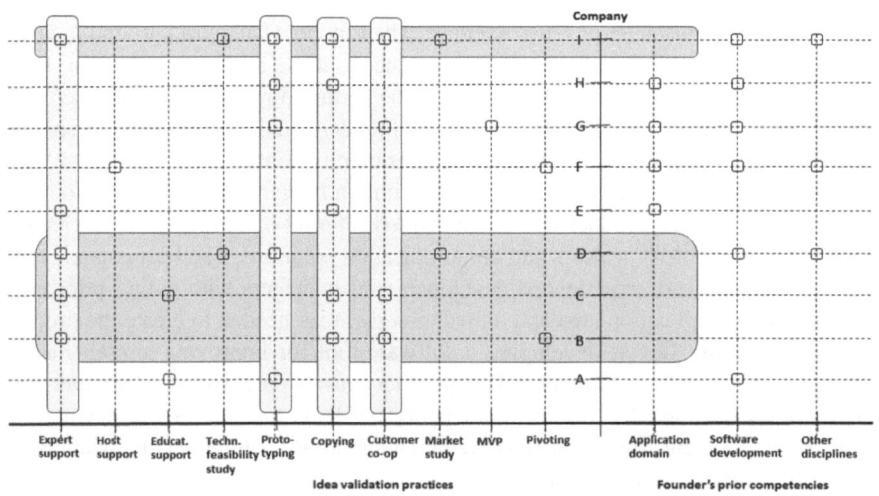

Fig. 1. Idea validation practices vs. founder's competencies

MVP, and pivoting, were in the research data strongly tied to the practices being more engineering-related. Practices from both categories were utilized in parallel, mutually supporting each other.

4.3   Effect of Prior Competencies on Idea Validation Practices

The results indicate that the founder's prior competencies in the application domain were the key difference between the case companies. The better the application knowledge competencies, the smoother the progress from idea to a product. Also, the palette of idea validation practices was the most focused, while the broadest variation of practices was in the cases when the founder did not have prior competencies in the application domain. In four out of five cases without application domain competencies, utilizing expert support belonged to the practices palette, broadened by copying existing products, customer cooperation, and prototyping.

Utilizing expert support was common for the three cases without prior competencies in software development. In all those cases, the experts' role was to compensate for the founder's missing competencies. Out of the six cases with existing software development competencies, expert support was utilized in two cases, both developing embedded products with highly specific technology.

Prior competencies in disciplines other than software were mainly relevant to companies that developed embedded products. Expert support was a common idea validation practice independent of existing competencies in the other discipline category,

The internal startup F differed from all other case companies by being self-sustained both in validating the idea and acquiring all necessary competencies from the host company.

5   Discussion

In this section, we discuss the findings of our research. First, the answers to the research questions are presented. Then, our findings are discussed in the context of development processes and requirement gathering. Finally, the relevance of our findings to the research and to practitioners is discussed.

5.1   Answering the Research Questions

Based on the results of the study, we conclude the following answers to our research questions:

RQ1: What practices are utilized when validating an idea in software startups?

From our case sample, we identified ten idea validation practices: close customer cooperation, MVP, copying existing products, market study, prototyping, technology feasibility study, pivoting, support from home company, support from educational institute, and expert support. We further found that copying existing products, prototyping, and utilizing expert support, together with customer cooperation, were the most often used practices in the cases.

Early and close customer cooperation was commonly utilized in our sample, especially in cases where the customer was easily identifiable and accessible.

In case companies A, D, and E, where the product was targeted to the mass market, close customer cooperation was not identified. That may indicate that following the recommendations proposed in [5–7, 10] may be difficult in a practical situation if good representatives of a customer base cannot be found.

In case companies F and H, late customer cooperation was identified. In both cases, the business-to-business (B2B) customer base was broad, and the companies had excellent competencies for developing and testing the product.

Possibly the most surprising practice for idea validation in our sample was copying existing products. Copying was identified in five out of nine companies. Copying was tied to business cases aiming at developing a cheaper or better product to compete with an existing product, developing a product for a specific customer base, broadening the use of known solutions to a new application area, or developing a local copy of a product already used in another country.

In our sample, the utilization of the methodology proposed by the lean startup method [5] was surprisingly small, although the interviews revealed that the approach was known. There may be several reasons for that. In cases where copying from existing products was utilized, the basics of the product idea, its business case, and the potential customers were probably already well enough known in early phases of the startup's evolution. Pivoting, as proposed in [5], was identified only in case companies B and F.

We separated prototyping from MVP according to the purpose. While an MVP's goal was early measuring of the customer value of an idea [5], prototyping was utilized for company internal validation and optimization of the technical solutions.

RQ2: In what ways do the prior competencies of the innovator/founder affect the idea validation practices?

The founder's missing competencies in the application domain and in software development led to the utilization of many idea validation practices in parallel.

The chart in Fig. 1 shows that expert support was a frequently utilized practice to compensate for the founder's missing competencies. It was utilized especially when embedded products were developed and when the founder did not have prior competencies in the application area or in software development.

Support from an educational institution and from the host company were utilized in companies A, C, and F when the founders studied or worked at the supporting organization.

Copying from existing products was utilized both when prior competencies in the application area existed and when they were missing. In the cases when copying was utilized, the dependency on the targeted business case was clearer than the dependency on the available competencies.

Close customer cooperation was an equally utilized practice independent of the prior competencies of the founder. However, in the cases of very competent founders and development teams, customer cooperation was first initiated at a later stage of the development.

In the sample, prototyping was a common practice for idea validation independent of other practices and the founder's prior competencies.

5.2   Idea Validation Process

The results of our study highlight the complexity of the idea validation process and thus confirm empirically the related findings of [1, 3, 8, 18]. A smooth and linear process from the idea to a product was identified in two cases, companies F and G. In company F, the reasons may have been a fairly clear business case for the IoT device and the host company's strong experience in developing such a product. In company G, the founder had direct work experience in the customer organization and hence excellent personal contacts. He also succeeded in deploying a simple but convincing MVP at a very early stage. The other companies faced different challenges and a nonlinear process during the idea validation.

The idea validation processes identified in our study in different case companies can be described as ad hoc, although the individual validation practices were well known ones in product development. The ad-hoc nature comes from three main elements derived from Sects. 4.2 and 4.3: (1) the combinations of different practices varied between the companies, (2) utilizing different practices was strongly context dependent, and (3) the founder's prior competencies affected the set of practices deployed. Thus, our empirical results are in line with the earlier findings of [1, 8, 18], and they don't allow us to determine any general process model for idea validation.

5.3   Idea Validation Practices and Requirements Gathering

As discussed above, the work done for refining and validating the original idea is a part of the overall product development process of a startup. In this section, we explore how the identified idea validation practices link to requirement gathering. As the framework for the exploration, we utilize the four-level requirement model proposed in [12]. In the model, the requirements are classified in four levels: goal, domain, product, and design.

Figure 2 shows the proposed research-data-based mapping of the identified idea validation practices onto the model.

At the goal level, requirements related to the business objective of the product are created and verified [12]. To gather the requirements of the goal level, copying and customer cooperation were utilized. Pivoting as defined in [5] is a retrospective decision and a sign that the targeted business case was not strong enough for continued development.

At the domain level, requirements usually focus on the key functionality of the product. It is important that the correct functionality is carefully recognized and the planned product's ability to support it is ensured [12]. As Fig. 2 shows, most idea validation practices, including copying, customer cooperation, expert support, technical feasibility study, market study, and MVP, were utilized at the domain level.

At the product level, requirements defining the product's physical and logical boundaries, its interfaces, and its inputs and outputs are described without focusing on the actual implementation [12]. For the requirements at this level, prototyping was used, and customer cooperation continued.

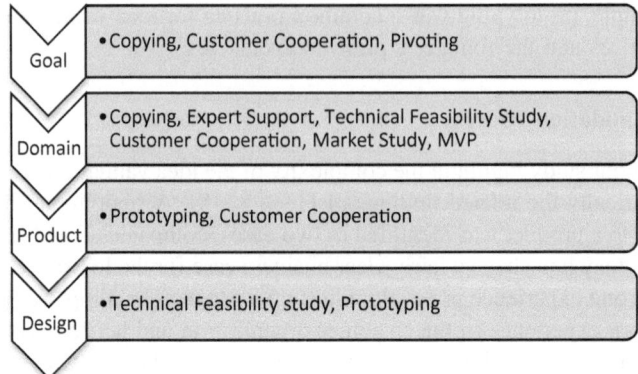

Fig. 2. Idea validation practices and requirement gathering level

At the design level, prototyping was continued. Company I, developing a demanding product, continued conducting small-scale trials separate from the main-stream prototype development. Thus, we include technical feasibility study in the idea validation practices for the design level.

Because of missing detailed research data, we do not map educational support and host company support onto the model shown in Fig. 2.

5.4   Validity Discussion

We discuss the validity of the study in terms of construct validity, internal validity, external validity, and reliability as described in [14]. Construct validity deals with taking full provisions in the data collection procedure so that the collected data line up with the research questions. We designed an interview guide before we conducted the interviews to ensure the interview questions covered the research topic and the research questions in a broad manner. Experienced people from the case companies were selected for the interviews based on the key informant technique.

Internal validity is mainly used for explanatory and causal studies in which causal relationship between outcomes and intervention is examined in order to find the explanation for a given condition or problem [14]. Our study explored phenomena in software startups without addressing causal relationships. Thus, we don't consider internal validity. External validity refers to whether the findings from the study can be generalized outside the studied cases. Our results are based on nine software startups in Europe. To generalize the results further empirical research across other regions and a bigger sample is needed.

Study reliability is concerned with how the data analysis depends on the particular researchers. In the initial phase, the first author created a case study protocol in order to have a systematic research procedure. The data analysis was performed by the first and second authors with the qualitative data analysis tool NVivo11 in order to ensure that various aspects of the idea validation process in the software startups were addressed.

5.5   Relevance to Academia and Practitioners

The results of this study reveal interesting viewpoints for academia and industry. Recently, startup research has focused on big innovations and methods for seeking them [5, 6]. Our results may, however, indicate that among the famous but few big innovation startups, there is a dense undergrowth of others creating business and furthering development, though in smaller steps. For academia, broadening the focus of research to that undergrowth may create valuable knowledge supporting the economic growth that takes place outside the big but few innovation cases.

From the practitioner's point of view, the study identified a set of idea validation practices that were deployed in real-life startups. The results highlight the complexity of the idea validation process, the importance for a startup to realistically recognize and acknowledge the competency weaknesses, and the importance of seeking ways to compensate for those weaknesses.

Though it is not reasonable to set any specific priority order onto the practices we identified, some general guidelines can be given. Close customer cooperation is recommended in cases where the potential customers are easily accessible and willing to cooperate. Close customer cooperation combined with active prototyping covers both the business-related and engineering-related issues of product development.

The value of following the recommendations of lean startup [5] was identified in our study, as well. A well-fitting MVP opened the business case of company G to a big institutional customer that otherwise might have been difficult to reach. Timely pivoting might have helped company A get back on track from the dead-end of its original product idea.

Our mapping of the identified idea validation practices onto the requirement gathering [12] highlights for practitioners the importance of conducting validation practices in an appropriate way, though no generic process covering the practices was defined.

6   Conclusions and Future Research

In this paper, we explored empirically the practices deployed in idea validation in software startups. We used a multiple case study method with nine software startups. To collect the data, we used semi-structured face-to-face interviews. During the data analyses, we found ten practices that affect the idea validation process. Of the ten practices, the most frequently utilized ones were copying existing products, cooperating closely with customers, utilizing expert support, and prototyping.

The results indicate that the case companies utilized the practices in varying, context-dependent ways. No uniform and systematic process from idea to product was identified. The results also indicate that the previous competencies and experiences of the founder affect the utilization of different practices. From those perspectives, our empirical study was in line with the prior literature, confirming our findings.

A finding of our study is that the founder's prior knowledge, skills, and competencies in software development and application area tend to make the process of moving from an idea to a product more linear and straightforward. In the opposite case, a key learning is the need to use all possible ways to fill the knowledge and competency gaps.

The research was based on several startup companies located in various regions across Europe. The results from this study need to be further empirically verified across other regions and a bigger sample of startups in order to validate the generalizability of our results. Other interesting future work would be to examine in more detail how the idea validation process continues to systematic requirement engineering.

Acknowledgements. This study was partly funded by TEKES as a part of the HILLA program. We thank the members of Software Startups Global Research Network, which supported this study, especially Anh Nguyen Duc and Pekka Abrahamsson, for their help in gathering the empirical data.

References

1. Paternoster, N., Giardino, C., Unterkalmsteiner, M., Gorschek, T., Abrahamsson, P.: Software development in startup companies: a systematic mapping study. Inf. Softw. Technol. **56**, 1200–1218 (2014)
2. Blank, S.A.: The four steps to the epiphany: Successful Strategies for Products that Win CafePress. com, (2005)
3. Giardino, C., Unterkalmsteiner, M., Paternoster, N., Gorschek, T., Abrahamsson, P.: What do we know about software development in startups? IEEE Softw. **31**, 28–32 (2014)
4. Giardino, C., Wang, X., Abrahamsson, P.: Why early-stage software startups fail: a behavioral framework. In: Lassenius, C., Smolander, K. (eds.) ICSOB 2014. LNBIP, vol. 182, pp. 27–41. Springer, Cham (2014). doi:10.1007/978-3-319-08738-2_3
5. Ries, E.: The lean startup: How today's entrepreneurs use continuous innovation to create radically successful businesses. Random House LLC (2011)
6. Steinert, M., Leifer, L.J.: "Finding One"s Way': Re-Discovering a Hunter-Gatherer Model based on Wayfaring. Int. J. Eng. Educ. **28**, 251 (2012)
7. Bosch, J., Holmström Olsson, H., Björk, J., Ljungblad, J.: The early stage software startup development model: a framework for operationalizing lean principles in software startups. In: Fitzgerald, B., Conboy, K., Power, K., Valerdi, R., Morgan, L., Stol, K.-J. (eds.) LESS 2013. LNBIP, vol. 167, pp. 1–15. Springer, Heidelberg (2013). doi:10.1007/978-3-642-44930-7_1
8. Coleman, G., O'Connor, R.V.: An investigation into software development process formation in software start-ups. J. Enterp. Inf. Manag. **21**, 633–648 (2008)
9. Crowne, M.: Why software product startups fail and what to do about it. Evolution of software product development in startup companies. In: IEEE International Engineering Management Conference, vol. 1, pp. 338–343 (2002)
10. Björk, J., Ljungblad, J., Bosch, J.: Lean Product development in early stage startups. In: IW-LCSP@ ICSOB. pp. 19–32 (2013)
11. Marmer, M., Herrmann, B.L., Dogrultan, E., Berman, R., Eesley, C., Blank, S.: The startup ecosystem report 2012. Technical report, Startup Genome (2012)
12. Lauesen, S.: Software Requirements: Styles and Techniques. Pearson Education, Upper Saddle River (2002)

13. Seppänen, P., Oivo, M., Liukkunen, K.: The initial team of a software startup, Narrow-shouldered innovation and broad-shouldered implementation. In: To be published in 22nd ICE/IEEE International Technology Management Conference (2016)
14. Runeson, P., Höst, M.: Guidelines for conducting and reporting case study research in software engineering. Empir. Softw. Eng. **14**, 131–164 (2009)
15. Cruzes, D.S., Dyba, T.: Recommended steps for thematic synthesis in software engineering. In: 2011 International Symposium on Empirical Software Engineering and Measurement (ESEM), pp. 275–284. IEEE (2011)
16. Giardino, C., Paternoster, N., Unterkalmstcincr, M., Gorschek, T., Abrahamsson, P.: Software development in startup companies: the greenfield startup model. IEEE Trans. Softw. Eng. **42**, 585–604 (2016)
17. Wang, X., Edison, H., Bajwa, S.S., Giardino, C., Abrahamsson, P.: Key challenges in software startups across life cycle stages. In: Sharp, H., Hall, T. (eds.) XP 2016. LNBIP, vol. 251, pp. 169–182. Springer, Cham (2016). doi:10.1007/978-3-319-33515-5_14
18. Klotins, E., Unterkalmsteiner, M., Gorschek, T.: Software engineering knowledge areas in startup companies: a mapping study. In: Fernandes, João M., Machado, Ricardo J., Wnuk, K. (eds.) ICSOB 2015. LNBIP, vol. 210, pp. 245–257. Springer, Cham (2015). doi:10.1007/978-3-319-19593-3_22
19. Selecting empirical methods for software engineering research. In: Shull F., Singer J., Sjøberg D.I.K. (eds.) Guide to Advanced Empirical Software Engineering, pp. 285–311. Springer, London (2008)
20. Marshall, M.N.: The key informant technique. Fam. Pract. **13**, 92–97 (1996)
21. Lethbridge, T.C., Sim, S.E., Singer, J.: Studying software engineers: data collection techniques for software field studies. Empir. Softw. Eng. **10**, 311–341 (2005)

Acquisitions and Growth of Software Startups: The Dual Role of Venture Capital as a Success Factor

Marcus Wagner[(✉)]

Augsburg University, Universitätsstr. 16, 86159 Augsburg, Germany
marcus.wagner@wiwi.uni-augsburg.de

Abstract. Innovation activities provide considerable challenges to small firms due to resource constraints. Conversely, large, established firms are often forced to buy technologies to remain innovative. This paper investigates the interplay of these two aspects in a specific software-based startup context. Based on structured interviews, the paper analyses what characteristics of startups and small firms and resources accessed through networking determine acquisition likelihoods and growth. This addresses a gap in the literature, namely understanding better the dual role of venture capital, specifically with regard to the type of innovation pursued by small firms and in its interplay with other determinants of growth and acquisition.

1 Introduction

Networking and other forms of co-operation have been suggested as key strategies of small firms and startups to acquire and leverage resources in order to circumvent liabilities of newness and smallness [1]. Specifically this concerns financial resource access in technology-intensive industries through networking to support startup growth. Importantly, resource endowments either generated within or sourced from outside a startup or small firm, such as financial means or innovations realised, potentially relate to both growth and acquisition chances. While studies have analysed separately determinants of growth [2] and acquisition chances [3], a joint analysis is more appropriate since becoming an attractive target may require different managerial actions than for realising a startup's growth potential, yet ex-ante growth and acquisition are equal outcomes [4]. At the same time, technology acquisitions become ever more important for large established firms in the semiconductor industry and other high-technology sectors, and are also increasingly easy due to novel markets for technology and technology brokers [5], which makes an integrated analysis of growth and acquisition potential even more relevant. Related to this, in the semiconductor industry levels of research and development (R&D) input are strongly affected by the highly cyclical nature of the industry, whose most severe downturn was 2000–2001. R&D expenditure has significantly dropped since then and not recovered up to the time of this empirical study. Furthermore, semiconductor firms' propensity to patent considerably increased in the USA in the 1980s, especially after the formation of a centralized appellate court in 1982 as a means of strengthening patent rights [6].

© Springer International Publishing AG 2017
A. Ojala et al. (Eds.): ICSOB 2017, LNBIP 304, pp. 18–31, 2017.
https://doi.org/10.1007/978-3-319-69191-6_2

Both trends, together with rapid technological change and the cumulative nature of innovation in the industry, make external technology sourcing through the acquisition of startups and small firms a frequent event, especially as concerns radical innovation [7]. Therefore, as will be detailed later, the electronic design automation (EDA) segment of the semiconductor industry (which focuses on chip design tools) offers an empirical context particularly suited to analysis of the joint determinants of growth of an acquisition, and to address the core research question: To what degree are the determinants for realising an entrant's growth potential the same as those that increase acquisition likelihood? Such joint analysis is a gap in the extant literature, and this paper contributes new empirical insights that extend the body of knowledge on this issue and sub-questions derived from it. The remainder of the paper is structured as follows: In the remainder of this section different theoretical perspectives on innovation in the electronic design automation industry are introduced and more detailed research questions are derived. Following this in the second section, the data and methodology used for the empirical analysis are described, and findings with regard to the activities that small firms or startups should pursue to increase their chances of becoming acquisition targets (such as the type of innovation to pursue) and interaction between this and growth determinants in the electronic design automation industry are reported. The final section draws conclusions with regard to the research questions, and outlines limitations of the empirical analysis and identifies future research needs. Overall, this paper in pursuing this sequence also contributes to the understanding of founders, investors and policy makers with regard to the financing of startups and its interaction with startup growth. As part of this it clarifies the role of finance-related networks for software startups based on a statistical analysis of a novel and detailed dataset of software startups.

1.1   Review of Extant Literature

This section derives research questions building on various theoretical perspectives such as the management, social networks, and economics literatures. The management literature develops important concepts, such as the distinction between radical and incremental innovation that have particular relevance in high-technology industries such as EDA. It also suggests that large established firms in particular may not be able or willing to carry out specific types of innovation, for example due to obstacles to an innovation from it not being invented by the firm itself, or challenges from lacking absorptive capacity [8, 9]. The social networks literature is relevant especially to how small firms and startups gain access to important resources such as capital [10]. Furthermore, it has been argued that partnering, intensive research collaboration and innovation networks may be needed to bring about radical innovation in the EDA industry [11].

Other relevant streams of scholarly work, especially as concerns acquisitions, are institutional and transaction cost approaches. These economic theories have proposed a number of reasons for acquisitions [12, 13]. Various studies have tested their empirical validity [14], and have explored links to the management literature on obstacles to innovation since, although acquisitions may be a very appropriate means for innovation, they are revealed in studies to be obstacles to innovation, especially in larger firms. Finally, both the management and economics literatures have extensively addressed the theme of firm growth [15]. The following paragraphs link theorising on networks and alliancing with theories of acquisition and growth to derive more detailed questions about the potentially joint determinants of the growth and acquisition.

A core aspect of note in the context of networks and alliancing is that they provide innovative startups and small firms with relevant competencies that they are lacking in [16, 17]. Specifically, small firms may sometimes not be capable of achieving growth by themselves, perhaps due to the limitations of newness and smallness which they often face [18], and therefore again would depend on networked activity. This particularly concerns the external sourcing of financial means to support expansion, which has been identified as the most frequent and most important activity in new ventures [19]. Venture capitalists use their own portfolio firms to help set up strategic alliances, especially in the case of early stage firms in their portfolios, which is likely to mitigate the weaknesses of newness and smallness significantly [20].

This result is regardless of the industries a venture capitalist specializes in and also links to the role of venture capital (VC) as a resource to be invested in R&D and patenting as a means to create intellectual property (IP) resources (since patent applications are enabled through financial resources). IP resources are in turn crucial to create competitive advantages and complementary assets that enable startups and smaller firms to establish themselves in product markets in the longer term [21]. Furthermore, the role of patents is highlighted as a means to create strong appropriation regimes that make it more difficult for incumbents to acquire entrants and foster alliances and more extensive innovation networks [22]. In relation to this, it is shown that startups and small firms with strong alliancing and networking activities experience higher growth rates [23]. On the other hand, other scholars find that acquired firms have larger stocks of accumulated knowledge (measured through patents) which suggests that a strong patent base can jointly influence growth and acquisition chances [3].

Finally, the commercialisation strategies of 118 startup projects were analysed with a focus on the choice between product market growth and acquisition [4]. Focusing on the high-technology sectors biotechnology, computer software, industrial machinery and equipment, electronic equipment and scientific instruments and using binary and multivariate probit models they find that patenting is insignificantly and VC engagement positively related to acquisition. In summary, alliancing and networking potentially determine both the growth and acquisition chances of startups and small firms and therefore need to be considered as one important determinant. Many reasons are suggested for technology acquisitions. From a transaction cost and institutional economic perspective, one of the main reasons for technology acquisition is that an innovation is organisationally radical because such innovation requires intensive learning and intellectual deliberation within an established firm [9, 24].

Other reasons for the incapacity of a large, established firm to carry out specific innovations are certain ideological views or conservative attitudes, a special case of which is the so-called "not-invented-here syndrome" [25–28]. Related to such failures of realising innovation are issues of communication channels and information filters that can aggravate a lack of absorptive capacity or resistance to innovation, or can hinder the development of internal and external networks that enable exploiting benefits from external innovation [24]. While such factors, attitudes or views may be subjective from an external point of view, they can therefore objectively deter inno-vation, especially within large established firms. In these instances, acquisition is a means of sourcing innovation externally to make up for lost time, yet absorptive capacity may be lacking either because new skills are required from larger firms (which essentially represents a problem of lacking human capital or capabilities) or because radically different organisational structures for R&D are required [29]. This is espe-cially important since it may imply that large firms tend to favor incremental over radical innovations.

It could be claimed that startups in the EDA industry have largely realised incre-mental innovations [11], which refers back to an argument made before in this section, namely that innovation networks are needed for radical innovation [30]. Larger firms, in acquiring a surviving or even fast-growing small firm, gain information that has been translated into appropriate strategies without having to address the various challenges that come with other forms of external technology sourcing, such as long-term strategic investments in alliances [31]. Linking this with other works on the emergence of dominant designs and the subsequent focus on process innovation in an industry one can also conclude that smaller firms are particularly likely to emerge in areas where the dominant design has not yet been established [32].

Finally, other scholars model the behaviour of small firms as stochastically drawing information on the market. Based on this information, they adjust their behaviour and strategies [33]. Those firms capable of learning based on new information are able to grow faster whilst those less capable have more difficulty surviving in the market and are more likely to be acquired by larger firms. However, this learning process unfolding over time can also explain why smaller firms that have managed to survive for some time in the market are acquired, as opposed to very young ones. Also because of the decreasing marginal effect of learning and information gains over time, the likelihood of being acquired decreases after some point, so that very old firms are less likely to be acquired (compared to exiting the market or concentrating on a niche with lower growth levels). The interaction of growth and acquisition determinants could basically be complementary or substitutive. For example, VC can provide additional resources to accelerate and enhance growth, but it could equally create a situation where investors push for a trade sale.

Similarly, the managerial and economic writings on industry life cycles suggest that growth initially decreases when firms become older [34]. On the other hand, after a shakeout has occurred in an industry, firm growth is likely to increase again due to the resulting oligopolistic market structures [35]. This suggests an inversely U-shaped relationship of firm age and growth. On the other hand, given the heterogeneity of startups and small (and younger) firms, less successful firms tend to grow more slowly and thus are more likely to become acquisition targets [36]. This suggests that firm age as a determinant could have opposing or similar association with growth and acqui-sition chances. Furthermore, it can be seen that firms make a strategic choice very early between a growth strategy focusing on recruitment and organisational development and a strategy aimed at building a patent portfolio [19].

One important aspect here is precisely how firm growth is measured. Whilst growth measures have been argued to be superior to profitability and similar performance measures [37], identifying which exact specification is the best growth measure is not intuitive, but the concurrent validity between relative and absolute measures, as well as between a 1-year and a 3-year time span, is relatively high, especially for employee growth. Despite the various linkages outlined here, a joint analysis of determinants for firm growth and acquisition is rare in the extant literature [38] and if only considers ex-ante acquisition chances in the context of university startups, but not ex-post actual acquisition likelihoods and their interaction with growth [39]. Another study coming close to this aim, analyses the innovation and growth effects of alliances in the semiconductor industry, but does not consider acquisition [40]. This study extends its analysis by considering acquisitions and actual acquisition likelihoods.

1.2 Development of Research Questions

The above considerations show that for incumbents acquisition can be another efficient means for firms to carry out innovation through acquiring successful startups or smaller firms in the industry, but that this may be at odds with small firms realising their growth potential. This raises the question of whether startups with particular characteristics, such as highly innovative ones, or those with VC support are more likely to be acquired.

On the other hand, given the argument that small EDA startups frequently come to a point where they do not realise their growth potential [11], for example due to lack of complementary assets or resource access, it matters if the determinants of acquisition chances are similar to or different from those determining firm growth. Based on insights derived from the extant literature, the following further research questions relating to whether there is an interaction between the determinants for firm growth and acquisition, and to what degree this is conflicting or complementary, shall be answered in the paper:

1. What association does firm age have with acquisition and firm growth?
2. Is organisational radicality of an entrant's innovation positively associated with acquisition and firm growth?
3. Is venture capitalist engagement positively associated with acquisition and growth?

2 Methodology

Next to the general technology and innovation-related reasons mentioned in the introduction, the EDA industry has additional features that make it a particularly suitable segment of the semiconductor sector for joint analysis of the determinants of acquisition and growth. Firstly, this is a very clearly defined market structure, and a number of small firms are active in the industry who are frequently acquired by larger incumbents. Furthermore, it covers a number of complex processes from chip design through to testing which enables a large variety of combinations of technological, organisational and economic radicality in innovations. In summary, EDA is therefore a very suitable industry for analysing the interaction of acquisition and growth. To gather data in this industry in order to address the above research questions, a key informant design was used, with the survey directed to either the founder or small firm owner or a general manager. This seemed appropriate given the success of this approach in similar settings [39, 41].

Therefore, structured interviews with key informants were used to gather primary data on innovation activities in the EDA. The aim of the interviews was to gather high-quality data on acquisitions chances and growth, and the characteristics of firms and their activities. Since personal interviews allow ongoing interaction, it is always possible to correct misunderstandings immediately and to ensure consistent ordinal ratings through immediate requests. A similar approach has more recently also been used in the context of telephone interviews with large firms which suggests its increasing relevance [42]. Of course a strong focus on data quality may reduce data quantity and can potentially make the resulting data set less representative.

This research incorporates several steps to reduce that risk. Firstly, 70 smaller and younger EDA firms were identified from the exhibitor list of the Design and Test Equipment (DATE) 2006 conference which took place 6-10 March 2006 in Munich. The selection formed the complete set of startups and small firms present at the conference. Given that DATE is known as the world's premier electronic design event [43], this initial population of firms is likely to be representative of startups and small firms in the EDA industry in general. The firms forming this population were approached for a structured interview during the conference. Of these, 32 provided information, resulting in a 42% response rate which is deemed acceptable to draw conclusions that are representative of the population, given the necessity to use face-to-face interviewing to survey the firms.

Finally, even though the number of observations is limited, given the high data quality resulting from the intensive data collection process, it is considered sufficient to enable quantitative analysis and generalizability across the software sector [44]. For example, another paper uses six explanatory variables with 28 observations, which is well below the ratio of observations to variables of this study [9].

Additionally, and in order to further ascertain the representativeness of the response sample, variables in our response sample were compared as far as possible with data from a sample of acquired firms in the EDA industry (n = 68) until end of 2005. Based on t-tests, for patenting (p = 0.67), firm age (p = 0.81) and VC investment (p = 0.30) no significant differences were found between these two samples. Given the two sets of firms are mutually exclusive, the analysis sample is considered sufficiently representative for the true population of all start-ups and small firms in the EDA industry that can potentially be acquired to safely continue with addressing the above research questions and deriving answers that are generalisable (Lee, and Baskerville 2003).

As concerns the dependent variables of the analysis, first, acquisition was measured as a binary variable taking the value of 1 if a firm in the sample was acquired until the end of the first quarter of 2013 (i.e. within the full seven years after the original survey) and 0 if not. Because measurement of actual acquisition was independent from the initial survey common method bias and endogeneity issues are minimised. Second, employee growth has been suggested as being superior to other measures of firm performance such as accounting profits [37], which is why this analysis utilises this measure.

In the following context, 3-year relative employee growth is used [45], since these were the most frequent measures and had higher concurrent validity than 1-year and

5-year periods [46]. Also growth as the second dependent variable is measured independent of the survey to avoid common method and endogeneity problems. For the multivariate analysis of the above research questions, a number of explanatory variables were derived from the literature to arrive at a parsimonious model by incorporating all those explanatory variables that have been proven significant for the dependent variables in question [39, 41]. These include the logarithm of the number of citation-weighted patents held by the respondents, whether a startup originated out of a university research context and a binary variable of whether or not the technology-oriented startups or small firms perceived their innovation to be organisationally radical. A significant positive correlation between the number of patents and a product innovation index can be shown, which suggests that information about patenting is a relatively robust indicator with high content and discriminant validity for technological radicality [47]. Whilst recent methodological research has shown that an adequate sample size required for a factor analysis crucially depends on the quality of the data (in turn rendering general rules of thumb for minimum sample sizes largely invalid), we make use of an exploratory factor analysis on different items (identified in the extant literature reviewed above) for the reasons why larger firms did not carry out an innovation carried out by our respondents [48–51]. From it, the second factor relating to 'low risk-taking/day-to-day' business is included as a control variable of differences across firms and respondents as concerns perceptions.

Additional variables in the multivariate regression are the age of the firm and its squared term, and whether or not a responding firm received VC investment prior to the interview. In the comparison sample of acquired EDA firms we used above to evaluate the representativeness of our analysis sample, the number of investors ($r = 0.58$, $p < 0.01$) and the diversity of different investor types ($r = 0.63$, $p < 0.01$) are both significantly associated with a binary variable of VC investments, which suggests that the latter can proxy well in our analysis for the network and alliancing effects identified in the literature review. To address the research questions (1) to (3), for the determinants of acquisition likelihood a binary logit and for firm growth an ordinary least squares (OLS) regression model is used. The former is the appropriate statistical model in the case of a binary dependent variable (which implies a non-normal distribution and thus non-applicability of the OLS model). Growth is a continuous dependent variable, for which OLS is the appropriate statistical model. Using growth (i.e. a change) in the context of the OLS estimation increases statistical power because it removes common source variation and so, similar to fixed firm effects, controls for at least some of the heterogeneity across firms can be addressed, which goes some way to mitigating the weaknesses of survey data in this respect [52]. Logit coefficients are reported as marginal effects. Concerning the demographics and descriptive statistics, the average age of a firm in the sample is 8.27 years (standard deviation: 6.26). Of the firms, 47% received VC investment and 27% were started out of academia. 53% of the small firms and startups interviewed stated that their innovation was organizationally radical. Finally, the logarithm of citation-weighted patents is on average 0.79 (standard deviation: 1.53). Given the Low risk/day-to-day value is a factor-score based on a principal component analysis, it is z-standardised with a zero mean and its standard deviation assuming unity. Table 1 provides the correlations in the data, suggesting that multi-collinearity is not a problem.

Table 1. Correlation of independent and dependent variables

Variables	1	2	3	4	5	6	7
1 Acquired (yes/no)							
2 Employee growth	0.23						
3 Age of the firm	0.16	0.07					
4 Log. of cit.-weight. patents	−0.09	−0.23	0.19				
5 Organisational radicality	−0.23	0.05	−0.17	−0.36**			
6 Venture capital (yes/no)	0.52**	0.43**	0.14	−0.04	−0.12		
7 Low risk/day-to-day	0.04	−0.02	0.13	0.14	−0.001	−0.15	
8 Academic startup (yes/no)	0.22	0.18	−0.03	−0.14	−0.11	0.11	0.34*

Notes: significance * $p < 0.10$; ** $p < 0.05$; *** $p < 0.01$; robust standard errors; n = 31

3 Results

Table 2 provides the results for the acquisition likelihood. As can be seen, in all models only VC engagement has a significant positive effect on this variable.

Table 2. Analysis of determinants for acquisition (yes/no)

Variables	Model 1	Model 2
Age	0.003 (0.011)	0.091 (0.086)
Age squared	–	−0.002 (0.002)
Logarithm of citation-weight. patents	−0.042 (0.052)	−0.054 (0.052)
Organisational radicality (yes → no)	−0.203 (0.218)	−0.168 (0.196)
Low risk/day-to-day	0.050 (0.096)	0.061 (0.098)
Venture capital (no → yes)	0.473*** (0.172)	0.476*** (0.166)
Academic startup (no → yes)	0.092 (0.199)	0.098 (0.178)
Pseudo-R^2	0.32	0.36
Wald Chi^2	11.38*	10.52*

Notes: significance * $p < 0.10$; ** $p < 0.05$; *** $p < 0.01$; robust standard errors, n = 31

As concerns determinants of employee growth, give the focus of the analysis is if drivers of acquisitions also affect growth, the same determinants are used in the OLS regression models for employee growth as the dependent variable reported in Table 3.

As can be seen in Table 3, for employee growth again only VC investment has a significant positive association in both model specifications. As a sensitivity test confirming the robustness of the findings these did not change in terms of significance and direction in variants of the model that only account for the long-term determinants of acquisition likelihood identified in prior research [39, 41], that is when omitting the low risk/day-to-day factor and the university startup dummy. All models also control for heteroscedasticity, which is the case when the error terms in the regression model

Table 3. Analysis of determinants for employee growth

Variables	Model 1	Model 2
Age	0.038 (0.143)	−1.131 (0.953)
Age squared	–	0.034 (0.026)
Logarithm of citation-weight. patents	−0.708 (0.531)	−0.437 (0.645)
Organisational radicality (yes → no)	0.562 (2.104)	0.013 (2.013)
Low risk/day-to-day	0.136 (1.128)	0.032 (1.183)
Venture capital (no → yes)	4.260* (2.182)	4.230* (2.270)
Academic startup (no → yes)	1.226 (2.483)	1.075 (2.470)
Adjusted R^2	0.25	0.30
F value	2.30*	5.20***

Notes: significance * $p < 0.10$; ** $p < 0.05$; *** $p < 0.01$; robust standard errors, $n = 31$

are not uncorrelated and uniform. This ensures for example that the OLS estimation yields efficient estimates even if error terms are correlated or do not have constant variance.

4 Conclusions and Discussion

The research in this paper addresses whether the trend towards the networked firm hinders startups and small firms from realising their growth potential. More specifically it analyses the degree of overlap between the determinants for acquisition and growth. Such a joint analysis has so far not been carried out in the literature and is possible here because of a personal interview approach that enables the recording of detailed acquisition and other information alongside growth data. The paper combines the theoretical lenses of institutional and transaction cost economics, social network theory, and competence- and resource-based perspectives in economics and management to address the above issue in an integrated manner. As concerns more specifically the first research question derived from the comprehensive and systematic review of different literatures relating to growth, alliancing and acquisitions, the results of the empirical analysis suggest that firm age has no significant association with acquisition likelihood and with firm growth. This suggests a substitutive relationship of this determinant for growth and acquisition. In response to the second research question on whether organisational radicality of an entrant's innovation is positively associated with acquisition and firm growth we find that for both, acquisitions and growth, organisational radicality has no significant effect, which suggests independence for this determinant with regard to growth and acquisition. The extent of patenting as indicator for the technological radicality of an entrant's innovation is also not associated with acquisition likelihood, nor with employee growth. This suggests again an independence of growth and acquisition with regard to this determinant. Finally, as concerns our third research question how VC engagement associates with acquisition and growth we find that VC engagement as an important direct and indirect measure of the extent of networking and alliancing (given its positive association with strategic alliances and its strong association with investor diversity and numbers), is positively associated with acquisition likelihood and employee growth in all specifications. This suggests strong complementarity for acquisition and employee growth for this determinant. In summary, the results suggest that the significant determinants of firm growth are identical to those that determine acquisitions. There are some that are potentially different, i.e. those determinants that are most relevant for acquisitions are of lesser relevance for growth. On the other hand VC engagement is positively associated with both growth and acquisition likelihood, in turn suggesting that external financial resources accessed through networking are generally important (directly and indirectly). The effect of VC engagement on employee growth is consistent with the finding that VC engagement early on leads entrants to a strategic choice that pushes recruitment growth [19]. If entrants are not supported by VCs, then financial resources are more limited, enabling only lower levels of recruitment. However, whilst venture capitalists initially support startups to help them realising their full growth potential, they later may reverse their preferences and push for an acquisition of by an incumbent in order to exit their engagement, especially when market or IPO conditions are adverse [4]. These key results seem generalisable to software-based industries at large, given that acquisitions enable a division of innovative labour leading to an overall more efficient institutional arrangement that also can be understood as a form of networked innovation. As concerns further generalizability, our findings also might apply more broadly if the conditions in another industry resemble those of software: a cumulative product that may impede the growth of young and small firms on their own and involvement of venture capital making trade sales and thus acquisition more necessary. Consistent with this, Table 4 indicates, based on the structured interviews of start-ups, that entrants themselves only rarely consider it to be possible to develop a larger market share on their own. This is consequently also important input for technology and industrial policies, especially as concerns technology entrepreneurship.

Table 4. Fate of small firms not acquired

Variable	Frequency	% of firms	% responses	% choices
Go out of business	17	54.8	53.1	50.0
Go into market niche	16	51.6	50.0	97.1
Merge with other small firm	1	3.2	3.1	100.0

Notes: '% of firms' and '% responses' sums are greater 100% since two or more choices were possible; '% choices' based on the cumulative sum of 'Frequency'

Next to identifying important determinants of firm growth and acquisitions, the analysis also finds some support for the concerns raised by other scholars [30], about levels of radical innovation being too low, and therefore points to the need to consider networking and co-operation as means for this latter type of innovation. Overall, the analysis presented here contributes to the literature by focusing on an element of networking which is crucial in the early stages of new ventures (namely the interaction with VCs) analysed simultaneously with other relevant determinants identified in the context of established theories such as the profiting-from-innovation framework [21]. It jointly addresses acquisition likelihoods and growth by means of an innovative research design and using several variables and model specifications to check the robustness of results in sensitivity analyses, especially as concerns technological radicality (going beyond binary patent thresholds), organisational factors, and firm size. Most importantly, it finds that venture capital matters for both, growth and acquisition, but with different motivations and hence differing support by venture capitalists for each strategy over time.

As concerns more provides guidance for entrepreneurs on how becoming an attractive target by suggesting this requires different managerial actions than realising a start-up's growth potential. This is due to the "fast second" strategy proposed in the management literature for incumbents, in which start-up acquisitions help them to mitigate innovation weaknesses. Managers of young and small firms should thus be considering their specific conditions to make the right choices. For practitioners, the paper thus contributes the important insight that as a resource accessed through networking venture capital determines both acquisition likelihood and growth. However, the motivation of venture capitalists for these latter two is not stable and hence over time their support for growth and their incentives for exiting through a trade sale shift, which, as the paper explains, needs to be accounted for by managers.

As an extension, in a next step a more detailed target perspective could be integrated in the frame of analysis [53], in order to better understand, when other networking factors are more relevant and when venture capitalist preferences change from growth motivations to supporting trade sales and hence acquisition. Furthermore, the analysis could address in more detail aspects of ecosystem evolution, as they have been discussed in the context of secondary software businesses [54] and of vertical industry structure, for example in the telecommunications sector [55].

Appendix: Interview Questions Used in the Analysis

Questions used in the structured interviews for calculation of the Low risk/day-to-day factor variable:

Large firms are so involved with the day-to-day requirements of their customers that they do not have resources for the innovation.

Large firms that lead the market are too risk-averse do carry out the innovation.

Question used in the structured interviews for calculation of the age of the firm:
When was your firm founded?

Question used in the structured interviews for identifying the fate of non-acquired companies:

What happens to start-ups that are not acquired after some years? Do these mostly go out of business and leave the market? Or do most of unacquired firms exist in small but lucrative market niches or merge with another small firm?

Question used in the interviews for identifying organisationally radical innovations:

Would you agree that compared to the competences of the top 3 firms in the industry) innovating your product requires new capabilities or skills of researchers (e.g. only recently taught at universities) or a different structure of R&D in a firm?

References

1. Freeman, J., Carroll, G.R., Hannan, M.T.: The liability of newness: age dependence in organizational death rates. Am. Sociol. Rev. **48**, 692–710 (1983)
2. Davidsson, P., Kirchhoff, B., Hatemi, J.A., Gustavsson, H.: Empirical analysis of business growth factors using Swedish data. J. Small Bus. Manage. **40**(4), 332–350 (2002)
3. Desyllas, P., Hughes, A.: The revealed preferences of high technology acquirers: an analysis of the characteristics of their targets. Cambridge J. Econom. **33**(6), 1089–1111 (2009)
4. Gans, J.S., Hsu, D.H., Stern, S.: When does startup innovation spur the gale of creative destruction? RAND J. Econom. **33**(4), 571–586 (2000)
5. Gambardella, A., Torrisi, S.: Does technological convergence imply convergence in markets? Evidence from the electronics industry. Res. Policy **27**, 445–463 (1998)
6. Hall, B., Ziedonis, R.: The patent paradox revisited: an empirical study of patenting in the U.S. Semiconductor Industry 1979–1995. RAND J. Econom. **32**(1), 101–128 (2001)
7. Linden, G., Somaya, D.: System-on-a-chip integration in the Semiconductor Industry: industry structure and firm strategies. Corp. Ind. Change **12**(2), 545–576 (2003)
8. Chakrabarti, A.K., Rubenstein, A.H.: Interorganizational transfer of technology – a study of adoption of NASA innovations. IEEE Trans. Eng. Manag. **23**(1), 20–34 (1976)
9. Henderson, R.: Underinvestment and incompetence as responses to radical innovation: Evidence from the photolithographic alignment equipment industry. RAND J. Econom. **24**(2), 248–270 (1993)
10. Birkinshaw, J., Van Basten Batenburg, R., Murray, G.: Venturing to succeed. Bus. Strat. Review **13**(4), 1–17 (2002)
11. Sangiovanni-Vincentelli, A.: The tides of EDA. IEEE Des. Test Comput. **29**(6), 5–74 (2003)
12. Grover, V., Purvis, R.L., Segars, A.H.: Exploring ambidextrous innovation tendencies in the adoption of telecommunications technologies. IEEE Trans. Eng. Manag. **54**(2), 268–285 (2007)
13. Morris, D.J., Hay, D.A.: Industrial Economics & Organisation – Theory & Evidence. Oxford University Press, Oxford (1991)
14. Bruno, A.V., Cooper, A.C.: Patterns of development and acquisitions for Silicon Valley Startups. Technovation **1**(4), 275–290 (1982)
15. Penrose, E.: The Theory of the Growth of the Firm. Oxford University Press, Oxford (1959)
16. Mowery, D.C., Oxley, J.E., Silverman, B.S.: Technological overlap and interfirm cooperation: Implications for the resource-based view of the firm. Res. Policy **27**, 507–523 (1998)
17. Gulati, R.: Managing network resources. Oxford University Press, Oxford (2007)
18. Stinchcombe, A.L.: Organizations and social structure. In: March, J.G. (ed.) Handbook of organizations, pp. 142–193. Rand-McNally, Chicago (1965)
19. Kaulio, M.A.: Initial conditions or process of development? Critical incidents in the early stages of new ventures. R&D Manag. **33**(2), 165–175 (2003)
20. Lindsey, L.: Blurring firm boundaries: the role of venture capital in strategic alliances. J. Finan. **63**(3), 1137–1168 (2008)
21. Teece, D.J.: Profiting from technological innovation: Implications for integration, collaboration, licensing and public policy. Res. Policy **15**, 285–305 (1986)

22. Pisano, G.: Profiting from innovation and the intellectual property revolution. Res. Policy **35**, 1122–1130 (2006)
23. Powell, W., Koput, K., Smith-Doerr, L.: Interorganizational collaboration and the locus of innovation: Networks of learning in biotechnology. Admin. Sci. Q. **41**(1), 116–145 (1996)
24. Henderson, R., Clark, K.: Architectural Innovation: The reconfiguration of existing product technologies and the failure of established firms. Admin. Sci. Q. **35**, 9–30 (1990)
25. Jelinek, M., Markham, S.: Industry-university IP relations: Integrating perspectives and policy solutions. IEEE Trans. Eng. Manag. **54**(2), 257–267 (2007)
26. Santoro, M., Chakrabarti, A.: Corporate strategic objectives for establishing relationships with university research centers. IEEE Trans. Eng. Manag. **48**(2), 15–163 (2001)
27. Geisler, E., Furino, A., Kiersuk, T.J.: Toward a conceptual model of cooperative research: Patterns of development and success in university-industry alliances. IEEE Trans. Eng. Manag. **38**(2), 136–145 (1991)
28. Katz, R., Allen, T.J.: Investigating the not invented here (NIH) syndrome: A look at the performance, tenure, and communication patterns of 50 R&D Project groups. R&D Manag. **12**(1), 7–19 (1982)
29. Cohen, W.M., Levinthal, D.A.: Absorptive capacity: a new perspective on learning and innovation. Admin. Sci. Q. **35**, 128–152 (1990)
30. Bingham, R.: In support of an EDATech: pooling resources for competitive advantage. IEEE Des. Test Comput. **20**(6), 74–75 (2003)
31. West, J., Gallagher, S.: Challenges of open innovation: the paradox of firm investment in open-source software. R&D Manag. **36**(3), 319–331 (2006)
32. Utterback, J.M.: Mastering the Dynamics of Innovation. Harvard Business School Press, Boston (1994)
33. Jovanovic, B.: Selection and the evolution of industry. Econometrica **50**, 649–670 (1982)
34. Klepper, S.: Entry, exit, growth and innovation over the product life cycle. Am. Econ. Rev. **86**, 562–583 (1996)
35. Klepper, S.: Firm survival and the evolution of oligopoly. RAND J. Econom. **33**(1), 3–61 (2002)
36. Jovanovic, B., MacDonald, G.M.: The life cycle of a competitive industry. J. Polit. Econ. **102**(2), 322–347 (1994)
37. Helfat, C., Finkelstein, S., Mitchell, W., Peteraf, M., Singh, H., Teece, D., Winter, S.G.: Dynamic Capabilities - Understanding Strategic Change in Organizations. Blackwell Publishing, New York (2007)
38. Wiklund, J., Shepherd, D.: The effectiveness of alliances and acquisitions: the role of resource combination activities. Entrepreneurship Theory Pract. **33**(1), 193–212 (2009)
39. Wagner, M.: Growth of university-based startups and acquisition as an exit strategy in academic entrepreneurship evidence from software-based ventures. Int. J. Entrepreneurship Small Bus. **12**(4), 39–412 (2011)
40. Stuart, T.: Interorganizational alliances and the performance of firms: a study of growth and innovation rates in a high-technology industry. Strateg. Manag. J. **21**, 791–811 (2000)
41. Wagner, M.: Acquisitions as a means of innovation sourcing by incumbents and growth of technology-oriented ventures. Int. J. Tech. Manag. **52**, 118–134 (2010)
42. Bloom, N., Kretschmer, T., Van Reenen, J.: Are family-friendly workplace practices a valuable firm resource? Strateg. Manag. J. **32**, 343–367 (2011)
43. Design Automation and Test Engineering (DATE) conference: DATE Press Preview. http://www.date-conference.com/. Accessed 5 Mar 2006
44. Lee, A.S., Baskerville, R.L.: Generalizing generalizability in information systems research. Inf. Syst. Res. **14**(3), 221–243 (2003)

45. Delmar, F., Davidsson, P., Gartner, W.: Arriving at the high growth firm. J. Bus. Ventur. **18**(2), 189–216 (2003)
46. Shepherd, D., Wiklund, J.: Are we comparing Apples with Apples or Apples with Oranges? Appropriateness of knowledge accumulation across growth studies. Entrepreneurship Theory Pract. **33**(1), 105–123 (2009)
47. Romijn, H., Albaladejo, M.: Determinants of innovation capability in small electronics and software firms in southeast England. Res. Policy **31**, 1053–1067 (2002)
48. MacCallum, R.C., Widaman, K.F., Zhang, S., Hong, S.: Sample size in factor analysis. Psychol. Methods **4**, 84–99 (1999)
49. MacCallum, R.C., Widaman, K.F., Preacher, K.J., Hong, S.: Sample size in factor analysis: the role of model error. Multivar. Behav. Res. **36**, 611–637 (2001)
50. Preacher, K., MacCallum, R.: Exploratory factor analysis in behavior genetics research: Factor recovery with small sample sizes. Behav. Genet. **32**, 153–161 (2002)
51. Costello, A.B., Osborne, J.W.: Best practices in exploratory factor analysis: four recommendations for getting the most from your analysis. Pract. Assess. Res. Eval. **10**(7) (2005). http://pareonline.net/pdf/v10n7a.pdf
52. Allison, P.D.: Change scores as dependent variables in regression analysis. Sociol. Methodol. **20**, 93–114 (1990)
53. Henkel, J., Rønde, T., Wagner, M.: And the winner is – acquired entrepreneurship as a contest yielding radical innovations. Res. Policy **44**, 295–310 (2015)
54. Tyrväinen, P., Warsta, J., Seppänen, V.: Evolution of secondary software businesses: understanding industry dynamics. In: León, G., Bernardos, A.M., Casar, J.R., Kautz, K., De Gross, J.I. (eds.) TDIT 2008. ITIFIP, vol. 287, pp. 381–401. Springer, Boston (2008). doi:10.1007/978-0-387-87503-3_22
55. Tyrväinen, P., Mazhelis, O. (eds.): Vertical Software Industry Evolution - Analysis of Telecom Operator Software. Springer-Physica, Heidelberg (2009). doi:10.1007/978-3-7908-2352-3

Governing Platforms in the Internet of Things

Maximilian Schreieck$^{(\boxtimes)}$, Christoph Hakes, Manuel Wiesche,
and Helmut Krcmar

Chair for Information Systems, Technical University of Munich,
Garching, Germany
maximilian.schreieck@in.tum.de

Abstract. The ambivalent paradigm Internet of Things (IoT) is gaining importance in today's industries. To manage the various devices built on different technologies and to apply complex event-triggered business rules to the data streams, platforms are necessary tools for almost all use cases. In the recent years, hundreds of vendors entered the intransparent IoT platform market, from small startups focusing on niches, to large enterprise vendors offering professional solutions. These platforms need tools to orchestrate the interactions between the different sides involved, so-called platform governance mechanisms. The purpose of this multiple case study analysis is to explore the platform governance mechanisms applied in IoT platforms. To achieve this goal, we explored the governance concepts of eight selected platforms in a multiple case study analysis, resulting in a description of the important aspects and differences regarding platform governance. Moreover, the four main trade-offs that platform vendors must be aware of are subsequently discussed. In a last step, an evaluation and discussion of the contribution to theory and practice is provided.

Keywords: Platform · Software ecosystems · Platform governance · Internet of things · IoT platform · Openness · Control · Boundary resources

1 Introduction

In the uprising Internet of Things (IoT), the concept of platforms has received a significant amount of attention in the recent years, leading to a large number of solutions that emerged with the purpose: to interconnect smart objects. In 2015, Amazon presented their "AWS IoT Platform" and IBM opened the new Watson IoT headquarter in Munich. Analysts state that the market for IoT platforms will grow to $1.6 billion by 2021 [1], underlining the economic importance of IoT. Beyond the context of IoT, platforms have transformed the way products and services are being consumed and managed to attract and lock-in large numbers of participants [2]. Today's most influential businesses are those that bring together two or more groups of entities in a platform ecosystem [3]. Governing the platform ecosystem, i.e. managing the collaboration of the different actors, has emerged as a key challenge and has thus been well discussed in recent literature on IT platforms [e.g. 4, 5].

Various studies compared platform governance mechanisms mainly in business-to-consumer (B2C) markets, such as in the field of mobile applications [6, 7] or digital payment [8, 9]. Nevertheless, there is no systematic research available regarding the

© Springer International Publishing AG 2017
A. Ojala et al. (Eds.): ICSOB 2017, LNBIP 304, pp. 32–46, 2017.
https://doi.org/10.1007/978-3-319-69191-6_3

governance structures of IoT platforms, even though their current high popularity and potential impact on the future Internet. Although, the IoT is a suitable empirical context to provide theoretical insights on some understudied issues in the literature on platforms. In the context of the IoT in general, the research and development challenges to create a smart world are enormous. Compared to other markets, the IoT is still in the very beginning when it comes to industry standards and established business models. Other unique characteristics of the IoT ecosystem are the particularly heterogeneous actors (e.g. end-users, device manufacturers, complementors, etc.) an unusual large number of 'sides' (see Chap. 4), and its proneness to platform-to-platform partnerships (see Chap 5). Those characteristics underline the specialty of this ecosystem and are of both theoretical and practical importance. Due to the fact that existing governance models do not always fit for this strongly diverse market, further research on the governance mechanisms in the IoT market is needed to determine the most important factors that most likely guarantee success to its provider.

The goal of this paper is to focus on this research gap by describing the ongoing development and to evaluate differences of the governance mechanisms in the emerging market of IoT platforms. Moreover, the strategic trade-offs that must be considered when those mechanisms are implemented will be analyzed. With the help of a multiple case study we identify exemplary causes and effects of those design decisions and help to underline the most important trade-offs of the governance implementations in the field of IoT platforms.

2 Background

This chapter provides the theoretical background for digital platforms, platform governance and platforms in the IoT.

2.1 Digital Platforms and Platform Governance

Platforms often serve as a core element of a larger business ecosystem which is built around it by the platform owner or vendor [10]. In this context, producers of complementary products and services are termed "complementors" [11], and all stakeholders interacting on the platform (the users or contributors) are commonly referred to as sides [12]. Thus, multi-sided platforms (MSPs) generate value by connecting two or more different parties who want to exchange products, services or information, in most cases complementors and customers [5].

The platform owner and the various sides involved form the platform ecosystem, which is typically characterized by indirect network effects: The attractiveness for its end-users is strongly correlated with the participation or the availability of offerings from the other side. Simply said, "the more users who adopt the platform, the more valuable the platform becomes to the owner and to the users" [10 p. 418]. A mall with no shops will not attract any customers, and a mall lacking customers will not attract any shops to open a subsidiary in it.

Organizations where platforms play a very important role are information technology-driven businesses. All major player from the IT industry like Microsoft,

Apple, Google, Amazon, IBM, Intel, Cisco, ARM and many other firms, build hardware and software products around platforms. They provide services for computers, smartphones or consumer electronic devices that serve as platforms in the regarding industry, forming business landscapes led by the platform owner [3]. From this technology-oriented perspective, platforms can further be defined as "a set of stable components that supports variety and evolvability in a system by constraining the linkages among the other components" [13 p. 3].

In contrary to the technical design, the functionalities for its users or the IT architecture of platforms, the goal of the platform governance is to orchestrate the communication between the different actors [14]. The interplay of the actors is orchestrated by the platform owner by means of platform governance, the "partitioning of decision-making authority between platform owners and [...] developers, control mechanisms, and pricing and pie-sharing structures" [5]. Governance has been identified as what holds ecosystems together at its core, beside the technical features it offers [7]. The right governance strategy brings together the actors on a platform and aligns their incentives making the ecosystem flourish [4]. However, as shown in recent literature reviews as for example by Sun, Gregor and Keating [15], IS research does not yet provide conclusive insights on how software platform ecosystems can be successfully governed, leaving practitioners to trial and error when they set up and run platforms. In an earlier studies [16, 17], we have identified and applied platform governance concepts (Table 1) which we will use as starting point for the analysis of the multiple case study in this paper. Applying these concepts often results in tradeoffs that have to be solved for specific platforms. For example, by enabling openness, a platform owner gives up control and thus needs to balance openness with suitable control mechanisms [4]. The concepts are therefore a first try to structure platform governance concepts and are reflected in the discussion.

Table 1. Concepts of design and governance of platform ecosystems [based on 16]

Concept	Aspects		Literature
Roles	• Number and order of sides • Ownership	• Distribution of power • Relationship to stakeholders	[3, 18]
Pricing and Revenue Sharing	• Achieving network effects • Barriers to market entry	• Subsidizing of one or more sides	[19, 20]
Boundary Resources	• Software tools (API, SDK) • Documentation	• Data	[6, 21]
Openness	• Granting access to technology	• Giving up control over technology	[4, 9]
Control	• Informal control mechanisms	• Formal control mechanisms	[22, 23]
Technical Design	• Modularity • Interfaces	• Compatibility	[13, 24]
Competitive Strategy	• Competition • Co-opetition, collaboration	• Absorption & Envelopment • Public Relations	[25, 26]
Trust	• Relationship complementor – platform owner	• Relationship end-user – platform	[27, 28]

2.2   Platforms in the Internet of Things

In the IoT, communication takes place among devices of multiple types. Already twenty years ago, machines have been connected via dedicated leased lines to allow communication between the different apparatuses. Back then, every single project has been an individual customer-specific end-to-end project, lasting six to twelve months, resulting in enormous costs. Hence, there was a need for a common standard application platform which hides the heterogeneity of the devices by providing a common working environment to them [29]. The fast-growing IoT market has not yet brought up a champion in the fight for the IoT software platform standard, even though Schlautmann, Levy, Keeping and Pankert [30] stated that the service enabler (i.e. platform provider) will likely occupy 30–40% share of the total value in the IoT value chain.

In the recent years, a lot of companies from different industries claimed to offer an "IoT Platform". But a closer comparison of those products and the concepts behind them reveals vast differences. Newcomer in the field of IoT platforms are confused by those complex offerings and dissimilarities, especially when confronted with so called "platforms" that only include single elements of a mature IoT platform.

In this paper, we define IoT platforms based on their capabilities. So called IoT Application Enablement Platforms (AEP) consist of seven building blocks [10]:

- **Connectivity & Normalization:** Device interface services that provide the needed abstraction and normalization to ensure that all devices can be interacted with.
- **Device Management**: Ensuring that functions like activation, configuration, device monitoring, and provisioning software updates are able to be fulfilled and maintained cost effectively.
- **Database**: Providing the foundation for applications and analytics, should be scalable for big data.
- **Event Processing & Action Management**: Set of business rules and logics defining what processes are triggered in response to specified events.
- **Analytics**: Both to extract the value from the data and to keep the user from drowning in too much monotonous information.
- **Visualization**: Enabling the users to recognize patterns and observe trends from dashboards.
- **External Interfaces**: Helping to connect to enterprise or consumer applications and third party systems.

3   Methodology and Cases

To provide an overview of the existing governance structures in the IoT, we apply the platform governance framework (Table 1) to eight different IoT platforms. To yield a robust and generalizable understanding of the platform governance concepts in the IoT, we aimed for a heterogeneous sampling [31] along the dimensions size (big players such as IBM vs. startups such as Cumulocity), target group (industrial such as Carriots vs. consumer oriented such as Arrayent) and breadth (industry specific such as TankTaler vs. generic such as Cumulocity). It was conducted with data collected from

117 publically available sources: archival data from existing case studies and publications, press releases, online news and information available on the company websites. In four cases where further information was needed, semi-structured interviews with the regarding IoT companies were used as additional sources. The guidelines for the interviews not only contained questions related to the research questions, but also covered topics that were derived from the business model canvas in order to get a full understanding of the platforms business strategy [32].

For analyzing the data from the interviews, the statements about different characteristics of the IoT platforms were systematically structured according to the platform governance framework. During the iterative coding procedure, the framework has been updated several times to fit this unique market. Finally, the data for each of the selected platforms has been compared in a qualitative data analysis in order to identify the similarities and key differences between them [33].

The eight platforms in the multiple case study are as follows. **Arrayent Connect Platform** was founded in 2005 and is the platform with the longest history in the multiple case study. Its customers are consumer brands, mostly from the smart home area, which are implementing IoT solutions in their products and systems. **AWS IoT** is a further module for Amazon's cloud services AWS (Amazon Web Services). Amazon takes a broad, industry-independent approach towards its users and heavily relies on the development expertise of its customers and their partners. **Carriots** is a proprietary cloud-based application enablement platform specially designed for the IoT. Since Carriots was one of the first movers in the IoT platform market, it holds expertise in almost all industry verticals. **CloudPlugs:** Even though the vendor markets its product as an industry-independent solution, almost half of their customers are settled in the telecommunications industry, using CloudPlugs for energy management, security or home automation solutions. **Cumulocity** is a platform that takes a horizontal approach in the market and focuses on enterprise customers that are looking for solutions to link and manage their connected machines or products. **TankTaler** is specialized in the Connected Car segment. The platform is the largest connected car platform in Europe and the only Hardware-specific IoT platform in the multiple case study. **ThingWorx** is a platform that has been merged by PTC with other solutions like Axeda or KepWare after their acquisition in the recent years. The IoT AEP is available either from cloud, on premise, federated or embedded, to fit the needs of any scenario in various industry segments. **Watson IoT Platform** is IBM's comparably young solution in the IoT market. The platform owner is offering extensions for the platform in the Bluemix catalogue.

4   Results on Governance Mechanisms

The analysis of the governance mechanisms of IoT platforms will be presented according to the dimensions from Table 1.

Roles. The number of sides varies between all analyzed platforms. One side that all platforms have in common is the end-user or customer side, since this is the focus group of all vendors that generate revenues. To promote their product and bring it closer to the potential customers, all platforms take advantage of their extensive partner networks. Hence, all platforms must not only deal with the customers, but also with the intermediary sales partners on the demand side. For example, Arrayent needs to convince customers that the Arrayent IoT platform for smart homes creates value for them. At the same time Arrayent needs to engage with sales channel partners to market the platform.

On the supply side, the side that potentially offers further functionalities or services to the customers, the strategies of the platforms vary dramatically. At present, most of the analyzed platforms do not offer a marketplace that enables trade between those two sides. Nevertheless, the platforms all use modules or services from partners and integrate them in their own product. As a peculiarity for IoT platforms, we identified the devices and device partners as an additional platform side. Many platform vendors work together with device manufacturers in order to guarantee a smooth integration and connection of the users' devices, or even provide their own specialized devices. Accordingly, Arrayent partners with device manufacturers such as Osram and Whirlpool.

It is difficult to say if the IoT platforms in the multiple case study are real MSPs. According to Hagiu and Wright [34], the direct interaction between the multiple sides sets MSPs apart from other business models like resellers or fully vertically integrated firms. Figure 1 depicts this theoretic description of the MSP model and compares it with the two platform models that we identified: A "standard" and an "advanced" IoT platform model.

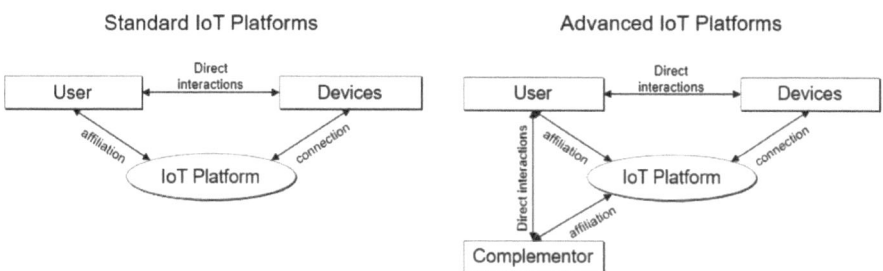

Fig. 1. The multi-sided platform model in theory and IoT practice [see also 34].

In this context, standard IoT platforms are those without marketplaces. Hence, complementors do not have access to the platform, and cannot offer further services for the platform user. The two sides of the standard IoT platforms are the users and the devices, but it is arguable if devices represent a side, since they are not humans or organizations and the interaction between the two sides needs to be evaluated completely different. Advanced IoT platforms involve marketplaces. Here, complementors can directly interact with users, and offer additional services to the demand side. We therefore categorized them as an MSP.

Regarding the order of sides, most platform vendors try to focus on the demand side first, before they open the platform for further developers. According to the mentioned lack of marketplaces on most IoT platforms, those platforms are still in the phase where they try to foster the user base, before opening their platform to the supply side.

Depending on the use case, the state of the ownership of the platform differs from case to case. For example, one platform vendor offers a "Private Edition" of his platform where customers deploy the platform in their own data center, and use the so called "white-labeled" platform to offer their own solutions under their own brand. In such cases, the ownership is passed over to the client in a special licensing model. In other, more prevalent cases, the customers can sign up to use the platform with all its services, but the ownership stays with the platform vendor the whole time.

Boundary Resources. All of the analyzed application enablement platforms offer APIs and SDKs as technical boundary resources for the platform users to enable a fast and smooth integration of their devices. Additionally, most of the platforms also have starter kits available. Regarding the social boundary resources, we identified an online documentation for all IoT platforms in the multiple case study. Most documentations also include step-by-step tutorials, guides and code samples that help developers to connect their devices, gateways or existing systems to the platform. Some platforms also offer video tutorials or webcasts. All platforms also offer a support or help center that serves as first point of contact in case a customer needs assistance. Besides two of the analyzed platforms, all platforms offer forums to support the exchange of information among their users and to make use of their technical knowledge by letting them reply to other users' questions.

Pricing and Revenue Sharing. Besides two of the analyzed platforms, all platforms offer a free trial of their platforms as part of their pricing model to achieve network effects and strengthen trust among their potential customers. For example, Cumulocity has introduced a 30 day trial access in 2016. Besides the free platform trials for the users, a subsidization of the sides could not be identified among the IoT platforms. The price for the end-users of the platforms depends on various factors, like the hosting option (cloud vs on-premises, if available), the number of devices or gateways that are connected, the amount of data traffic and data storage used, the application area, as well as subscriptions to further optional functionalities and applications. The individual and industry specific solutions that Cumulocity offers, illustrate that pricing is also specific to customers and their deals rather than standardized. The governance mechanism of revenue sharing is only applicable for platforms that either offer a white-labeling or that have a dedicated application marketplace. Here, third-party developers can sell their own applications for the platform and share the respective earnings with the platform owner that is responsible in setting up and maintaining the marketplace.

Openness. The openness of IoT platforms can be analyzed among two dimensions: The openness of the platform towards its users and towards third-party developers. The former highlights the platforms' degree of openness by granting access to new users. All platforms except one allow the self-registration of new users, upon which they can directly start using the platform. Only one platform is more restrictive concerning the accessibility of the platform, since the vendor must be contacted first.

In terms of openness towards third-party developers, each platform takes a different approach. TankTaler is not open for external developers to sell platform extensions to the platform users. The Cumulocity platform enables the extension of the platforms' functionalities through applications uploaded by the users, but does not offer a marketplace. Other vendors such as Carriot and CloudPlugs offer dedicated application marketplaces for platform extensions or plan to do so.

Control. For an AEP without an application marketplace, the examination of the applied control mechanisms as proposed by Tiwana, Konsynski and Bush [35] is rather problematic: Since there is no input or output on the platform but the data streams from and towards to the devices, the control aspects applied on the platforms are not related to the traditional platform governance mechanisms. Among the IoT platforms that offer a marketplace, we identified formal control mechanisms such as output control, input and process control. For example Amazon's AWS platform implements customer ratings as output control.

Technical Design. All platforms that offer an application marketplace require a possibility to integrate additional applications. On the contrary, there are platforms available that allow the extension of its functionalities by external applications, but do not offer a dedicated marketplace for such. Besides the APIs, some platforms even offer more dedicated interface solutions in order to integrate the platform to existing systems or other ecosystems. For example, Cumulocity's solution can be integrated with other SaaS products via Zapier, a service that connects diverse SaaS web applications. On the identified application marketplaces, a variety of applications is available that supports the communication of the regarding IoT platform with external systems. All platforms in the multiple case study analysis offer a wide range of device connectivity. Next to the communication via Ethernet or Wi-Fi, other types like cellular, satellite or low power/short range communication (e.g. Bluetooth, ZigBee, etc.) are regularly supported. Common communication protocols among these platforms include HTTP and MQTT.

Competitive Strategy. To promote their IoT platforms and to publish news and updates, all of the analyzed vendors use an array of media channels for advertisement. Social media accounts, blogs, and e-mail newsletters are among the most common ways to raise the attention of potential clients. Furthermore, all listed platforms use specialized trade fairs to get in touch with their users and to sell their solutions to potential customers. All identified application marketplace vendors situated themselves in the conflict of absorption by offering their own extensions and applications on their marketplaces. For example, IBM offers various own applications such as analytics applications on the BlueMix platform. Those applications stand in competition to the third-party developers' offerings, and hence lead to direct competition between the platform owner and the complementors. On the other hand, absorption might be an important part of the monetization model of the platform vendors, as observed on other platforms (e.g. Android, see [36]). All platform owners underline the high importance of their strategic partnerships. Collaboration seems to be of much higher importance in the IoT platform market than fighting against the competitors.

Trust. All IoT platforms in the multiple case study analysis provide information regarding the security of their solutions (e.g. data security, security certifications or redundancy) separately. For most IoT platforms, reference cases of well-known customers are a good measure to strengthen trust among potential future users and to show-off expertise in the industry. For example, Cumulocity offers rich descriptions of existing use cases on their website. The free trial of the platform, as well as the available starter kits are further instruments that aim on reducing the perceived risk and strengthen the trust in the offered solutions. Enabling customer ratings and user reviews of the platform extensions are two instruments to strengthen trust, and have been identified on one platform marketplace.

The trust between the user and the complementor is also an important factor with a high influence on the platform's success. Anyhow, the platform owner can only support the sides to help build this trust at the most, therefore this issue has not been further examined in this study.

5   Discussion on Governance Trade-Offs

In the previous chapter, the platform governance mechanisms identified in the multiple case study analysis have been explained in detail. In this chapter, the four main strategic trade-offs of IoT platform providers will be examined to get a better understanding of what impact the strategic decisions in the governance models have on the business model (Table 2). The relevant literature for each of the trade-offs is provided in the following discussion.

Table 2. Governance trade-offs in IoT platforms (Source: own analysis based on [16]).

Trade-off	Description
Vertical vs. horizontal market approach	Focus on use cases across different industries with less specialized functionality or on industry-specific use cases with highly specialized functionality
Degree of openness	Degree to which the platform is open to third-party contributions in terms of technological openness as well as mechanisms applied to control the third parties
Complexity of partner networks	Balance between keeping power within a complex network of partners and expanding the network through building trust in reliable business partners
Compatibility to IoT standards	Approach to either embraces as many standards as possible or to focus on single or even a self-developed standard for IoT data and processes

Vertical vs. horizontal market approach. All IoT platforms in the multiple case study can be categorized as either horizontal or vertical platform regarding their market approach. A vertical market is one in which all customers are in one particular industry [37]. Some IoT platforms specialized on particular IoT segments and market their services towards the regarding focus group. In contrast, a horizontal market is one in which all customers use a product with a common goal, regardless of what industry they are operating in [37]. In the case of IoT platforms, the common goal of the platform users is to connect their "things" with the IoT and to profit from the resulting enhanced opportunities. The most platforms in the multiple case study follow a horizontal market approach. They try to reach customers from different industry segments with various problems and requirements.

"While a lot of the action is happening at the vertical application level, the ultimate prize for many ambitious players in the space is to become the software platform upon which all vertical applications in the Internet of Things will be built" [38]. Hereby Turck [38] emphasizes the high aim for IoT platforms to not only address customers from one vertical, but several or all verticals to become the platform leader in the IoT. The eight platforms in the multiple case study directly compete against each other, since they are all open to mostly all IoT segments. Thus, the potential market is bigger, compared to the specialized, vertical IoT platforms. In the same time, competition for horizontal platforms is tougher due to the high number of competitors.

Degree of openness. The degree of openness towards the platform complementors is another strategic governance trade-off that IoT platforms must deal with. According to the preceding findings, we derived four stages of openness towards platform complementors:

1. **Closed**: In terms of openness towards third-party developers, closed platforms do not allow any kind of participation of complementors in the platform ecosystem.
2. **Participation possible**: In the second stage of this model, a participation for external developers is not precluded on the platforms, but an open marketplace is not (yet) available. Hence, the degree of openness is higher compared to the closed platforms, but not as high as on platforms that offer an application marketplace.
3. **Marketplace with tight control**: IoT platforms that include a marketplace on which third-party developers can offer additional services. The restrictions for platform complementors to offer and sell extensions can be categorized as tight control mechanisms on all examined IoT platforms.
4. **Marketplace with loose control**: An even higher stage of openness is imaginable in the model with more loose control mechanisms towards the platform complementors.

In IoT platforms, reasons to opt for openness differ from standard MSPs. Positive network effects that represent one main reason to open MSPs [4] are not as strong in the IoT market due to the market's high degree of fragmentation. Still, openness helps to co-create value within the partner network and trigger innovation. Since this strategic choice might change in the future, the degree of openness is not a fixed value, but rather an evolution in the lifecycle of IoT platforms.

Complexity of partner network. The IoT platform owner must deal with various stakeholders in his ecosystem. Platform providers form the core of the ecosystem and supply the critical building blocks for their partners [10]. Understanding the roles of business partners in the platform ecosystem is important for understanding the ecosystem development [12]. Among the various IoT platforms in the multiple case study analysis, we identified four distinct groups of partners in the platform ecosystem.

Platform partners can act as resellers. Resellers offer another company's platform to potential customers and get a share for the generated revenue. In some cases, the customers do not even notice that the platform is from another company, as some platform vendors offer so-called "white-labeling" solutions. In such cases, the platform will be rebranded and gets a new look and feel per the reseller's corporate identity. For some companies, this is the only sales channel for the platform, since there is no way for end-users to subscribe to the services of the platform directly.

The second group of potential partners in an IoT platform ecosystem are the **device integrators.** Those can either be device manufacturers, building devices especially for the platform or helping IoT platforms to connect their devices with the platform. Device integrators can also be third-party developers that program device-unique interfaces or platform extensions that make it easier for the platform users to connect their devices to the platform. In some cases, the platform owner directly offers such interfaces, in other cases such extensions are offered by external developers.

The third group of partners in the IoT platform partner ecosystem identified during the multiple case study analysis are the **platform complementors**. Those partners help the platform owner to build features as services for the platform users. Usually, those applications are then offered (for free or paid) on the platform's marketplace to the demand-side of the platform.

Finally, the **infrastructure providers** form the fourth group of partners that are relevant to an IoT platform vendor. In most cases, the data of IoT platforms is hosted on external servers of the platform vendors' business partners. Often other components of the IT infrastructure are not part of the core business of the platform vendor and are therefore sourced from partners.

Keeping this complicated partnering network stable comes with a difficult balance between keeping power (by holding the number of partners on a low level) and trust in reliable business partners and expanding the network. This is an important trade-off for every analyzed IoT platform.

Compatibility to IoT standards. It is a complex task to decide which of the competing technologies in the IoT fits best for a specific (business) goal and almost impossible to predict which standard will evolve and will be future-proof. Researchers even claimed that the lack of standardization and device heterogeneity is keeping the IoT from further growth [12]. Especially for horizontal platforms, which promise to be open for all possible IoT devices, keeping track of all available interfaces and connection types is a very hard to manage task. Those platforms need to offer a wide range of interfaces for their users and to apply to new standards in order to stay competitive and to satisfy their customers' needs. Possible strategies for platform owners to tackle this problem are described in the following.

One way to address the mentioned problem of volatile standards in the IoT is to integrate all technologies through interfaces and the support of all possible communication protocols. This would satisfy all platform users and lead to a superior competitive position of the platform in the market. Unfortunately, this is an almost impossible task, since new IoT-related standards and updates for existing technologies are published almost daily. Keeping track and supporting all of those different interfaces would require a massive amount of manpower and hence result in very high personal and maybe also licensing costs.

Another possible strategy for platform owners is to specialize on one or more IoT industries or use cases. Especially in the industrial IoT, the amount of used protocols is still very large, but the customer requirements are at least more similar.

Partnering with experts and specialized companies in the addressed IoT segment (e.g. SIs in the regarding industry) might also be a solution to outsource the problem of the volatile IoT standards. On the downside, this might lead to a high dependency on the business partners and experts.

In order to create more power to enforce the global adoption of specific already supported standards, IoT platforms already form or join alliances. The downside of this strategy is that unwanted knowledge transfer to competitors could happen due to the strong cooperation that is needed to reach the common goal.

The acquisition of specialized competitors is another strategy for platform owners that helps companies to acquire not only experts but also knowledge about specific IoT standards within a very short time. This strategy is intimately connected with high costs and therefore high risks.

Last but not least, the introduction of marketplaces for interfaces is another approach to outsource the problem of the changing IoT standards. Third-party contributors could develop fitting interfaces for the platform and would get a revenue share for each sold extension. Initial high setup costs for the marketplace and the support around it are a disadvantage of this strategy.

Contributions to theory and practice. The trade-offs we derive contribute to literature on platform governance and help practitioners in the IoT market. In literature, platform governance has been analyzed for various different platforms mainly in B2C markets such as mobile applications [6] or digital payment [8, 9]. However, B2C markets exhibit a simpler structure than the heterogeneous, multi-layered IoT market. It is therefore worthwhile to analyze how established mechanisms of platform governance can be applied and what trade-offs arise in their implementation.

We confirm trade-offs that are discussed in the B2C context and extend existing findings. First, we show that the trade-off between vertical and horizontal integration [34] is even more relevant in the IoT market than in standard MSPs as the IoT technology is highly complex extending to different layers from the devices to the applications. Second, we contribute to the ongoing discussion on the right degree of openness that platform owners need to identify [4, 9]. We not only confirm the relevance of the trade-off but also define specific degrees of openness for IoT platforms, referring to both the technology and provider level [9]. Future research could compare different IoT platforms that focus on a specific degree of openness and compare their success. Third, we discuss the value of partner networks in IoT markets that has rarely been analyzed for B2C markets [26]. The findings might prove useful for markets that are less complex but also prone to value cocreation on platforms through partnerships such as in the area of enterprise research systems [39]. Lastly, we open up the discussion on how to handle the issue of complex and heterogeneous standards in the IoT markets. As standards will dynamically evolve over the next years, future research could engage in longitudinal case studies on successful strategies to cope with standards.

Other issues for future research projects are, first, the comparison of the analyzed governance mechanisms in different markets and to focus on each of the four trade-offs to deepen the understanding of the governance challenges. This could be done with in-depth case studies that provide richer insights than a multiple case study does. Second, it would be worthwhile to reconsider the initial structure of governance mechanisms that we used as basis for our study. For example, Gulati, Puranam and Tushman [40] provide a framework that differentiates governance along the dimensions open vs. closed boundaries and high vs. low stratification. This would also be applicable to the IoT context and could help to generalize our findings. Third, our study does not specifically focus on governance of infrastructure providers and device manufacturers in IoT platforms as greater access to the cases would be necessary. This is a follow-up question for exploratory case studies which grant deeper access to the technological ecosystem of the IoT platform in focus. For practice we first show how established governance mechanisms such as boundary resources or control are applied in the IoT market. We thereby provide an overview on relevant decisions a platform owner has to make when establishing an IoT platform. Second, we illustrate main trade-offs that emerge when making these decisions. Our discussion on these trade-offs provides starting points for practitioners how to resolve them for their platform.

Acknowledgement. We thank the German Federal Ministry for Economic Affairs and Energy for funding this research as part of the project 01MD15001D (ExCELL).

References

1. Scully, P., Holbrook, K., Glynn, P.: The Rise of IoT Platforms. IoT Analytics (2016)
2. Smedlund, A., Faghankhani, H.: Platform orchestration for efficiency, development, and innovation. In: Forty Eighth Hawaii International Conference on System Sciences, Hawaii, pp. 1380–1388 (2015)
3. Eisenmann, T., Parker, G., van Alstyne, M.: Platform Strategies for two-sided markets. Harvard Bus. Rev. **84**(10) (2006)
4. Boudreau, K.: Open platform strategies and innovation: granting access vs. devolving control. Manag. Sci. **56**, 1849–1872 (2010)
5. Tiwana, A.: Platform Ecosystems: Aligning Architecture, Governance, and Strategy. Morgan Kaufmann, Amsterdam (2014)
6. Eaton, B., Elaluf-Calderwood, S., Sorensen, C., Yoo, Y.: Distributed tuning of boundary resources: the case of Apple's iOS service system. MIS Q. **39**, 217–243 (2015)
7. Manner, J., Nienaber, D., Schermann, M., Krcmar, H.: Six principles for governing mobile platforms. In: 11th International Conference on Wirtschaftsinformatik Proceedings, Leipzig (2013)
8. Kazan, E., Damsgaard, J.: An investigation of digital payment platform designs: a comparative study of four european solutions. In: Twenty Second European Conference on Information Systems, Tel Aviv (2014)
9. Ondrus, J., Gannamaneni, A., Lyytinen, K.: The impact of openness on the market potential of multi-sided platforms: a case study of mobile payment platforms. J. Inf. Technol. **30**, 260–275 (2015)
10. Gawer, A., Cusumano, M.A.: Industry platforms and ecosystem innovation. J. Prod. Innov. Manag. **31**, 417–433 (2014)

11. Teece, D.J.: Explicating dynamic capabilities: The nature and microfoundations of (sustainable) enterprise performance. Strateg. Manag. J. **28**, 1319–1350 (2007)
12. Toivanen, T., Mazhelis, O., Luoma, E.: Network analysis of platform ecosystems: the case of internet of things ecosystem. In: Fernandes, João M., Machado, R.J., Wnuk, K. (eds.) ICSOB 2015. LNBIP, vol. 210, pp. 30–44. Springer, Cham (2015). doi:10.1007/978-3-319-19593-3_3
13. Baldwin, C.Y., Woodard, C.J.: The architecture of platforms: a unified view. In: Gawer, A. (ed.) Platforms, Markets and Innovation. Cheltenham, UK (2009)
14. Hein, A., Schreieck, M., Wiesche, M., Krcmar, H.: Multiple-case analysis on governance mechanism of multi-sided platforms. In: Nissen, V., Stelzer, D., Straßburger, S., Fischer, D. (eds.) Multikonferenz Wirtschaftsinformatik, pp. 1613–1624. Universitätsverlag Ilmenau, Ilmenau (2016)
15. Sun, R., Gregor, S., Keating, B.: Information technology platforms: conceptualisation and a review of emerging research in the IS discipline. In: Twenty-Sixth Australasian Conference on Information Systems, Adelaide (2015)
16. Schreieck, M., Wiesche, M., Krcmar, H.: Design and governance of platform ecosystems: key concepts and issues for future research. In: Twenty-Fourth European Conference on Information Systems, Istanbul (2016)
17. Schreieck, M., Wiesche, M., Hein, A., Krcmar, H.: Governance of nonprofit platforms – Onboarding mechanisms for a refugee information platform. In: SIG GlobDev Ninth Annual Workshop, Dublin (2016)
18. Bakos, Y., Katsamakas, E.: Design and ownership of two-sided networks: implications for internet platforms. J. Manag. Inf. Syst. **25**, 171–202 (2008)
19. Armstrong, M.: Competition in two-sided markets. Rand J. Econ. **37**, 668–691 (2006)
20. Evans, D.S.: Economics of vertical restraints for multi-sided platforms. SSRN Electron. J. (2013)
21. Bianco, V.D., Myllarniemi, V., Komssi, M., Raatikainen, M.: The role of platform boundary resources in software ecosystems: a case study. In: IEEE/IFIP Conference on Software Architecture, Sydney (2014)
22. Evans, D.S.: Governing bad behavior by users of multi-sided platforms. Berkeley Technol. Law J. **27**, 1202–1249 (2012)
23. Ghazawneh, A., Henfridsson, O.: Balancing platform control and external contribution in third-party development: The boundary resources model. Inf. Syst. J. **23**, 173–192 (2013)
24. Visnjic, I., Cennamo, C.: The gang of four: acquaintances, friends or foes? Towards an integrated perspective on platform competition. SSRN Electron. J. (2013)
25. Brandenburger, A.M., Nalebuff, B.J.: Co-opetition: 1. A revolutionary mindset that combines competition and co-operation; 2. The game theory strategy that's changing the game of business. Doubleday, New York, NY (1998)
26. Mantena, R., Saha, R.L.: Co-opetition between differentiated platforms in two-sided markets. J. Manag. Inf. Syst. **29**, 109–140 (2012)
27. Hurni, T., Huber, T.: The interplay of power and trust in platform ecosystems of the enterprise application software industry. In: Twenty Second European Conference on Information Systems, Tel Aviv (2014)
28. Nambisan, S.: Information technology and product/service innovation: a brief assessment and some suggestions for future research. J. Assoc. Inf. Syst. (JAIS) **14**, 215–226 (2013)
29. Nakhuva, B., Champaneria, T.: Study of various internet of things platforms. Int. J. Comput. Sci. Eng. Surv. **6**, 61–74 (2015)
30. Schlautmann, A., Levy, D., Keeping, S., Pankert, G.: Wanted: Smart market-makers for the "Internet of Things". Prism (2011)

31. Yin, R.K.: Case study research: Design and methods. Sage publications, Thousand Oaks, California (2013)
32. Osterwalder, A., Pigneur, Y.: Business model generation: a handbook for visionaries, game changers, and challengers. Flash Reproductions, Toronto (2010)
33. Huberman, A.M., Miles, M.B.: Data management and analysis methods. In: Handbook of Qualitative Research. Sage Publications, Thousand Oaks (1994)
34. Hagiu, A., Wright, J.: Multi-sided platforms. Int. J. Ind. Organ. **43**, 162–174 (2015)
35. Tiwana, A., Konsynski, B., Bush, A.A.: Platform evolution: coevolution of platform architecture, governance, and environmental dynamics. Inf. Syst. Res. **21**, 675–687 (2010)
36. The Information. https://www.theinformation.com/Google-s-Confidential-Android-Contracts-Show-Rising-Requirements
37. Gust. http://blog.gust.com/what-is-the-difference-between-a-vertical-and-a-horizontal-market/
38. TechCrunch. http://techcrunch.com/2013/05/25/making-sense-of-the-internet-of-things/
39. Ceccagnoli, M., Forman, C., Huang, P., Wu, D.J.: Cocreation of value in a platform ecosystem: the case of enterprise software. MIS Q. **36**, 263–290 (2012)
40. Gulati, R., Puranam, P., Tushman, M.: Meta-organization design: rethinking design in interorganizational and community contexts. Strateg. Manag. J. **33**, 571–586 (2012)

Software Business Development

Pricing of Data Products in Data Marketplaces

Samuel A. Fricker[1,2(✉)] and Yuliyan V. Maksimov[1]

[1] i4Ds Centre for Requirements Engineering,
University of Applied Sciences Northwestern Switzerland (FHNW),
Windisch, Switzerland
{samuel.fricker,yuliyan.maksimov}@fhnw.ch
[2] Software Engineering Research Laboratory (SERL-Sweden),
Blekinge Institute of Technology, Karlskrona, Sweden
samuel.fricker@bth.se

Abstract. Mobile computing and the Internet of Things promises massive amounts of data for big data analytic and machine learning. A data sharing economy is needed to make that data available for companies that wish to develop smart systems and services. While digital markets for trading data are emerging, there is no consolidated understanding of how to price data products and thus offer data vendors incentives for sharing data. This paper uses a combined keyword search and snowballing approach to systematically review the literature on the pricing of data products that are to be offered on marketplaces. The results give insights into the maturity and character of data pricing. They enable practitioners to select a pricing approach suitable for their situation and researchers to extend and mature data pricing as a topic.

Keywords: Data pricing · Data marketplace · Systematic literature review

1 Introduction

With the rise of Mobile Computing and the Internet of Things, massive amounts of data are being produced [1]. Already today, a substantial portion of the population owns a smartphone that is packed with sensors. In the near future, Internet nodes with sensing capabilities are expected to reside in almost any everyday thing. The data, analyzed with big data analytics and machine learning, offers an opportunity to bring about breakthroughs in processing images, video, speech, and audio [2]. Data of importance are generated by industrial vendors, private citizens, or the government [3]. Politics and executive floors of global businesses underline the importance of such data [4].

Marketplaces are enablers for the exchange of data [5]. A *data marketplace* is a platform on which dataset can be offered and accessed [3]. Marketplaces enable trade by offering services for buying and selling data, finding datasets, and obtaining access to vendors. Often cited examples are the Microsoft Azure Marketplace, Xignite, Gnip, AggData, and Cvedia. Data that are being offered may be static archives or online streams of new data. Different modes of access may be offered, e.g. whole repositories, APIs for answering queries, or subscriptions. We call such variants *data products*.

According to an early survey of data vendors, estimating the value of data and setting the right price for a data product offering is a key challenge [6]. For vendors, the

© Springer International Publishing AG 2017
A. Ojala et al. (Eds.): ICSOB 2017, LNBIP 304, pp. 49–66, 2017.
https://doi.org/10.1007/978-3-319-69191-6_4

pricing is part of the value-creation with data. For customers, wrong pricing makes data unattractive. While overviews of the pricing of software products exist [7], there is no consolidated overview of the state-of-the-art for pricing data products.

Given the drastic changes that the software industry is undergoing at this moment with the move towards 'smart everything everywhere,' it is critical that a better understanding of the business with data is obtained. It is urgent that the so far young and small research area is being developed, especially because it has hardly been discussed in the domain of software business. The lack of consolidation limits the uptake of good practice by practitioners and hinders the planning of research in this area.

This paper offers an overview of the current research in the pricing of data for data marketplaces. It utilizes a systematic approach to identifying, screening, analyzing, and synthesizing the research literature. The paper describes the research on data pricing, the contexts in which data pricing was investigated, and the maturity of the area. For owners of data products, the results offer guidance of how to do pricing. For researchers, the results offer insights into the knowledge frontier and knowledge gaps for planning research in data pricing. We intend to utilize the results for building support for data pricing into the Bonseyes marketplace (www.bonseyes.com).

The paper is structured as follows. Section 2 gives an overview of the research methodology. Section 3 describes the results of reviewing the research literature. Section 4 discusses the obtained results. Section 5 summarizes and concludes.

2   Research Methodology

The study aimed at consolidating the research on the pricing of data products offered on marketplaces. To achieve this aim, we used a systematic approach to reviewing the research literature. We used the following steps to conduct the review. (1) Identify and screen the start set of primary studies with a database search. (2) Identify and screen the final set of primary studies with snowballing. (3) Evaluate the quality of the research based on full texts. (4) Extract and analyze the data for answering the research questions.

We used the snowballing guidelines proposed by Wohlin [8] for paper identification. The snowballing helped us to avoid many false positives that would have been generated by a database search string that is too inclusive. For screening and research quality evaluation, we used the guidelines provided by Kitchenham and Charters [9]. The data extraction and analysis step followed the systematic mapping recommendations of Petersen [10]. We chose to follow Petersen because the results presented by the included papers did not allow any meta-analysis with quantitative statistic methods.

To guide our systematic review, we asked the research questions shown in Table 1. RQ1 is intended to overview how far the state-of-the-art has advanced and where the research gaps are. We followed the ideas of Ivarsson and Gorschek to assess the maturity of the research with the strength of the empirical evaluation [11]. RQ2 is intended to obtain an overview of pricing from the data vendor's perspective. To understand pricing, we were first interested in what the products were that were priced and which contexts these products targeted. We then described the rules for determining prices, the *pricing models*, and the mechanisms used for applying these rules.

Table 1. Research questions.

Research Question	Description
RQ1: How mature are the researched pricing models?	Maturity is a concern in technology transfer from academia to industry [11]. Maturity is important for practitioners to decide about the adoption of technology, such as pricing models, and for researchers to further mature the technology
RQ2: How do vendors price data?	The pricing of data is the concern being addressed by the presented research. The answer to this RQ should inform practitioners adopting pricing for the data they offer, trade, or buy and researchers that aim at improving the state-of-the-art
RQ2.1: Which contexts did the pricing models target?	A context offers the frame for offering and exploiting technology. The contexts for the pricing of data comprise the domains in which the data would be used, the types and storage of data, and scenarios for exploiting that data
RQ2.2: What kinds of data products were being priced?	A data product is the packaging of data that get a price tag attached. We expect the definition of the data products to consist of the price metrics (i.e. a definition of what is being priced), the quality attributes that are being considered for product definition, and the characteristics of the market for which the product is defined
RQ2.3: What pricing models were evaluated?	A pricing model is a set of the rules established for defining prices. A pricing model describes how product and context variables are considered to achieve aims of interest, such as profit optimization
RQ2.4: What mechanisms were proposed to determine a price?	To sell data to a customer the final price for the instance of the data product must be determined by applying a pricing model. With the answer to this RQ, we give an overview of how the pricing model is used to determine a final price

2.1 Research Process

Start set of primary studies. We built the start set of papers with a keyword search for primary studies in Scopus. Scopus was selected because it offers the largest number of abstracts and citations in science and technology. We searched title, abstract, and keywords fields with the string *"data marketplace"* on January 20, 2017. The string constrained the population while leaving the intervention, comparators, outcomes, and contexts open [9]. These latter parts were used in the analysis for RQ2. We constrained the search to *marketplace*, leaving terms like *databases* and *repositories* out, because of our interest in business with data and not warehousing. The search yielded 181 papers.

We screened the papers based on title, abstract, and meta-information. Following Kitchenham's recommendations [9], we developed the selection criteria based on the research questions and practical issues. We maintained a list of excluded studies together with the reasons for exclusion. Table 2 shows the inclusion and exclusion criteria that resulted from this process. The two authors assessed the exclusion of primary articles by seeking consensus. After screening, the start set of papers contained 11 papers.

Table 2. Study selection criteria (based on the research questions* and practical reasons**).

Inclusion criteria	Exclusion criteria
- Proposal, evaluation, and discussion of a vendor's pricing of data*	- Short papers of up to 4 pages** - Study report superseded by an ensuing report of the same study** - Customer or market maker's view of pricing instead of vendor's view* - Costing, e.g. for cost minimization of data management* - Units of analysis other than the pricing of data, e.g. market policies* - Analyses of data value or other variables, rather than data pricing*

Final set of primary studies. We did backward and forward snowballing by looking at the reference lists of the papers in the start set and by using Scopus to identify papers that cited the papers in the start set. The backward snowballing yielded 66 additional relevant papers. The forward snowballing yielded 6 additional papers that cited the start set. The small number was due to the inclusion of many recent papers in the start set.

We again screened the papers by studying their title and abstract and applying the same selection criteria. After screening, the final set of papers contained 18 papers.

Quality Assessment. We assessed the quality of the so far selected papers with the aim of including only those with research quality sufficient to extract data and answer our research questions reliably. Table 3 shows the quality assessment criteria that we derived from Kitchenham [9] and applied to the full text. Papers with a score of less than 0.6 got removed from further consideration, leaving us with 15 papers for the data extraction and analysis step.

Data Extraction. To answer our research questions, we extracted data with the data extraction form shown in Table 4. The table declares what we extracted, defines how we abstracted the extracts, and offers details about the data extraction.

Data Analysis. We followed the suggestions from Petersen [10] to systematically map the research literature and aggregate the results. Table 4, column *"Values"* describes categorization schemes that we used for classifying the papers. Our analysis focused on giving an overview of the categories and how common publications were for each category. This analysis made it possible to see which categories have been emphasized

Table 3. Quality assessment criteria.

Quality Criterion	Assessment Question	Evaluation approach	Score
Fulfillment of aims	How well does the research address its original aims?	Identify the aims from the abstract and introduction and compare with the research	1.0: perfect match 0.5: partial or vague match 0.0: no match
Clarity of background	How clear are the underlying theory and assumptions?	Evaluate the background and related work sections if it fits the performed research	1.0: well-defined and strong fit 0.5: partial fit 0.0: unclear or not fitting
Quality of the sample	How credible are the data that are used for the research?	Evaluate the data used for validating theories or models	1.0: representative real-world data 0.5: data well described 0.0: unclear what data was used
Credibility of the research	How clear is the chain of evidence?	Evaluate the match between the method section, data, analysis, and analysis results	1.0: clear and traceable 0.5: partial chain. 0.0: unclear chain of evidence.
Clarity of synthesis	How clear is the link of analysis results and the related work to the discussed contribution and implications?	Evaluate the traceability of the discussion to the presented results and background literature	1.0: contribution and both traces clear 0.5: contribution vague or only one trace clear 0.0: no discussion or unclear connection with results and related work

and which categories represent gaps in the research. Instead of bubble plots, we used tables and networks to give a visual representation of research focus and intensity.

Some values were not defined with a predefined categorization scheme. Here, we developed the categories inductively by following a conventional content analysis approach [16]. We let insights about categories emerge by studying the papers. We then gave an overview of these categories and defined their meaning with a synthesis of the relevant data extracted from the papers. The results represent a proposal of a categorization scheme that is grounded in the research that we have reviewed.

Table 4. Data extraction form (*: values determined inductively)

Property	Values	Description
RQ1: Pricing Model Maturity		
Research method	Formal analysis, simulation, laboratory validation, real-world validation	The type of research method influences the readiness of the researched entity. E.g., the European Horizon2020 research program connects research methods[a] to technology readiness levels
Dataset	No data, synthetic data, synthetic data of justified industrial size, industrial data	The dataset used for analysis or validation influences the readiness of the researched entity. E.g., a synthetic dataset limits the credibility of the research results in comparison to the use of a full-scale industrial dataset
RQ2.1: Contexts		
Domain	A vertical market like Smart City, Business Administration, or Linguistics.	Different verticals may have different norms, standards, and practices. Trading of data may need to take such contextual factors into consideration
Type of data*	See column 'Type of Data' in Table 7.	Different types of data may require different types of pricing models to make data sharing attractive
Data exploitation scenario*	See column 'Data Exploitation Scenario' in Table 7.	Different data exploitation scenarios may require distinct types of pricing models to make data sharing attractive
Storage mechanism*	See column 'Storage' in Table 7.	Different types of data storage require different types of pricing models to make data sharing attractive
RQ2.2: Data Products		
Market structure	Perfect competition, oligopoly, monopoly, monopsony	The number of sellers, intermediary market-makers, and buyers influences the market structure and the way the sellers and buyers behave [12]
Price metrics	Free, charging of single requests, volume packages, access to specific data-types, time-based subscription	The price metrics define the unit by which pricing is applied to data product [13]. We use the two taxonomies of metrics described by Muschalle [6] and by Sarkar [14]

(continued)

Table 4. (*continued*)

Property	Values	Description
Data quality attributes	Accuracy, completeness, time (currency, timeliness, volatility), consistency, other	Data quality is critical in any application using the data and in the processes supported by the data. Data quality may be characterized by a range of attributes [15]
RQ2.3: Pricing Models		
Aims of pricing model*	Internal consistency of pricing model, fairness of prices, profit maximization, social welfare maximization	To understand the rationales behind a pricing model, one must understand its aims
Pricing model*	Price function with desired properties, game theoretical pricing approach	The categories and description of the pricing models
Pricing variables*	Price of views, price of tuples, customer profile, data quality, customer bid, data usage, cost of the data	The variables used in the pricing model to determine a price
RQ2.4: Pricing Mechanisms		
Price determination mechanism*	Algorithm, pricing function	The mechanism used by a party to determine the price for an offer of a data product.
Evaluation results*	Polynomial time (PTIME), Pseudo-PTIME, NP-Complete, N/A	The results of evaluating the pricing mechanism in terms of computational complexity.

[a]https://ec.europa.eu/research/participants/data/ref/h2020/wp/2014_2015/annexes/h2020-wp1415-annex-g-trl_en.pdf.

2.2 Threats to Validity

Kitchenham and Charters suggest the following four criteria for assessing the quality of a systematic literature review [9]: completeness of the literature search, clarity of paper inclusion, transparency of the study quality assessment, and adequacy of the description of the basic studies. These quality criteria were also used by tertiary studies to judge the quality a secondary study like this literature review, e.g. [17].

Our research process used a hybrid approach for literature search: keyword database search followed by snowballing. The combination of the two techniques allowed us to obtain a reasonable sample of the literature. The search efficiency of 6% is a figure that can be found in other literature reviews [8]. For increasing the confidence, one could further increase the start set of primary studies with a wider search string or validate the obtained set of papers with experts in the data marketplace and pricing domains. A consultation of experts could also give us insights about publication bias [9], about which we cannot make any statement with our research process.

We made explicit the inclusion and exclusion criteria that we applied. The criteria were discovered and documented during a pilot search as rationales for our inclusion and exclusion decisions. Inclusion and exclusion were decided by seeking consensus between the two authors. A limitation is that we applied the inclusion and exclusion criteria on titles and abstract only. Thus, we assumed that the authors succeeded to accurately reflect the contents of their papers in title and abstract.

For the study quality assessment, we used explicit rubrics with clear scoring instructions. The scoring results were developed, reviewed, and discussed by both authors and reflect the consensus of the two parties.

Due to the imposed space limitations, we could not offer a comprehensive description of each study. Instead, we decided to list the included papers in the appendix, enrich the analysis with syntheses of the data extracted from the papers, and established traceability of the syntheses to the source papers. This approach allows the reader to appreciate the overall meaning of the papers and obtain details by consulting the cited papers.

3   Results: Pricing of Data Markets

3.1   Quality Assessment

Most papers scored well in the quality assessment, yet no paper in the final set reached a score of 1.0. Of the well-scoring papers, all fulfilled the research aims and offered a clear overview of the research background.

The *quality of sample* and *clarity of synthesis* indicators were difficult to meet. The *quality of sample* indicator was difficult to meet because many papers used formal proofs instead of data for the evaluation or experimented with synthetic data. Few papers used real-world empirical data. *Clarity of synthesis* was hardly met because most papers offered only a limited synthesis of the obtained results with the rest of the literature. Table 5 gives an overview of the detailed scores.

Table 5. Quality assessment of the included studies (italics: papers scoring below 0.6).

Paper	Assessment score	Fulfillment of aims	Clarity of background	Quality of sample	Credibility of Research	Clarity of synthesis
P04 Koutris 2015	0.9	1	1	0.5	1	1
P06 Kushal 2012	0.9	1	1	1	1	0.5
P09 Niyato 2016	0.9	1	1	1	1	0.5
P05 Koutris 2013	0.8	1	1	0.5	1	0.5
P08 Li 2014	0.8	1	1	0.5	1	0.5
P10 Stahl 2016	0.8	1	1	0.5	1	0.5
P11 Tang 2013 Get	0.8	1	1	0.5	1	0.5
P12 Tang 2013 Right	0.8	1	1	0.5	1	0.5
P13 Tang 2015	0.8	1	1	0.5	1	0.5
P01 Balasubramanian 2015	0.7	1	1	0	1	0.5
P02 Golrezaei 2014	0.7	1	1	0.5	0.5	0.5
P03 Jiang 2015	0.7	1	1	0	1	0.5
P07 Li 2012	0.7	1	1	0.5	0.5	0.5
P14 Tang 2016	0.7	1	1	0	1	0.5
P15 Wu 2010	0.7	1	1	0	1	0.5
P16 Balazinska 2013	*0.5*	*1*	*1*	*0*	*0.5*	*0*
P18 Shen 2016	*0.5*	*0.5*	*1*	*0.5*	*0*	*0.5*
P17 Shapiro 1998	*0.3*	*0*	*1*	*0*	*0.5*	*0*

Three papers scored below the threshold of 0.6 points: P16, P17, and P18. In addition to the two quality indicators that were difficult to meet overall, the three papers scored low in the *credibility of the research* and partially did not meet the stated research aims.

3.2   RQ1: Maturity of the Pricing Models

Most research was of conceptual nature and employed formal analysis or simulation of the proposed pricing models for validation. However, none of the pricing models has been validated in the real world or by deploying it in a laboratory environment. P06 was the only study which used real-world industrial data. P05 did a simulation with synthetic data of industrially relevant size. The other simulations used a random synthetic dataset or did not define the used data. Table 6 gives an overview.

Table 6. Maturity of the pricing models (top-left: low maturity, bottom-right: high maturity).

Dataset research method	No Data	Synthetic data	Synthetic and industrial size	Industrial
Formal analysis	P01, P02, P04, P07, P08, P09, P10, P11, P13, P14, P15			
Simulation	P03	P12	P05	P06

3.3   RQ2: Pricing of Data

RQ2.1: Contexts Targeted by the Pricing Models. Table 7 gives an overview of the domains and types of data considered by the papers. While many domains were covered, some evident ones were missing. When using the Horizon2020 program as a reference[1], the domains of health and wellbeing, food and agriculture, and energy appear to be of relevance but were not considered.

Also, the data being traded and the scenarios of how these data would be exploited are broad. Four papers, P02, P03, P09, and P13, consider the use of sensor data, which could be generated in mobile sensing and Internet of Things contexts. One paper, P08, considers pricing for personal data, a type of data that is sensitive and subject to strict regulations. One paper, P09, considers the exploitation of data for machine learning, a basis for building systems that enable smart decision-making and control.

Eight papers are unspecific in the application domain or data exploitation scenario. For example, P12 just states that the data was intended for decision-making. The lack of specificity also means that the papers do not report any evaluation of their approaches or, in the case of P06, apply their pricing approach on a diversity of data as broad as demographics, weather imagery, DNA sequences, sales and marketing analytics, and financial records.

In most of the papers, the authors assume that data is uploaded to the market maker's cloud for making that data available for trade. Such upload may be efficient for

---

[1] https://ec.europa.eu/programmes/horizon2020/en/h2020-section/societal-challenges.

Table 7. Contexts.

Domain	Type of data	Paper	Storage	Data exploitation scenario
Cities	Sensor data	P02	Cloud	Traffic and waste management
		P03	Edge	Environment management
		P13	Cloud	City management
Business management	Demographic data	P07	(not stated)	Financial assessments
	Personal data	P08	Cloud	Monetization
	(unspecific)	P14	Cloud	Market research and advertisement
		P12	Cloud	Decision-making
Engineering	(unspecific)	P01	Cloud	(no scenario defined)
Consumer	Newsfeed	P15	(not stated)	Social networking
Linguistics	Linguistic data	P05	Cloud	Text analysis and translation
(unspecific)	Sensor data	P09	(not stated)	Machine learning
		P06	Cloud	(no scenario defined)
		P10, P11, P14	(not stated)	(no scenario defined)

the market maker but could reduce transparency and control of the transactions for the data vendor. One paper assumed the opposite approach, edge computing, in which the data is controlled by the data vendor. Six papers did not state any assumption about where data would be stored.

RQ2.2: Data Products being Priced. The papers covered a broad variety of product definitions. Table 8 gives an overview. Many papers assumed, explicitly or implicitly, a monopoly market structure where the data provider does not care about competing providers. We judged a paper to consider a monopoly implicitly if it assumed that the offered product is so far differentiated that the pricing model does not need to consider competing offerings. Four papers considered a duopoly situation where two data providers compete. No paper generalized a duopoly to an oligopoly situation. Two papers, P05 and P08, considered a monopsony situation, where a buyer requests data from many data providers. We judged a paper to consider a monopsony if the pricing did not consider interactions between multiple customers. Only one paper studied a market situation with a perfect competition where anybody could trade with anybody.

Most papers studied data products with usage- or request-based price metrics, where charging takes place on a fine-grained level. The variants were pay-per-use or unit, pay-per-query or view, or customer-proposed prices. One volume-based pricing model was investigated, step pricing where the customer pays for a given volume of data. Three papers studied flat fee products that allow all data to be accessed without

Table 8. Data product definitions (*: papers comparing multiple products).

Price metrics market	Single requests	Volume packages	Time-based subscription	(not stated)
Monopoly	P01*, P15*: pay-per-use P06*: per-unit P04, P07, P12, P13: query- or view-based P10, P11, P14: customer-proposed price	P06*: step pricing	P01*: unrestricted use P09: subscription fees P15*: flat fee	P02
Duopoly	P01*: pay-per-use P06*: per-unit	P06*: step pricing	P01*: unrestricted use	P02
Oligopoly				
Monopsony	P05, P08: query-based			
Perfect Competition				P03

restriction, either continuously or as part of a time-based subscription. The papers P02 and P03 did not state any price metrics used to define the data product.

Three papers compared the attractiveness of usage and flat fee products, P01 and P06 in both monopoly and duopoly market structures, and P15 in a monopoly market structure alone.

A subset of the papers utilized quality in the product definition and, consequently, as an attribute for pricing. Table 9 gives an overview.

Table 9. Quality attributes used in the product definition and pricing model.

Quality attribute	Paper	Quality metrics
Time	P02	Delay: Delay may influence the perceived value of a data product
	P05	Aging: Data may need to be updated because it gets incorrect over time
	P10	Freshness: a price should be defined depending on how new the data is
Accuracy	P08	Perturbations: noise for deteriorating aggregated data quality for privacy
	P11	Accuracy: distance and likelihood of deviation from the true value
Completeness	P10	Completeness: parts of the data may be missing
	P14	Completeness: incompleteness may be traded for discounted prices
Consistency	–	–

In these papers, quality played a role in price setting, delivering value, and managing privacy. Quality differences may influence a customer's perceived value of a data product. Thus, reduced quality was a counterpart for price reductions: "you pay what you get." Also, quality was considered to deteriorate over time. Thus, data needed to be updated to be of high value or prices be reduced. Quality, finally, was a trade-off with privacy. Perturbations were introduced into the data to avoid unwanted disclosure of information. Alternatively, price increases were used to compensate for disclosure.

RQ2.3: Pricing Models. We identified three approaches to researching pricing models. Some papers designed a price function with desired properties. Most of these papers addressed a single-vendor situation (monopoly). Other papers casted pricing into game theory to identify an optimal pricing approach in a competitive situation. Most of these papers addressed a multi-vendor situation (duopoly and monopsony). A final set of papers compared constellations of price metrics and market to select pricing approaches. Most of these papers addressed both, single-vendor and multi-vendor situations.

Figure 1 gives an overview of the pricing models for the *single-vendor situation*. We used the function symbol to depict papers designing a price function. The dice symbol was used to denote a game-theoretic analysis.

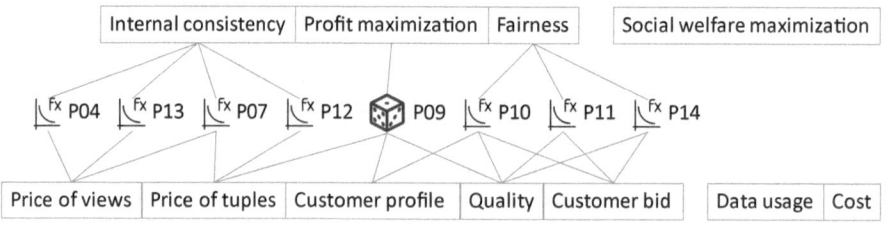

Fig. 1. Papers researching pricing models for single-vendor situations.

The papers proposed and evaluated pricing models for achieving internal consistency of the pricing function, profit maximization, and fairness between customers and vendors. *Internal consistency* meant monotonicity of the pricing function (i.e. higher prices mean more data), usage or volume-based prices are not higher than the price of the whole database, non-disclosiveness (i.e. impossible to infer unpaid query answers), and freedom from arbitrage (i.e. all ways to obtain an insight have the same price), freedom from discounts (i.e. the prices are maximal), and freedom from regret (i.e. all sequences to obtain an insight have the same price). *Profit maximization* meant pricing models that maximized the data vendor's profitability. *Fairness* meant a fair trade-off between quality and price.

Within the single-vendor context, three groups of pricing models could be discerned: customer bid-based pricing, view-based pricing, and tuple-based pricing. *Customer bids* were answered by compensating low bids with the delivery of low-quality data. The compensation was motivated by the customers' understanding that with just a little money only low quality can be bought. For the vendors, the compensation was an aspect of fairness. *View-based pricing*, a variant of usage-based pricing, was based on the idea that the customers' queries could be answered with predefined data views that are stored in the vendor's database. P07 called this approach *deductive pricing*. The price for a query is the price of the cheapest set of views needed to answer the query. *Tuple-based pricing* is another variant of usage-based pricing. Its idea is to charge access to rows in a database. P07 called this approach also *inductive pricing*.

Figure 2 gives an overview of the pricing models for *multi-vendor situations*. Again, the same symbols were used for price function designs and game-theoretic analyses.

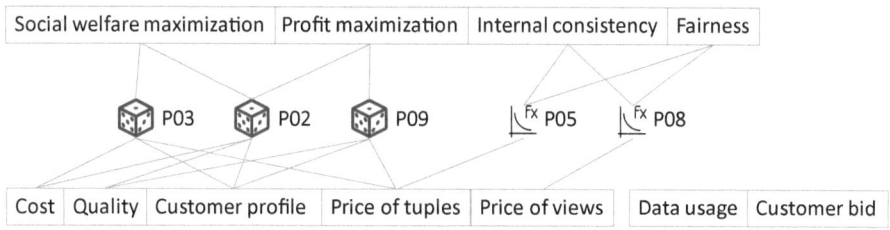

Fig. 2. Papers researching pricing models for multi-vendor situations.

The papers proposed and evaluated pricing models for the additional goal of maximizing social welfare as well as the already mentioned goals of profit maximization, internal consistency, and fairness goals. *Social welfare maximization* meant to maximize the sum of all customers' payoffs. *Profit maximizations* and *internal consistency* had the same meaning as before. *Fairness* meant now a fair split of revenue among sellers.

Two groups of pricing models could be discerned: pricing models that aimed at internal consistency and fairness, and game-theoretic approaches for maximizing social welfare or profit. The *design of the pricing functions* resembled the view- and tuple-based pricing models studied in the monopolistic context, but now extended with a mechanism to fairly compensate a multitude of sources for the data they provided. The *game-theoretic approaches* allowed parties to decide about the role they wanted to adopt in the marketplace, how pricing tactics would affect the equilibria in the market, and how to compute the optimal price.

Figure 3 gives an overview of pricing model comparisons. We used the tick-box symbol to denote these papers that aimed at offering decision support for selecting an appropriate pricing model. The shaded dices and function indicate secondary contributions of the papers. For example, P01 used game theory to study the duopoly situation.

All three papers compared pricing approaches with the aim of profit maximization. P01 and P06 made this comparison for both the monopoly and duopoly situations. P15 did it for the monopoly situation only. P06 studied arbitrage for the pricing function, thus pursued the secondary goal of achieving internal consistency of the pricing.

According to the three papers, a monopoly requires a different approach for a good product definition than a duopoly. For a monopoly, the papers conclude that usage-based pricing of data is attractive. The pricing may be fine-grained or package-based; the

Fig. 3. Papers comparing pricing models.

granularity of the price steps does not matter. Thus, no clear preference can be established between usage or volume-based pricing. In a duopoly, the two competing data vendors should offer complementary product definitions, or the profits will rapidly erode to zero.

RQ2.4: Price Determination. Most papers proposed equations or algorithms to calculate prices. Only in P01, P02, and P03, we could not identify any specific price determination mechanisms that could be used by a data vendor. Table 10 gives an overview.

Table 10. Price determination mechanisms for data vendors.

Price determination	Paper	Specific result	Complexity
Algorithm	P04	Pricing for chain queries	PTIME
		Pricing for cyclic queries	PTIME
	P06	Multi-step pricing	PTIME
	P07	Cell-based or regret-free inductive pricing	PTIME
		Deductive pricing for continuous price functions	PTIME
	P10	Knapsack pricing	Pseudo-PTIME
	P12	Approximate pricing	PTIME
	P13	Rewriting-based pricing	NP-Complete
	P11	Fair quality distortion	N/A
	P14	Uniform or binary tree sampling	PTIME
Pricing functions	P08	Basic and synthesized pricing	NP-Complete
	P09	Globally optimal pricing	N/A
	P15	Vendor's generic optimization problem	N/A
	P05	ILP-formulation for some conjunctive queries	PTIME

P04, P05, P07, P12, P13, and P14 suggested that pricing is NP-complete in general. Also, P8 suggests that consistency checking of arbitrary price point setting is NP-complete. However, as Table 10 shows, algorithms for specific cases may be designed that are less complex and offer tractable pricing. The algorithms that may be executed in polynomial time (PTIME or Pseudo-PTIME) were considered tractable.

Some of the pricing functions may be formulated so that they can be solved as differential equations or by a solver, e.g. an Integer Linear Programming (ILP)-Solver.

4 Discussion

This paper has contributed the first systematic review of research on pricing for data products, thus helping to enable business with the massive amounts of data generated by Mobile Computing and the Internet of Things. Fifteen papers were analyzed that proposed or evaluated pricing models for data product vendors. While earlier work has introduced pricing metrics [14] as well as the structure of a marketplace and its participants [6], no systematic overview had been given of the models and mechanisms used for pricing. The here presented research enables marketplace owners and data vendors to plan how to generate revenue and profit from data. Such thinking is important to make the potentially vast amount of data created by billions of humans and devices available for the development of smart systems and services.

Section 3 gave an overview of the objectives for pricing data products and the attributes that could be considered as inputs for a pricing model. The results suggest that data vendors seek profit maximization and consistency of the pricing model. Further concerns are social welfare and fairness. Some pricing attributes could be used for value-oriented pricing [13] and cover the customer profile, the data usage, and customer bids. Other attributes consider the cost side of data and include the cost of data provision and the price of tuples or views. A special role plays quality of the data that, according to the reviewed research, is a means acceptable for customers to relate to prices.

The here presented research also identified concrete advice on how to act when discovering a competitive situation (i.e. achieving complementarity of product definitions) and what the pricing models are that should be preferred when offering unique data (i.e. usage-based pricing rather than a flat subscription fee).

While the pricing models are appealing from a conceptual point-of-view, the calculation of prices remains challenging. Good pricing model should exhibit a variety of characteristics, such as monotonicity, boundedness, non-disclosiveness, and freedom from arbitrage, discount, and regret. Price determination is NP-complete in general. Only for special cases, approaches of polynomial complexity were proposed.

We have constrained our review to papers that discuss pricing of data products for use in data marketplaces from a vendor's perspective. This strict scope excluded studies that focused purely on value and cost of data without having used these attributes for pricing the data. Also excluded were papers that studied the data consumer's or market maker's perspective, e.g. of procuring data at a minimal cost. Future reviews should expand towards value and cost aspects of data including the customers' view.

Research on pricing for data products is still in its infancy. Most research we identified features microeconomic modeling and formal analysis of the pricing models. When using the 9-level European Horizoon2020 technology readiness (TRL) model as a benchmark, such research is positioned at TRL2 only. Four papers went as far as TRL3 by offering a simulation-based evaluation of the pricing models. With our search, we could not identify any paper at a higher TRL that would have reported applications of pricing in relevant environments. This disconnect of research from practice is surprising as several data marketplaces have been launched (c.f. Section 1) and are confronted with pricing questions. Real-world research is urgently needed to understand the applicability and impact of the pricing models. The work of Schomm could represent a starting point and offer guidance for such practical applications [3].

Also, the surveyed pricing models were developed for simple market situations only. Considered were the monopoly where competition could be ignored and the duopoly where competition is a gameplay between two adversaries. Such simplification is attractive because it makes formal analysis feasible. From a practical perspective, it would be important to understand how to design and differentiate data products to make the offering so unique that it could be considered a monopoly or at least complementary to existing products. Software product management offers such product strategy advice for software products [7]. It would be interesting to understand whether and how such advice can be transferred and applied to data products.

5   Summary and Conclusions

This paper has offered a systematic review of the literature on pricing models for data marketplaces. The papers were identified first with a keyword-based search in Scopus and then complemented with forward and backward snowballing. From initially 181 papers 11 papers were selected for snowballing. The snowballing step yielded 18 papers that were assessed for research quality. 15 papers made it in the final set of papers.

11 papers offered formal analysis of pricing models, while 4 additional papers went as far as simulating the formal models. Cities, business management, engineering, consumer, and linguistics were the contexts addressed by the pricing models. Usage-based, volume-based, and flat fee pricing models were proposed or evaluated for single-vendor and multi-vendor situations. The pricing models aimed at profit maximization, internal consistency, fairness, and social welfare maximization. Pricing attributes included customer bids and profile, data usage, quality, the price of views or tuples, and cost. Price calculation is NP-hard with PTIME approaches existing for special cases.

Our results offer an overview of what in the domain of data pricing has been researched and where the gaps are. It serves as a compact advice for anybody who seeks incentives and rewards for data sharing. However, the presented results should be used with caution. Research is needed to validate the models in the laboratory and real-world settings.

Acknowledgments. The presented work was funded by the European Union's Horizon 2020 research and innovation program under grant agreement No. 732204 (Bonseyes) and by the Swiss State Secretariat for Education, Research and Innovation (SERI) under contract number 16.0159. The opinions expressed and arguments employed herein do not necessarily reflect the official views of these funding bodies.

Appendix: Bibliography of Included Papers

P01   Balasubramanian, S., Bhattacharya, S., & Krishnan, V.: Pricing information goods: A strategic analysis of the selling and pay-per-use mechanisms. Marketing Science, 34(2), 218-234 (2015)

P02   Golrezaei, N., & Nazerzadeh, H.: Pricing Schemes for Metropolitan Traffic Data Mar-kets. 3rd International Conference on Data Management Technologies and Applications, Vienna, Austria (2014)

P03   Jiang, C., Gao, L., Duan, L., & Huang, J.: Economics of peer-to-peer mobile crowdsensing. 2015 IEEE Global Communications Conference (GLOBECOM), San Diego, CA, USA (2015)

P04   Koutris, P., Upadhyaya, P., Balazinska, M., Howe, B., & Suciu, D.: Query-based data pricing. Journal of the ACM (JACM), 62(5), 1-44 (2015)

P05   Koutris, P., Upadhyaya, P., Balazinska, M., Howe, B., & Suciu, D.: Toward practical query pricing with QueryMarket. 2013 ACM SIGMOD International Conference on Management of Data, New York, NY, USA (2013)

P06   Kushal, A., Moorthy, S., & Kumar, V.: Pricing for data markets. Technical Report (2012)

P07   Li, C., & Miklau, G.: Pricing Aggregate Queries in a Data Marketplace. 15th International Workshop on the Web and Databases 2012 (WebDB), Scottsdale, AZ, USA (2012)

P08   Li, C., Li, D. Y., Miklau, G., & Suciu, D.: A theory of pricing private data. ACM Trans-actions on Database Systems (TODS), 39(4), 1-28 (2014)

P09   Niyato, D., Alsheikh, M. A., Wang, P., Kim, D. I., & Han, Z.: Market model and optimal pricing scheme of big data and Internet of Things (IoT). 2016 IEEE International Conference on Communications (ICC), Kuala Lumpur, Malaysia (2016)

P10   Stahl, F., & Vossen, G.: Fair Knapsack Pricing for Data Marketplaces. 20th East European Conference on Advances in Databases and Information Systems (ADBIS), Prague, Czech Republic (2016)

P11   Tang, R., Shao, D., Bressan, S., & Valduriez, P.: What you pay for is what you get. 24th International Conference on Database and Expert Systems Applications (DEXA), Prague, Czech Republic (2013)

P12   Tang, R., Wu, H., Bao, Z., Bressan, S., & Valduriez, P.: The price is right. 24th International Conference on Database and Expert Systems Applications (DEXA), Prague, Czech Republic (2013)

P13   Tang, R., Wu, H., He, X., & Bressan, S.: Valuating Queries for Data Trading in Modern Cities. 2015 IEEE International Conference on Data Mining Workshop (ICDMW), Atlantic City, NJ, USA (2015)

P14   Tang, R., Amarilli, A., Senellart, P., & Bressan, S.: A Framework for Sampling-Based XML Data Pricing. Transaction on Large-Scale Data-and Knowledge-Centered Systems XXIV, 9510, 116-138 (2016)

P15   Wu, S. Y., & Banker, R. D.: Best pricing strategy for information services. Journal of the Association for Information Systems, 11(6), 339-366 (2010)

P16   Balazinska, M., Howe, B., Koutris, P., Suciu, D., & Upadhyaya, P.: A discussion on pricing relational data. Search of Elegance in the Theory and Practice of Computation. In: Search of Elegance in the Theory and Practice of Computation. 167-173, Springer (2013)

P17   Shapiro, C., & Varian, H. R.: Versioning: the smart way to sell information. Harvard Business Review, 76(6), 106-114 (1998)

P18   Shen, Y., Guo, B., Shen, Y., Duan, X., Dong, X., & Zhang, H.: A pricing model for Big Personal Data. Tsinghua Science and Technology, 21(5), 482-490 (2016)

References

1. Atzori, L., Iera, A., Morabito, G.: The internet of things: a survey. Comput. Netw. **54**(15), 2787–2805 (2010)
2. LeCun, Y., Bengio, Y., Hinto, G.: Deep learning. Nature **521**(7553), 436–444 (2015)
3. Schomm, F., Stahl, F., Vossen, G.: Marketplaces for data: an initial survey. ACM SIGMOD Record **42**(1), 15–26 (2013)
4. Schwab, K., et al.: Personal data: the emergence of a new asset class. World Economic Forum (2011)
5. Koutsopoulos, I., Gionis, A., and Halkidi, M.: Auctioning data for learning. In: IEEE 15th International Conference on Data Mining Workshops, Sydney, Australia (2015)
6. Muschalle, A., Stahl, F., Löser, A., Vossen, G.: Pricing approaches for data markets. In: International Workshop on Business Intelligence for the Real-Time Enterprise (2012)
7. Kittlaus, H.-B., Clough, P.: Software Product Management and Pricing. Springer, Heidelberg (2009). doi:10.1007/978-3-540-76987-3
8. Wohlin, C.: Guidelines for snowballing in systematic literature studies and a replication in software engineering. In: 18th International Conference on Evaluation and Assessment in Software Engineering (2013)
9. Kitchenham, B., Charters, S.: Guidelines for performing systematic literature reviews in software engineering. In: EBSE Technical Report (2007)
10. Petersen, K., Feldt, R., Mujtaba, S., Mattson, M.: Systematic mapping studies in software engineering. In: 12th International Conference on Evaluation and Assessment in Software Engineering (2008)
11. Ivarsson, M., Gorschek, T.: Technology transfer decision support in requirements engineering research: a systematic review of REj. Requirements Eng. **14**(3), 155–175 (2009)
12. Frank, R., Cartwright, E.: Microeconomics and Behaviour. McGraw-Hill Education, London (2013)
13. Nagle, T.T., Hogan, J.E.: The Strategy and Tactics of Pricing: A Guide to Growing More Profitably. Pearson Prentice Hall, Upper Saddle River (2006)
14. Sarkar, P.: Data as a Service - Framework for Providing Re-Usable Enterprise Data Services. Wiley, Hoboken (2015)
15. Battini, C., Scannapieco, M.: Data Quality: Concepts, Methodologies and Techniques. Springer, Heidelberg (2010). doi:10.1007/3-540-33173-5
16. Hsieh, H.F., Shannon, S.E.: Three approaches to qualitative content analysis. Qual. Health Res. **15**(9), 1277–1288 (2005)
17. Nurdiani, I., Börstler, J., Fricker, S.: The impact of agile and lean practices on project constraints: a tertiary study. J. Syst. Softw. **119**, 162–183 (2016)

Knitting Company Performance and Board Interlocks

An Exploration with the Finnish Software Industry

Sami Hyrynsalmi[1]([⊠]), Arho Suominen[2], Jukka Ruohonen[3], Marko Seppänen[1], and Antero Järvi[3]

[1] TTY Pori, Tampere University of Technology, Tampere, Finland
{sami.hyrynsalmi,marko.seppanen}@tut.fi
[2] VTT Technical Research Centre of Finland, Innovations, Economy, and Policy, Espoo, Finland
arho.suominen@vtt.fi
[3] Department of Future Technologies, University of Turku, Turku, Finland
{juanruo,antero.jarvi}@utu.fi

Abstract. A board of directors is a supreme organism of a modern company. Often, a single board member has a place in several companies' management teams. This is called a board interlock and its impact on a single board member, companies and the economics on the whole has been studied for decades. However, there is a lack of understanding how software companies' board of directors interlock as the field is driven by knowledge and relations more heavily than the other fields. Therefore, well-connected board members could be a vital competitive advantage for companies. This study presents a quantitative analysis of 262 Finnish software companies, their boards and performance. The results show that neither high board interlocks nor foreign board members are remarkably related on the performance of companies. The implications of the findings are discussed and future research inquiries are proposed.

Keywords: Board interlock · Software industry · Finland

1 Introduction

A worn out idiom states that no organization can survive alone in the modern hyper-connected business era [20]. Networks, ecosystems, communities, complementors *et cetera* have been argued to be a key for the survival of modern companies regardless of their sector [14]. Therefore, it is not surprising that connectivity of a company's board of directors and its impact on the firm's performance have been studied exhaustively in prior literature [6,16,25].

In extant literature, there are both empirical evidence as well as arguments for the advantages and disadvantages of board interlocks. Board interlocks have been seen as elitist [26], legally suspicious [24], serving only personal benefits [7] as well as also bringing new connections and best practices for the use of a company [19].

© Springer International Publishing AG 2017
A. Ojala et al. (Eds.): ICSOB 2017, LNBIP 304, pp. 67–81, 2017.
https://doi.org/10.1007/978-3-319-69191-6_5

Also empirical studies on the impact of board interlocking to the performance of a company have yielded contradictory results. For example, Santos et al. [25] showed that a high degree of board interlocking impacts negatively on firms' performance in Brazil, whereas Horton et al. [11] found exactly the opposite in the United Kingdom.

However, a majority of existing studies handle all industries similarly, often failing to separate different fields. That is, the variety of the results might be explained by the industrial structure—e.g. the relative importance of financial, human and social capital in different industrial sector—of the studied country rather than the phenomenon itself. For the knowledge-intensive software industry, only a little attention has been given on boards of directories and their connections. We hypothesize that connections and experiences of a board member in the software industry is linked to good performance of a software firm due to the intangibility of software and value of knowledge. Thus, in this research paper, we focus first on the following question:

RQ1 *Are board interlocks associated with the economic performance of Finnish software companies?*

In addition, business networks and ecosystems are nowadays often international. For example, first time in 2012, half of the Finnish software companies have international revenue and nearly one fifth have significant international revenue [23]. Also, due to the internationalization of software businesses, we are assuming that there are increasing number of foreigners serving in boards of directors. A foreigner in the board is expected to be better networked and have more experienced than a domestic board member. This should be also visible in performance of a company. Therefore, we are secondly focusing on the question:

RQ2 *Are Finnish software companies with board of directors including foreign members performing better than companies managed by exclusively domestic boards of directors?*

Regarding the theoretical frameworks, this study leans towards *theory of social capital* by [3]. The theory explains that there are value in informal and formal relationships. That is, well-connected board members might be able to open new venues and offer new connections that can be vital for a company. In addition, well-connected board members can be more experienced and, thus, be able to help the company better. In this study, we focus only on formal connections and study how well-connected directors help software companies perform better.

To answer the presented question, we perform a quantitative study of selected software firms. As the dataset, we use 262 Finnish software companies, their executives, board members and financial key figures. The financial information is queried from Orbis database. This study contributes mainly on the on-going discussion on the impacts of board interlocks in companies' performance and shed lights on software companies board of directories composition and board interlocks in Finland. This study is among the first address this effect in a specific industrial domain and in software industry.

Remaining of this work is structured as follows. Section 2 presents related work and the central concepts. The following Sect. 3 clarifies the used research approach and it is followed by results in Sect. 4. The final two sections discuss the implications and limitations of the results, and conclude the study, respectively.

2 Background, Related Work and Motivation

Board interlocking, or *interlocking directorate*, refers to a practice where a member of a company's board of directors or top management serves in several boards or top management teams [24,26]. As there are for example possibilities for misuses in competition, board interlocking has received attention mainly from the view-points of antitrust and business ethics (c.f. [24]).

From another point-of-view, board interlocking can be seen as a positive *social capital* [3] resource for a company. Well-networked members of a board can bring valuable connections for the company's use. In addition, members who serve in multiple boards are likely more experienced, being able to better support company. Along these lines, Hao et al. [9], among others, have observed that companies with connected boards of directors are more likely to use relative performance evaluation for CEO compensation. In addition, Clarysse et al. [2] show that high-tech startups are likely to bring complementary human capital to the board of directors with outsider board members.

While the basic theoretical underpinnings are thus relatively clear, empirical studies on the impact of board interlocking have yielded contradictory results. On one hand, Santos et al. [25] find that board interlocking is a frequent phenomenon in Brazilian companies, but with a negative impact upon a company's value, especially when the degree of interlocks is high. Similarly, Loderer and Peyer [17] find that board interlocking impacts a firm's value negatively (cf. also [8]), and Fich and White [7] noted that it mainly serves board members, not the shareholders. In addition, Fich and Shivdasani [6] showed that busy board members—those with three or more directorships—have a negative impact on companies' performance.

On the other hand, for example Mol [19] points out that board interlocking might benefit all networked companies by bringing competitive advantages on giving access to resources, clients, new methods and innovations. In addition, Heracleous and Murray [10] argue that interlocking directorate should provide value for all companies in a network, but it depends on the type of the network how directors should mediate. Horton et al. [11] were among the first to show that better-connected executive or outside director is, his or her firm would achieve greater benefits in future. Similarly, Larcker et al. [16] find that best-connected boards outperform worst-connected boards in their large data set. Pombo and Gutiérrez [22] reached similar results in their study in Columbia. Stuart and Yim [27] showed that well-connected boards are more likely to be targets of private equity -backed take-private transactions. Finally, Intintoli et al. [15] argue that overall well-connected board seems to be beneficial for protecting interests of the company's shareholders.

Despite of many general board interlock studies, only a handful has been done in the scope of software industry. Narrowing even more down to Finnish software industry, there are two recently published studies on board interlocks. Peltonen and Rönkkö [21] studied Finnish software companies' board interlocks with cluster analysis. From their dataset of 2008–2009, they identified six interlock clusters: (i) Rapidly expanding international ventures, (ii) Early-stage international ventures, (iii-iv) Private and public sector venture capitalist dyads, and (v-vi) International and non-international dyads. Their study is explorative and they did not analyze the impact of board interlock to the companies' performance.

In a more recent study, Suominen, Rilla, Oksanen, and Still [28] used social network analysis methods to study board interlocks of Finnish digital game companies. They start with the hypothesis that small, well-connected and swiftly growing industry would have a dense board interlock graph. By using data sets from the years 2013 and 2015, they find the opposite; the board interlock network was sparse and the formal board relationship does not seen to have a role in Finnish game industry. Suominen et al. [28] did not focus on performance of the game companies.

To summarize, extant literature have showed both positive and negative implications of board interlocking. Whereas the 'positive side' leans towards social and human capital theories in order to explain that well-connected and experienced directors are beneficial for a company, the 'negative side' argues that multiple directorships mainly benefits a well-connected board member by a higher compensation and better future career options. Existing literature have showed statistical support for both that interlocking directorate harms and benefits companies.

Interestingly, we find only a few studies specifically focusing on software industry. As stated by Cusumano [5], *"software is not like other businesses"*. Due to, e.g., the intangibility of software, zero reproduction costs, electronic distribution and high dependence on knowledge [1,12,13], social and human capital might be more valuable than financial or natural capital. For example, it has been shown that formal and informal network relationships are crucial for small software firms' internationalization process [4]. Therefore, the importance of well-connected and experienced boards of directors could be especially beneficial in the software industry.

The motivation for this study can be summarized with the following observations:

- Founding a software company requires a little financial capital: successful software companies have been founded in garages and building a modern software product can be done with cheap laptops and rented servers. However, due to this, competition is tight as anyone with enough skills can found a firm and replicate used business model. In this kind of market, good connections to the paying customers can be more valuable than excellent technical implementation.

Therefore, well-connected board can be a competitive advantage for a software company.

- As an intangible product, software is easy to transfer from a country of origin to all over the world. However, as all software vendors can easily transfer their products, differentiation from competitors can be hard. Thus, we hypothesize that foreign members in boards of directors could perhaps foster entry into foreign markets and this effect might be observable in performance of software companies.
- Finally, existing studies have reported contradicting results on either that board interlocking benfits [11,15,16,22] or harms [7,8,17,25] the company.

Thus, this study pays a special attention to board interlocking and its impacts on software industry. We address whether software companies with well-connected board of directors perform better or not and whether foreign board member influence on the performance. In addition, as the full-scale studies, focusing on all companies in a given country, have yielded contradictory results, this study offers an alternative strategy by focusing on a single market domain.

3   Research Approach, Data and Method

This study uses Finnish software industry as a case study population. This decision is justified by existing research on the case study country (e.g. [21,28]) offering the possibility of qualitative reflections. In addition, the researchers are familiar with the selected industry and country, enabling a more in-depth analysis. Finally, the Finnish software industry is well studied: Finnish Software Industry Survey has ran eighteen times[1].

We collect, prepare and analyze data for this study in six phases. At the first phase, the aim is to create a dataset of Finnish software companies. As there is no easy way to identify all Finnish software companies through e.g., NACE REV. 2 classification, we use a proxy measure for creating a representative sample. We acquire a list of Finnish software companies from the member page[2] of *Ohjelmistoyrittäjät ry* (Finnish Software Industry and Entrepreneur Association). In total, the parsed list contained 289 companies. Naturally, this data source contains only members of the association and provides only a limited view on the Finnish software companies. A clear limitation is that we can presume member companies are more established, both in revenue and age. The data acquaintance was done in the middle of February 2016.

In the second phase, we enriched the data by querying financial and board information from the Orbis database by Bureau van Dijk. The database contains financial information of more than one hundred million companies globally. We queried the companies from the database based on company name. The search

---

[1] Software Industry Survey. https://www.softwareindustrysurvey.fi.
[2] Finnish Softawre Industry & Entrepreneurs Association, Members. https://ohjelmistoyrittajat.fi/en/members.

resulted in retrieval of 287 companies. The search is a fuzzy matching implemented by the data provider and the sample gathered was manually checked.

In the third phase, we created a dataset of all Finnish companies. This data is later used to search if board members or executive officers have other affiliations than the one in a software company. The data was searched from the Orbis database, limiting the search to privately-held Finnish companies. For each company, names of board members and executive officers where extracted. Orbis data does not allow us to separate board members and executive officers. However, we use the list provided from Orbis as board member data. In total, the data of 288,581 companies are included in the final dataset. The Statistics of Finland reports that at the end of 2015, there were 360,051 registered companies in Finland[3]. This leaves roughly 72,000 companies that are not accounted in Orbis. However, the extent of this dataset is argued to be substantial enough for the analysis.

In the fourth phase, we create a matching dataset of Finnish individuals using *Avoindata.fi* (literally, *open data*) service that list Finnish first names and surnames. If a board member's surname was not found in the *Väestötietojärjestelmän suomalaisten nimiaineistot* provided by *Väestörekisterikeskus*[4], we assumed that the member is foreigner. Due to privacy issues, the service publish only surnames that have more than 20 living individuals in Finland. Thus, this data sets certain limitations into the research. For example, rare surnames can be classified as foreigners.

In the fifth phase, two variables—international and network size—were created using a Python script. The Python script was used to match the surnames of software companies against the Finnish surnames to identify individuals that would not be Finnish. In practice, the script created a dichotomous variable 'international' for each company. The variable is set as true if the surname of even one of the members of the company board or its executives is not listed in the Finnish surname database. The variable 'network size' counts the sum of board members and executives directorship positions in the full set of Finnish companies. It uses the full name of individuals in the matching. That is, we calculate for all board members of software companies' the number of directorship positions they have in Finland. Finally the continuous variable is the mean of the affiliation counts of each individual associated with a company.

In the sixth phase, the data for the software companies is complemented with data on company performance. Research has pointed towards several financial data variables as good performance indicators [18]. Partly due to the fact that the majority of the companies in the sample are not publicly listed, this study uses 'Profit Margin', 'Return on Assets' (ROA), 'Current Ratio' (CR) and 'Operating Revenue' (OR) as indicators of a company's economic performance. The dependent variables are controlled for yearly variation by using a three year

---

[3] Tilastokeskus, Yritysten rakenne- ja tilinpäätöstilasto http://tilastokeskus.fi/tup/suoluk/suoluk_yritykset.html.

[4] Väestötietojärjestelmän suomalaisten nimiaineistot. https://www.avoindata.fi/data/en/dataset/none. Licensed with Creative Commons Attribution 4.0.

mean for each variable. Companies that did not have data for three years, were excluded from the analysis. This reduced the sample to 262 companies.

Finally, the data was analyzed looking at the internationalization of the company executives and board as independent variables. The dependent variables are the four company performance indicators, and network size is used as a control variable. In addition, to evaluate the goodness of our internationalization identification strategy, we evaluated a dozen companies. Out of those, only a few had clear a false positive match caused by either a rare or compounded surname.

4   Results

The dataset is sufficiently small for an analytical exploration both in terms of size (262 firms) and dimensions (six variables). From the dataset, 97 firms were classified as 'internationals' and 165 as 'domestic'. Thus, the results are presented with four simple plots. In each plot, a y-axis represents a given economic performance measure, while the average number of board intelocks is always given on the x-axis. These simple scatter plots provide a tentative answer for RQ1. For answering to the question about international board members (RQ2), the scatter plots are further conditioned according to whether or not a board is exclusively domestic, only comprised of members with Finnish surnames.

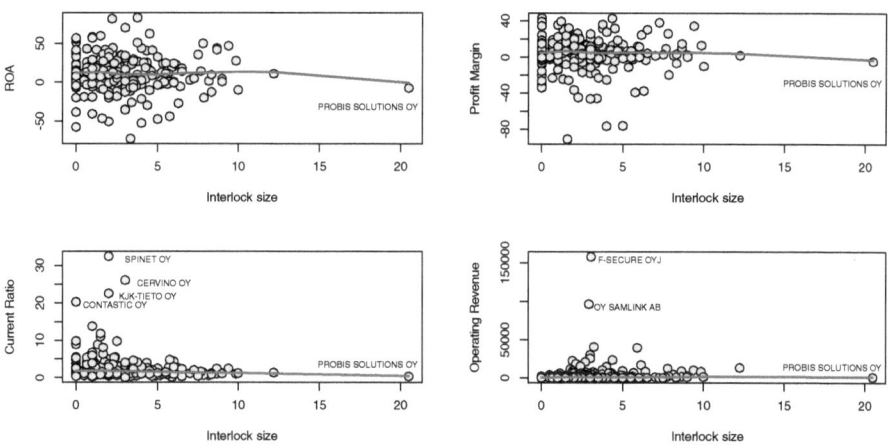

Fig. 1. ROAs, current ratios, profitmargins, and operating revenues for all companies (three-years average)

Given these preliminary notes, the results for RQ1 are shown in Fig. 1 and for RQ2, the results are summarized in Figs. 2, 3, 4, and 5 for the ROAs, current ratios, profit margins, and operating revenues, respectively. The following points can be used for disseminating the figures.

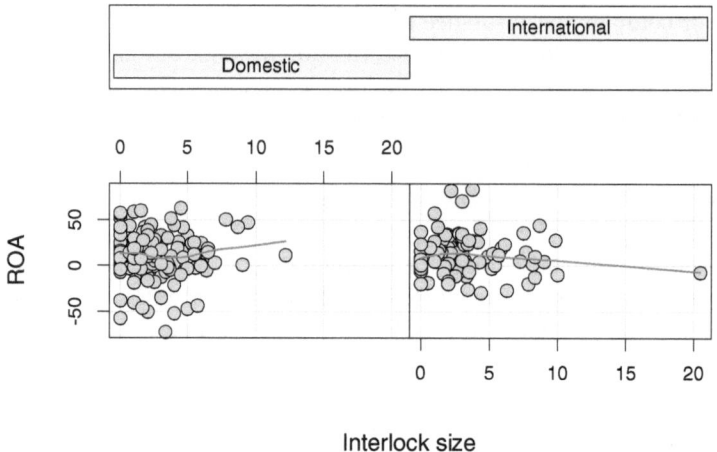

Fig. 2. ROAs, Interlocks, and International Board Members

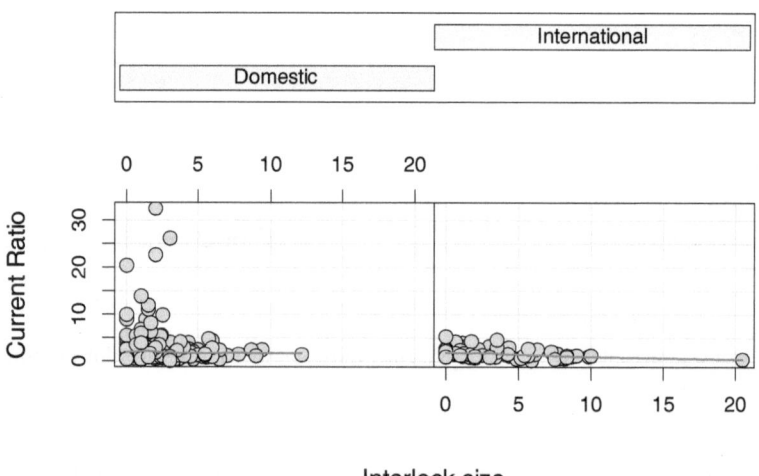

Fig. 3. Current Ratios, Interlocks, and International Board Members

Given a board that is:

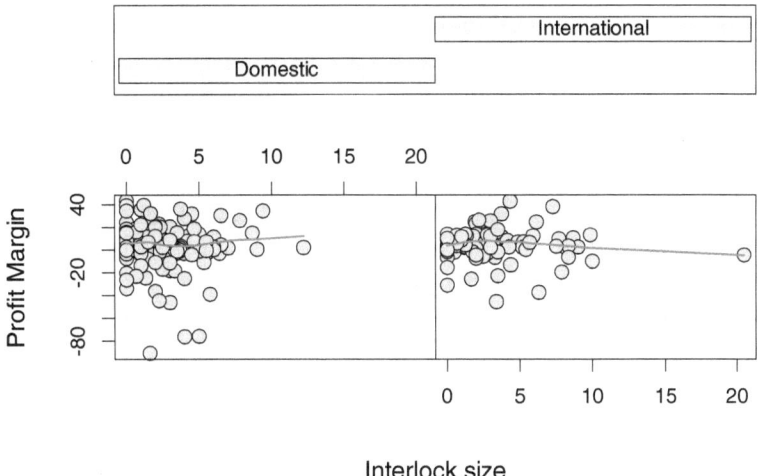

Fig. 4. Profit Margins, Interlocks, and International Board Members

Given a board that is:

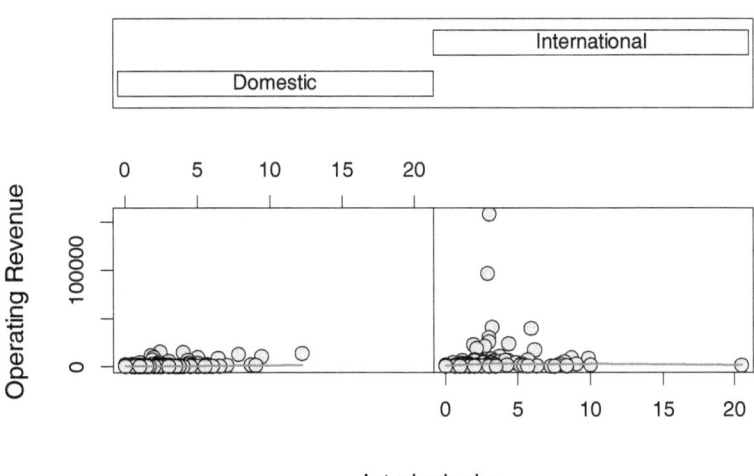

Fig. 5. Operating Revenues, Interlocks, and International Board Members

- The foremost observation is clear: the interlock sizes are not statistically associated with any of the four economic performance measures (Fig. 1). Even when polynomial regression lines are used for accounting potential non-linearities, the resulting lines are flat. Thus, it seems reasonable to conclude that nationwide board interlocks are not generally associated with economic performance of the sampled Finnish software companies.
- When focusing on the conditioning upon whether the boards are exclusively domestic, it becomes evident that there are no notable differences in terms of ROAs and profit margins, as can concluded by comparing the y-axes of the two scatter plots in Figs. 2 and 4. In contrast, the current ratios of a few companies with fully national boards are notably higher when compared to boards staffed also with international members. An analogous but reverse conclusion applies to the operating revenues shown in the y-axes of Fig. 5. This observation also warrants a further point.
- All figures indicate the presence of outliers. These outlying companies also distort the results regarding international boards, although removing the outliers does not strengthen the negligible statistical association between the four economic performance measures and the interlock sizes. In particular, the operating revenues in Fig. 5 are substantially higher for two outlying companies that both have also international board members. These outliers correspond with F-Secure and Samlink. The former company operates in the domain of cyber security, while the latter provides business-to-business service for banking, insurance, and related sectors.

To summarize, on one hand, the amount of nationwide board interlocks provides no noteworthy statistical power for explaining the economic performance of the sampled Finnish software companies. On the other hand, the economic variables vary to some extent according to whether the boards contain also international members. The latter observation is particularly noteworthy with respect to a few outlying companies.

5 Discussion

This study seek answers to the two questions: Whether well-connected boards of software companies are performing better or worse than the rest (RQ1), and whether or not foreigners in the board of directors is associated with better performance of companies (RQ2)?

To answer RQ1, we did not find any evidence that the interlock sizes would be statistically associated with any of the four economic performance measures used. That is, we did not find that interlocking would have either positive or negative impacts on the firms' performance.

To answer RQ2, we showed that the performance measures vary to some extent according to whether the boards contain international member or not. This observation is mainly related to current ratios and operating revenues; however, the effects are opposite – international boards have higher operating revenues whereas national boards have higher current ratios. Nevertheless, the outliers remain interesting cases for further studies.

The results have certain implications for on-going academic discussions. First, this study contributes to a long-running debate on whether high board interlocking impacts positively or negatively to the company's performance. Prior studies have showed support for both relations. In this study, we did not found any robust statistical associations—that is, high board interlocking sizes seem not to have major impacts on the performance of Finnish software companies. This can be associated some aspect of the software industry, which was not uncovered in the scope of this study, but warrants further analysis.

Looking to explain prior positive associations between board interlocks and company performance, we might question the temporal aspects of the data gathered. For example, it can be that well-connected directors are lured to well-performing or promising companies, which then creates a virtuous cycle. Further qualitative and quantitative work are needed to fully understand the impacts and limitations of interlocking directorate. In addition, in our data gathering process, Orbis data limits the study by providing no historical information on board members, although financial data is provided up to the 10 last years.

We were expecting that either well-performing stable companies would have foreigners in their board of directors or quickly growing companies would have acquired foreigner investors and board members. However, when outliers are excluded, we find only a little, if any, statistical association. A further research could be targeted to investigate these outliers if they can suggest some indication on the direction of relationship between foreign member and firm performance. While companies with international board or executive members were performing a little better than companies with fully domestic directors in current ratios whereas an opposite result was found in operating revenues. Nevertheless, the differences remain small. When the few notable outliers are taken into account, there is a substantial difference in operating revenue and these companies seem to support our starting expectation.

For practitioners, this study gives some suggestions. Statistically it seems that there are no differences whether the board members are highly or lowly interlocked. This might seem to be counter-intuitive as one would easily assume that highly interlocked board members would have higher social and human capital, and thus be able to support company better than ones with lower social capital. Board interlocks is expected to improve social capital by, e.g., offering a connection to other board professionals who are well-connected, which might open new opportunities for both the person and the company. Highly connected board members' social capital is increased by, e.g., increasing experiences faster with more directorships. Therefore, well-connected board members should bring some benefits for also company. However, we did not found strong and clear statistical correlation to show that the number of board interlocking would be associated with performance.

In addition, of course board members can be motivated by other reasons than helping the company. There are existing studying suggesting that 'busy' board members do not help companies as well as the others. A busy member is defined as one who have three or more directorships at the same time. However, at least our analysis did not show that having more interlocking directorships would harm companies. Nevertheless, the basic underpinning is clear: having too many positions mean that one cannot concentrate well on every task at hand and, therefore, some of those tasks might not be handled with enough attention. Another further research theme would thus be the quality of board work. There may exist differences in the level and activity of board work and this might be a stronger explaining factor to firm performance.

Naturally, there are some limitations to our research that should be taken into account. First, our strategy to select software companies based on the membership and existence of a profile page in a local advocacy group limits our attention to active, well-performing companies.

Second, we used an open data service to identify foreigners in boards of directors. The used approach has limitations as, e.g., rare surnames are not listed which might have generated some 'false positives'. We noted in the evaluation, for example, that double-barrelled surnames (e.g., when two surnames are joined with a hyphen after a marriage) cause false positives in our matching strategy. However, our identification approach is usable for a large-scale quantitative study and some small error margin, thus, can be accepted.

Third, Finland remains a small, isolated Nordic country with a language spoken by only few and that resembles only little the other languages spoken in the area. Thus, it can be that there are smaller numbers of foreigners available to serve in boards of directors and therefore there could be a higher number of highly interconnected board members. Further work is needed to replicate the analysis in other countries and with other industries. Fourth, Orbis data limits our capabilities to extract only board members and to get historical data for the individuals associated with the company. This makes showing the impact of a new board member challenging, as we can not attribute a specific performance gain to a person. We should also note, that our study looks at top management as a whole whereas prior research has focused on board interlocks either purely in board of directors or executives.

Nevertheless, this study opens new avenues for future inquiries. For example, a majority of existing work focus only on formal, observable, ties between board members and companies. Social capital theory identifies also informal ties, which can be even more stronger and meaningful for performance of a company than formal ones. Further work should study the importance of informal connections such as those created in clubs and software industry associations.

In addition, most of the interlocking directorate studies are based on a single snapshot of a time. There are only a handful of studies (e.g. [8]) presenting longitudinal analysis on the impacts of board interlocking. Further studies should pay attention to model long time implications of having board interlocks. Finally, our dataset have outliers that differ remarkably from the remaining set. Whereas we did not focus on analysing those in this study, a qualitative analysis of outliers could reveal interesting alternative approaches and working patterns.

Finally, this study tried to focus on a smaller segment of Finnish industry in order to avoid the possible pitfalls of previous studies. However, it might be that there are small clusters inside our set of data – thus, in further work, we should cluster the companies and study the impact of board interlocking inside these clusters. For example, companies, that are seeking to growth quickly, could benefit more from well-connected board members than already established companies. In addition, in further studies the meaningfulness of the performance indicators should be analyzed with care.

6   Conclusions

This study addressed the impacts of board interlocks to the performance of software companies. We used a set of 262 Finnish companies, their directors and financial indicators in a quantitative analysis. First, the results show that board interlocks do not seem have either positive or negative correlation on the companies' performance. Second, we showed that having a foreign board member correlates with a better performance of a company only when the performance is evaluated with operating revenues. An opposite effect was found with current ratios. However, there are remarkable outliers in the dataset. Nevertheless, these are contradicting results when compared to the extant literature. However, there are certain limitations in restricting the study population to a single country and therefore future work is needed to replicate the results with a larger dataset. Nevertheless, this study might help scholars to better understand the impacts of board interlocks in software industry and provide some suggestions for the practitioners.

References

1. Almor, T., Hashai, N.: The competitive advantage and strategic configuration of knowledge-intensive, small- and medium-sized multinationals: a modified resource-based view. J. Int. Manag. **10**(4), 479–500 (2004)
2. Clarysse, B., Knockaert, M., Lockett, A.: Outside board members in high tech start-ups. Small Bus. Econ. **29**(3), 243–259 (2007)
3. Coleman, J.S.: Social capital in the creation of human capital. Am. J. Sociol. **94**, S95–S120 (1988)
4. Coviello, N., Munro, H.: Network relationships and the internationalisation process of small software firms. Int. Bus. Rev. **6**(4), 361–386 (1997). http://www.sciencedirect.com/science/article/pii/S0969593197000103
5. Cusumano, M.A.: The Business of Software: What Every Manager, Programmer, and Entrepreneur Must Know to Thrive and Survive in Good Times and Bad. Free Press, New York (2004)
6. Fich, E.M., Shivdasani, A.: Are busy boards effective monitors? J. Finance **61**(2), 689–724 (2006)
7. Fich, E.M., White, L.J.: Why do CEOs reciprocally sit on each other's boards? J. Corp. Finance **11**(1–2), 175–195 (2005)

8. Friel, N., Rastelli, R., Wyse, J., Raftery, A.E.: Interlocking directorates in Irish companies using a latent space model for bipartite networks. Proc. Natl. Acad. Sci. U.S.A. **113**(24), 6629–6634 (2016)
9. Hao, Q., Hu, N., Liu, L., Yao, L.J.: Board interlocking networks and the use relative performance evaluation. Int. J. Acc. Inf. Manag. **22**(3), 237–251 (2014)
10. Heracleous, L., Murray, J.: Networks, interlocking directors and strategy: toward a theoretical framework. Asia Pac. J. Manag. **18**(2), 137–160 (2001)
11. Horton, J., Millo, Y., Serafeim, G.: Resources or power? implications of social networks on compensation and firm performance. J. Bus. Finance Account. **39**(3–4), 399–426 (2012)
12. Hyrynsalmi, S.: Letters from the War of Ecosystems – An Analysis of Independent Software Vendors in Mobile Application Marketplaces. Doctoral dissertation, University of Turku, Turku, Finland, http://urn.fi/URN:ISBN:978-952-12-3144-5, TUCS Dissertations No 188
13. Hyrynsalmi, S., Suominen, A., Knuutila, T.: A discussion of software product conceptualizations. In: Seppänen, M., Mäkinen, S., Ortt, R.J., Hosni, Y. (eds.) Proceedings of the 5th European Conference on Management of Technology EuroMOT 2011, pp. 226–240. Tampere University of Technology (2011)
14. Iansiti, M., Levien, R.: Strategy as ecology. Harvard Bus. Rev. **82**(3), 68–78 (2004)
15. Intintoli, V., Kahle, K.M., Zhao, W.: Board connectedness and board effectiveness (July 22, 2015). SSRN
16. Larcker, D.F., So, E.C., Wang, C.C.: Boardroom centrality and firm performance. J. Account. Econ. **55**(2–3), 225–250 (2013)
17. Loderer, C., Peyer, U.: Board overlap, seat accumulation and share prices. Eur. Financ. Manag. **8**(2), 165–192 (2002)
18. Männiste, M., Hazak, A., Listra, E.: Typology of european listed companies reactions to global credit crunch: cluster analysis of share price performance. In: 3rd International Conference on Information and Financial Engineering, pp. 565–569 (2011)
19. Mol, M.J.: Creating wealth through working with others: interorganizational relationships. Acad. Manag. Executive **15**(1), 150–152 (2001)
20. Moore, J.F.: Predators and prey: a new ecology of competition. Harvard Bus. Rev. **71**(3), 75–86 (1993)
21. Peltonen, J., Rönkkö, M.: Board interlocks in high technology ventures: the relation to growth, financing, and internationalization. In: Tyrväinen, P., Jansen, S., Cusumano, M.A. (eds.) ICSOB 2010. LNBIP, vol. 51, pp. 163–168. Springer, Heidelberg (2010). doi:10.1007/978-3-642-13633-7_14
22. Pombo, C., Gutiérrez, L.H.: Outside directors, board interlocks and firm performance: empirical evidence from colombian business groups. J. Econ. Bus. **63**(4), 251–277 (2011)
23. Pussep, A., Schief, M., Weiblen, T., Leimbach, T., Rönkkö, M., Buxmann, P.: Results of the German Software Industry Survey 2013. Technische Universität Darmstadt, August 2013
24. Sallinger, L.M. (ed.): Encyclopedia of White-Collar & Corporate Crime. SAGE Publishing, Thousands Oaks (2005)
25. Santos, R.L., di Miceli da Silveira, A., Barros, L.A.: Board interlocking in brazil: directors' participation in multiple companies and its effect on firm value and profitability. Latin Am. Bus. Rev. **13**(1), 1–28 (2012)

26. Scott, J. (ed.): Corporate Business and Capitalist Classes, 3rd edn. Oxford University Press, New York (1997)
27. Stuart, T.E., Yim, S.: Board interlocks and the propensity to be targeted in private equity transactions. J. Financ. Econ. **97**(1), 174–189 (2010)
28. Suominen, A., Rilla, N., Oksanen, J., Still, K.: Insights from social network analysis - case board interlocks in finnish game industry. In: Proceedings of the 2016 49th Hawaii International Conference on System Sciences HICSS 2016, pp. 4515–4524. IEEE Computer Society, Washington (2016)

Modeling Strategic Complementarity and Synergistic Value Creation in Coopetitive Relationships

Vik Pant[1(✉)] and Eric Yu[1,2]

[1] Faculty of Information, University of Toronto, Toronto, Canada
vik.pant@mail.utoronto.ca, eric.yu@utoronto.ca
[2] Department of Computer Science, University of Toronto, Toronto, Canada

Abstract. This paper proposes an approach for modeling and analyzing strategic complementarity in software businesses. The primary research objective is to develop an approach for representing and reasoning about synergistic value creation in software enterprises and ecosystems. This agenda is based on the increasing importance of complementarity as a concern within software organizations and their networks. It recognizes the prevalence of coopetition, as a common practice, in the software industry where businesses cooperate and compete simultaneously in open source communities, standards-setting bodies, and software ecosystems. It focuses on complementarity since it is a critical motivator for coopetition among software businesses. This study offers an approach for comparing alternate combinations of software products for assessing their abilities for synergy creation with reference to the concept of added value. It evaluates the sufficiency of this approach by applying it to an industrial case study from management literature. It also identifies a direction for future research for this line of inquiry.

Keywords: Complementarity · Coopetition · Software business · Strategy · Synergy

1 Introduction

Software enterprises and ecosystems rely on simultaneously cooperative and competitive relationships to achieve their collective as well as individual business objectives. It is common for software businesses, from global conglomerates to nascent startups, to engage in coopetitive behaviors towards each other. Such behaviors can be observed in dealings between software businesses in open source communities, standards-setting bodies, and software ecosystems [1]. Moreover, software businesses coopete with each other individually as well as through their partnerships and alliances with other firms – which are themselves coopetitive. Therefore, such software ecosystems [2], partner networks and alliance constellations have multifaceted relationships with each other where cooperation and competition exist concomitantly at the individual and collective levels. Furthermore, coopetition between enterprises can only be expected to increase as larger numbers of enterprises transform themselves from pipeline-driven business models to platform-oriented business models. This is because a key contributor to the

© Springer International Publishing AG 2017
A. Ojala et al. (Eds.): ICSOB 2017, LNBIP 304, pp. 82–98, 2017.
https://doi.org/10.1007/978-3-319-69191-6_6

growth of coopetition in the software industry is the presence of complementarity between many software businesses.

Software business (SB) research focuses on the corporate strategies of software companies. It is concerned with the study of business models of software enterprises to identify their sources of value creation for organizational stakeholders. SB frameworks are intended to explain various facets of a software business such as its product strategy, revenue logic, distribution model, and service implementation model [3]. Such frameworks can be applied to examine different types of software businesses including "pure software product business, enterprise solution system business, and software service business" [4]. These frameworks are designed for analyzing software businesses and hence they are useful for understanding the "relation between a business model, business logic and business strategy" of software companies [5]. Complementarity motivates coopetition, which is an increasingly common feature of inter-organizational relationships between software enterprises and ecosystems. Thus, by illuminating this important concept, this paper furthers understanding into business models and strategies of software businesses.

The rest of the paper is organized as follows. The next section of this paper outlines our research objectives and expected contributions to the study of complementarity. It lists the core facets of strategic complementarity that must be accommodated by any framework that is designed to support the analysis of synergy. The third section presents a model of strategic complementarity and synergistic value creation that is based on an industrial case study from the software industry. The fourth section discusses the key facets of strategic complementarity that are relevant for modeling and analyzing it. The fifth section covers future work and conclusions. The references in this paper are listed in the sixth section.

2   Analyzing Strategic Complementarity Between Actors

Complementarity is a key characteristic of coopetition [8]. Complementarity is also referred to as synergy which is colloquially described as the whole being greater than the sum of its parts [6]. Tee & Gawer [9] assert that "complementarity refers to the combined returns from the combination of two or more assets, with some combinations resulting in higher value creation than other combinations." Similarly, Kyriakopoulos & Moorman [10] claim that "complementarity refers to the degree to which the value of an asset or activity is dependent on the level of other assets or activities." Milgrom & Roberts [11] credit Edgeworth for introducing this concept into economics, where it has been studied extensively. They note that the notion of complementarity can be applied to inputs, such as goods and services, as well as activities [12]. In their influential work on coopetition theory, Brandenburger & Nalebuff explain that a "complementor" is an actor that makes a focal actor more valuable/attractive to a buyer/seller when that buyer/seller can buy/sell from/to both actors rather than when it can only do so with one of them alone [13].

The effects of complementarity can be observed in a variety of enterprise functions ranging from marketing and sales to production and distribution. Examples of the former include goods/services that are regarded by consumers as being more valuable together than separately. For instance, Barquera et al. [14] and Ng et al. [15] claim that coffee and milk are complements. Examples of the latter include economies of scope wherein it is cheaper for a firm to manufacture/deliver goods/services jointly in comparison to manufacturing/delivering each good/service individually. For instance, Tsuji [16] asserts that economies of scope can be found in "department stores which offer consumer loans" and "electric appliances makers which produce PCs". Complementarity is a key motivation for participation in software ecosystems by rival vendors.

Following [29], we distinguish between the concepts of *value added* by an actor, and *added value* of an actor in a multi-party economic relationship. Reasoning about strategic complementarity between actors requires the ability to analyze three main factors which are resources/assets/objects, value added by each actor, and added value of each actor. A resource/asset/object refers to an entity associated with some value, benefit, or utility for a stakeholder. Value added by an actor refers to the incremental addition of some value, benefit, or utility by that actor. Added value of an actor refers to the worth of that actor in terms of value, benefit, or utility creation in a multi-party economic relationship. In analyzing complementarity, the notions of value added and added value are viewed from the perspective of the stakeholder that is the beneficiary of synergy.

Modeling is widely used in IS engineering, and recently has been extended to deal with strategic management (SM) concerns. IS researchers have incorporated theories from SM into modeling frameworks to reason about strategic decisions [7, 31]. For example, in our earlier work, we analyzed inter-organizational competition that resulted from resource conflicts [6]. Similarly, Santos [34] proposes Power Models that are useful for understanding the relationships between different actors in an ecosystem by applying ideas about power from the SM literature. Driven by their proliferation in industrial practice and prominence in SM literature – ideas from coopetition theory are starting to appear in IS publications. However, complementarity, which is a prime driver of coopetition, has not been integrated into modeling frameworks in a structured and systematic manner. The absence of such integration "make it difficult for requirements engineers to validate low-level requirements against the more abstract high-level requirements representing the business strategy" [32]. In this paper we use modeling to analyze strategic complementarity.

3   Example: Complementarity Between Windows and Pentium

3.1   Analyzing Strategic Complementarity in the Wintel Alliance

A widely-studied example of complementarity and coopetition is the case of Wintel (i.e., Microsoft Windows operating system on Intel x86 chipsets) [17]. Throughout the 1990s, Microsoft and Intel simultaneously competed and cooperated with each other [18]. They cooperated to achieve their common goal of establishing Wintel as the de facto standard in personal computing [19]. This joint objective comprised of enlarging the market for Windows on x86 by competing with vendors of substitute products, such as Apple and Motorola [20]. However, Microsoft and Intel also had their private goals of maximizing their individual shares of the collective value created by the Wintel alliance [21]. This created a, "kind of interfirm dynamics which allow the competing firms involved to manage a partially convergent interest and goal structure" [22].

Brandenburger & Nalebuff [13] suggest that complementarity between Windows and Pentium motivated the coopetitive relationship between Microsoft and Intel. The basic reason for the presence of this complementarity was that a customer (i.e., PC user), with a specific set of requirements, could do more by using these products together rather than separately. For example, a PC user could get better performance in Windows with Pentium because Intel had optimized that chipset for Windows and Microsoft had implemented the MMX multimedia instruction set from Intel into Windows [18]. If this user chose a different operating system (e.g., Linux) on Pentium or Windows on a different chipset (e.g., K6) then that user would have foregone the performance improvements that stemmed from the co-optimization of Windows and Pentium.

However, while Wintel offered performance advantages to a PC user (compared to substitutes of Windows and Pentium) it also locked that user into a relationship with proprietary vendors. Microsoft and Intel charged premium prices and this translated into higher costs for that user. Conversely, if this user chose a different operating system or chipset then they would have saved money but would not have benefited from the performance advantages of Wintel. This was just one of many tradeoffs that vendors (such as Microsoft, Intel, Apple, and AMD) had to analyze to develop persuasive value propositions for their target customers.

As this example indicates, reasoning about complementarity requires the ability to evaluate the objectives of an actor (e.g., PC user), the options that are available to meet those objectives, and the impact of those options on those objectives. Each alternative can impact the satisfaction or denial of an actor's goals differently since there are trade-offs between those options. The satisfaction of an objective leads to realization of benefits for an actor while its denial impairs such benefit realization. Therefore, to understand the presence and extent of complementarity between entities the individual and collective effects, of those entities, on value creation must be compared. This can be done using text, as was done in this sub-section, as well as by using models, as is done in the following sub-section.

3.2 Reasoning About Strategic Complementarity in the Wintel Alliance

In this paper, we use two modeling languages, i* and e3value, in combination to analyze strategic complementarity between Microsoft Windows and Intel Pentium. i* is explained by Lucena et al. in [27] and e3value is explained by Souza et al. in [28]. These authors depict metamodels of i* and e3value in [27, 28] respectively. i* (distributed intentionality) is a socio-technical modeling language that can be used to represent the intentional structure of an actor as well as its strategic relationships with other actors. It is useful for analyzing complementarity because it supports comparing the impact of alternatives on objectives via links between means and ends.

Figures 1a, 1b, and 1c show the impact of different combinations of operating systems and chipsets on the satisfaction of various objectives of a home user of personal computer (PC). Figure 1d presents a composite model of alternatives available to a home user for personal computing. i* is a goal modeling language and the main conceptual entities in i* are goals, tasks, resources, and softgoals. Within the scope of each actor, a *goal* is a state of affairs that an actor intends to achieve in the world. For example, in Figs. 1a, 1b and 1c, the goal of a home user is to buy a PC. A *task* is a means for achieving an end which refers to satisfying a goal. For example, in Figs. 1a, 1b and 1c, a home user can buy Windows on Pentium, Windows on other chipset, or other operating system on Pentium to satisfy its goal of buying a PC. A *resource* is a physical or informational object that is required to achieve some goal or perform some task. For example, in Fig. 1a, a home user procures Pentium from Intel and obtains Windows from Microsoft.

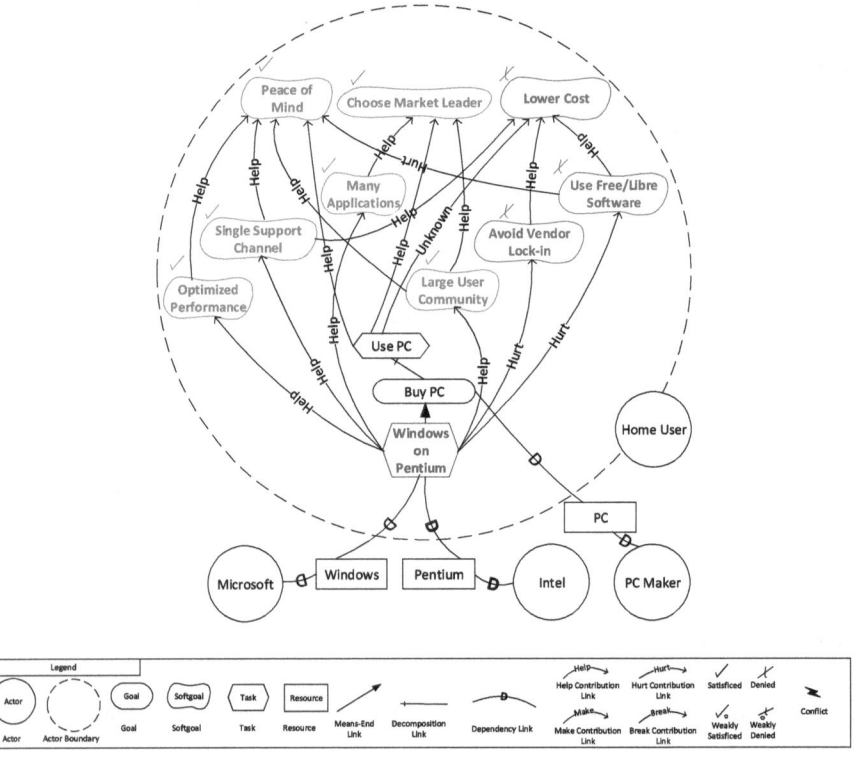

Fig. 1a. i* SR diagram showing adequacy of Wintel.

A *softgoal* is a quality objective or nonfunctional requirement that does not have well defined satisfaction criteria. The fulfilment of a softgoal is judged subjectively from the perspective of an actor through elaboration and refinement. For example, in Figs. 1a, 1b and 1c, the requirements of a home user are represented as softgoals. This is because their satisfaction is judged subjectively from the perspective of that home user. Figure 1a shows those requirements that are satisfied/denied if the home user chooses Windows on Pentium. Figure 1b shows those requirements that are

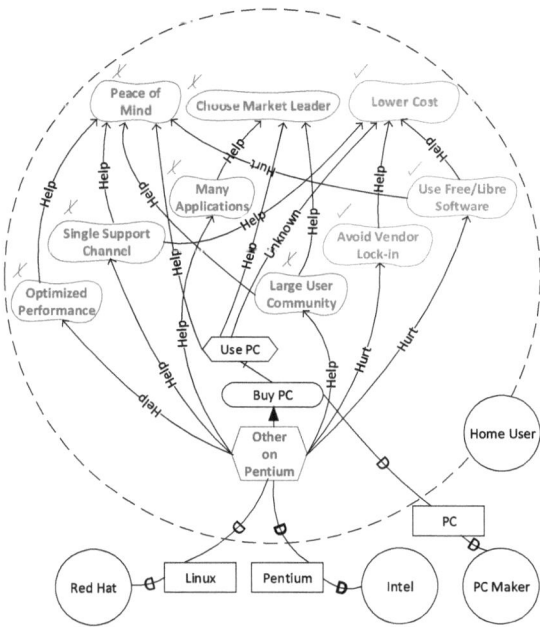

Fig. 1b. i* SR diagram showing adequacy of other operating system on Pentium.

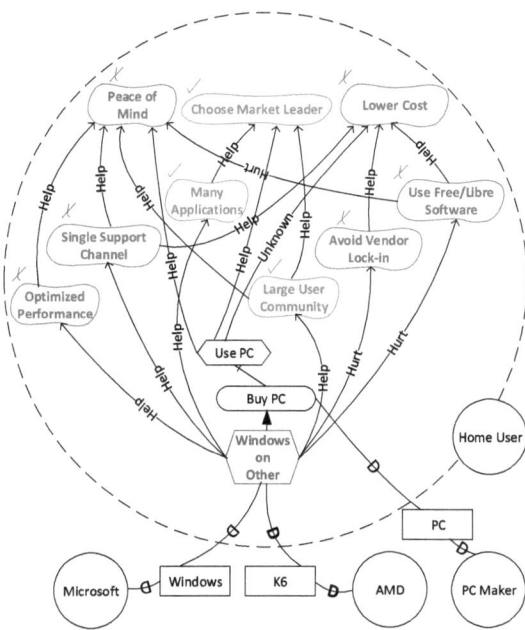

Fig. 1c. i* SR diagram showing adequacy of Windows on other chipset.

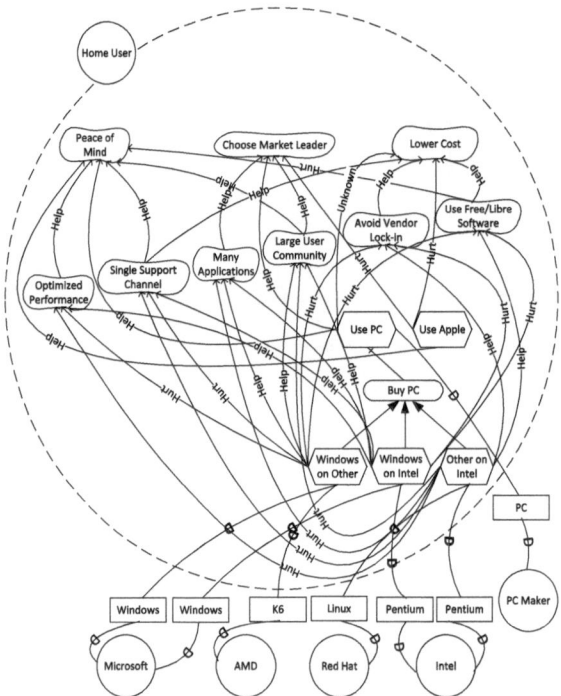

Fig. 1d. i* SR diagram showing all three alternatives.

satisfied/denied if the home user chooses an operating system other than Windows (e.g., Linux) on Pentium. Figure 1c shows those requirements that are satisfied/denied if the home user chooses Windows on a chipset other than Pentium (e.g., K6).

These entities are connected via means-ends links, decomposition links, dependency links, and contribution links. *Means-ends links* relate a goal to one or more tasks such that the completion of any of those tasks achieves that goal. For example, in Figs. 1a, 1b and 1c, Windows on Pentium, other operating system on Pentium, and Windows on other chipset are examples of alternate means that satisfy the same goal of buying a PC. *Decomposition links* relate a task to other elements such that the fulfillment of all those elements is required to perform that task. For example, in Figs. 1a, 1b and 1c, a home user needs to buy a PC before it can use that PC. Contribution links denote various types of impacts (such as help, hurt, etc.) that different entities have on softgoals. For example, in Fig. 1a, buying a PC that runs Windows on Pentium helps a home user benefit from optimized performance as well as access to a large user community.

Dependency links are used to express the intentional relationships between actors based on the goals, tasks, resources, and softgoals that an actor depends on from another actor. An actor that depends on another actor is termed a depender, an actor on which another actor depends is termed a dependee, and the object of the dependency between actors is termed a dependum. For example, in Fig. 1a, a home user depends on

Intel to procure Pentium and Microsoft to obtain Windows. In the diagrams in this paper, we have omitted dependencies from the vendors to the home user (i.e., for money) to simplify the visual presentation and interpretation of these diagrams.

A comparison of Figs. 1a, 1b and 1c shows that Windows on Pentium satisfies the overall requirements of a home user better than Windows on other chipset or other operating system on Pentium. Thus, Windows and Intel are more valuable together for a home user than Windows and Pentium separately because neither Windows and a different chipset nor another operating system and Pentium can meet a home user's PC requirements as optimally as Windows and Pentium can jointly. This demonstrates the presence of complementarity between Windows and Pentium and points out the reasons for the existence of that complementarity. It should be noted that while these i* diagrams allow us to depict the presence of complementarity between Windows and Pentium—they do not allow us to depict the magnitude of surplus from that synergy.

e3value is a value modeling language that can be used to represent networks that are setup to facilitate economic exchanges between organizations. It is useful for analyzing complementarity because it can be used to compare the individual and collective value creation effects of entities. In e3value, the main conceptual entities are actors, value objects, value ports, value interfaces, value transfers, value transactions, and value activities.

An *actor* is an economically independent entity (e.g., Microsoft) that transfers *value objects* (e.g., Windows) to other actors (e.g., home user) in return for objects (e.g., money) of benefit/utility from them. *Value ports* (e.g., catalog) are used by an actor (e.g., Microsoft) to offer (e.g., Windows) or demand (e.g., money) value objects from other actors (e.g., home user). *Value interfaces* are groupings of value ports (e.g., sale) that represent economic reciprocity such that all the value ports in a value interface exchange value objects or none of them do. *Value transfers* are used to connect two value interfaces (e.g., buy, sell) and *value transactions* (e.g., procurement) group value transfers such that all the value transfers in a value transaction occur or none of them do. Actors perform *value activities* (e.g., sell software) to create economic profits.

In this paper, we use a slightly extended e3value notation, in Figs. 2a and 2b, to analyze the magnitude of complementarity between Windows and Pentium. The concepts of *willingness-to-pay (WP)* and *opportunity cost (OC)* are relevant for analyzing complementarity. WP refers to the maximum resources (e.g., money) that an actor (e.g., home user) will voluntarily relinquish in exchange for another resource (e.g., operating system, chipset). OC refers to the minimum resources (e.g., money) that an actor (e.g., Microsoft, Intel) will voluntarily accept to relinquish another resource (e.g., Windows, Pentium). The logics of WP and OC hold because a rational and self-interested actor cannot be expected to give up a more valuable resource in exchange for a less valuable resource but that it will gladly give up a less valuable resource in exchange for a more valuable resource [29].

We have extended the standard e3value notation slightly by inscribing the identifiers of actors, market segments, and value activities within their respective boundaries. We have also specified the content of a value exchange above the arrow that represents it. The value can specify a range (expressed as inequalities) rather than a fixed quantity. Figure 2a shows the separate value constellations of Intel and Microsoft wherein each of these vendors provide their products, Pentium and Windows, to a home user

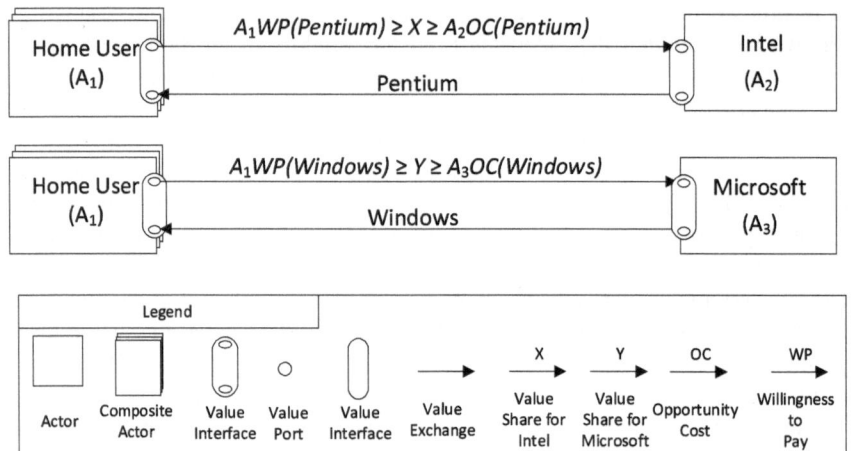

Fig. 2a. e3value diagram of separate value constellations of Microsoft and Intel.

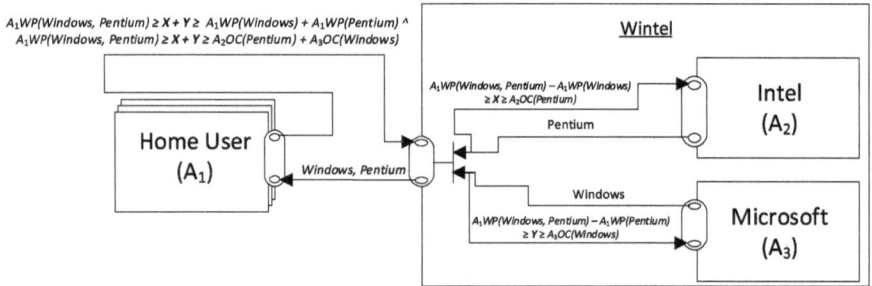

Fig. 2b. e3value diagram of Wintel's value constellation.

separately. The upper sub-diagram in Fig. 2a shows that Intel delivers a Pentium chip to a home user who pays Intel an amount that is less than or equal to that home user's WP for Pentium and is greater than or equal to Intel's OC for selling Pentium. The lower sub-diagram in Fig. 2a shows that Microsoft delivers Windows operating system to a home user who pays Microsoft an amount that is less than or equal to that home user's WP for Windows and is greater than or equal to Microsoft's OC for selling Windows.

Figure 2b shows the joint value constellation of Wintel wherein the home user gets the Microsoft operating system and the Intel chipset together (i.e., Windows on Pentium). In this case the WP of a home user for Windows and Pentium together is greater than the sums of their WP for Windows and Pentium separately. This is the case, because comparing Figs. 1a, 1b and 1c leads to the conclusion that Windows and Pentium are complements such that a home user is willing to pay more for an offer that combines their value propositions than one that keeps them apart. Both Windows and Pentium are more beneficial to a home user and offer greater utility to that home user when they are together than when they are separate. This difference between a home user's WP for Windows as well as Pentium jointly and the sum of a home user's WP for Windows as well as Pentium separately can be regarded as surplus from synergy. This is additional value that is present within a joint value constellation of Microsoft and Intel but is absent from the individual value constellations of these vendors.

In the scenario depicted in Fig. 2a, calculating the amount of value that is acquired by Microsoft and Intel in their separate value constellations is relatively straightforward. This is because the upper bound of value that Microsoft and Intel can appropriate individually is constrained by a home user's WP for their respective products alone (i.e., Windows, Pentium). In Fig. 2b, however, calculating the upper bound of value that Microsoft and Intel can appropriate from their joint value constellation is relatively complicated. This is because both Microsoft and Intel can stake their respective claims on the surplus from synergy that is generated by their partnership. While neither Microsoft nor Intel will, under most circumstances, voluntarily accept an amount that is lower in value than their OC for Windows and Pentium respectively – the presence of surplus creates the possibility for them to appropriate an amount that is greater in value than a home user's WP for Windows and Pentium respectively.

Added value is relevant for determining the upper bound on the amount of value that Microsoft and Intel can appropriate from for themselves from the Wintel constellation. The reason that this is the case is because if an actor appropriates an amount of value greater than this limit then the amount of value remaining for the other actors to appropriate becomes lower than their OCs. In such a case those other actors would be worse off by participating in such an economic relationship and they would be better off by abstaining from it [29]. This logic describes the paradox of joint value creation and individual value appropriation within coopetition wherein firms are "cooperating to create a bigger business 'pie,' while competing to divide it up" [13]. Hence, being able to analyze complementarity is a crucial requirement for managing coopetitive relationships.

Added value is calculated by subtracting the economic value of the relationship without the focal actor from the economic value of the relationship with all the actors [29]. The formulae for calculating added value is denoted in Fig. 2b above the arrows representing the value transactions from the composite actor, Wintel, to its constituent actors, Microsoft and Intel. These formulae above the inbound value transaction for Microsoft/Intel indicate the upper bound on the value that Microsoft/Intel can appropriate for itself from Wintel. Thus, added value is a home user's WP for Windows and Pentium (i.e., value of the economic relationship with all the actors involved) less that home user's WP for Pentium/Windows (i.e., value of the economic relationship without the focal actor). These formulae also specify the lower bound on the amount of value that Microsoft/Intel will voluntarily accept as their OCs for Windows/Pentium respectively.

As this modeling-supported reasoning shows, i* is useful for understanding the causes of complementarity while e3value is useful for determining the extent of complementarity. i* and e3value explain different aspects of strategic complementarity between actors and together they can represent more facets of synergistic value creation than either of them can depict alone. Specifically, "i* goal models complement the e3value models by revealing the strategic reasoning (i*) behind the value exchanges (e3value)" [25]. Due to such compatibility, i* and e3value have been used jointly to depict strategic relationships between actors in the scholarly literature [25, 26]. This is also consistent with the recommendation from Bleistein et al. [32] that, "depending on the needs, several languages can also be used together in a complementary way".

The steps for reasoning about the Wintel case can also be applied to analyze the complementarity between other software businesses and networks such as software ecosystems. The first step involves the development of actor and goal models using i* to explain the strategic rationales and strategic dependencies between software businesses and focal stakeholders. The second step involves comparing these models to identify the relative impact of each alternative on the satisfaction of stakeholder requirements. The third step involves the development of e3value models of separate and joint value constellations of software businesses to measure the magnitude of complementarity between them. The next section presents an abstraction of the concepts in this section to aid in the reuse of these steps. It focuses on the modeling of the concepts of value added by an actor in isolation and added value of an actor to a multi-party economic relationship.

4 A Method for Modeling and Analyzing Strategic Complementarity and Synergistic Value Creation

4.1 Value Added by an Actor in a Value Chain

Value added is an intuitive concept that is defined by [30] "as revenue minus the cost of purchased inputs." Consider Figs. 3a and 3b that show a market in which a consumer (A_1) buys a finished product (O_2) from a vendor (A_2) and that vendor (A_2) procures raw materials (O_1) from a supplier (A_3). A_2 performs an activity (C_1), by applying its competences and combining its resources, to transform O_1 (that it has procured from A_3) into O_2. A_1 decides to buy O_2 from A_2 by compensating it with X resources since O_2 is useful for A_1. While the following exposition discusses the relationship between A_1 and A_2 _ such a relationship holds likewise between A_2 and A_3. This is because, just as A_2 is a vendor that sells O_2 to A_1 which is its customer – similarly A_3 is a vendor that sells O_1 to A_2 which is its customer.

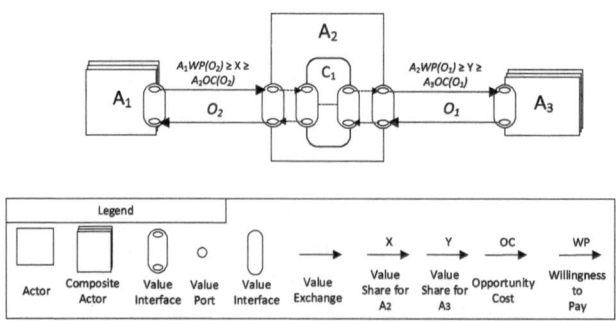

Fig. 3a. e3value diagram of A_2's value constellation.

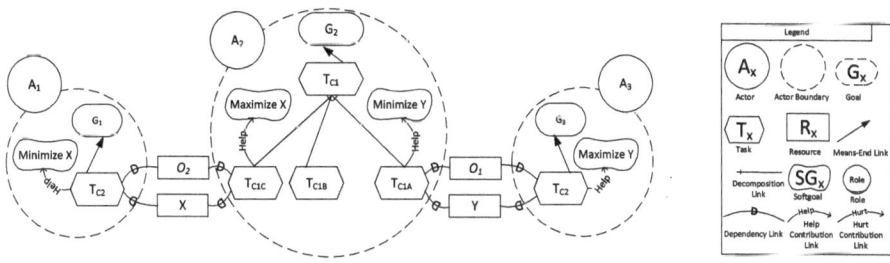

Fig. 3b. i* Strategic Rationale (SR) diagram showing willingness-to-pay and opportunity cost.

In this market, two economic factors impose an upper and lower bound on X/Y respectively. The upper bound is dictated by the customer (A_1/A_2) while the lower bound is determined by the vendor (A_2/A_3) such that X/Y is determined through a process of bargaining and negotiation between A_1/A_2 and A_2/A_3. Figure 3a denotes the upper/lower bounds in the formula above an arrow representing value exchanges, which are X and Y, between A_1 and A_2 as well as A_2 and A_3 respectively. In this example the value added by A_2 is X – Y. We focus on the relationship between A_1 and A_2 to discuss these upper/lower bounds on X but this logic is equally relevant in the relationship between A_2 and A_3.

The maximum amount of resources that A_1 is willing to pay A_2 is less than or equal to the maximum benefit, utility, or value that A_1 can obtain from O_2. This upper bound refers to the concept of '*willingness to pay*' that was discussed in Sect. 3. This WP is noted in Fig. 3a as $A_1WP(O_2)$. A_1 is unwilling to pay an amount higher than A_1WP (O_2) because doing so would mean that A_1 would give away more resources for O_2 than what A_1 considers it to be worth. Conversely, however, A_1 is willing to pay A_2 an amount less than $A_1WP(O_2)$ for O_2 because that would mean that A_1 is underpaying A_2 by giving away fewer resources for O_2 than what A_1 considers it to be worth. A rational and self-interest seeking economic actor is willing to underpay for a resource because doing so creates a perceived surplus. However, that actor is unwilling to overpay for a resource because doing so creates a perceived deficit for that actor.

The minimum amount of resources that A_2 is willing to accept from A_1 is greater than or equal to the maximum amount of resources that A_2 can obtain from O_2 through an alternate use (e.g., selling it to someone else). This lower bound refers to the concept of '*opportunity cost*' that was discussed in Sect. 3. This OC is noted in Fig. 3a as $A_2OC(O_2)$. A_2 is unwilling to accept an amount less than $A_2OC(O_2)$ because doing so would mean that A_2 would get fewer resources by selling O_2 to A_1 than it can by applying it to some other use. Conversely, however, A_2 is willing to accept an amount from A_2 that is greater than $A_2OC(O_2)$ for O_2 because that would mean that A_2 is getting more resources for O_2 from A_1 than it would from the next best alternative use of O_2. Figure 3b shows the structure of such bargaining and negotiating between A_1/A_2 and A_2/A_3.

4.2   Added Value of an Actor to a Multi-party Economic Relationship

Added value is different from value added because while the latter represents economic margin (i.e., difference between revenues and purchased inputs), the former denotes the worth of a party in a multi-party economic relationship. In the context of a specific player, added value refers to the "value created by all the players in the vertical chain minus the value created by all the players in the vertical chain except the one in question" [29]. Consider Figs. 4a, 4b and 4c that show a market in which a consumer (A_1) buys two products from two vendors – O_1 and O_2 from A_2 and A_3 respectively. A_1 can use O_1 and O_2 individually (i.e., without each other) or it can use them jointly (i.e., with each other).

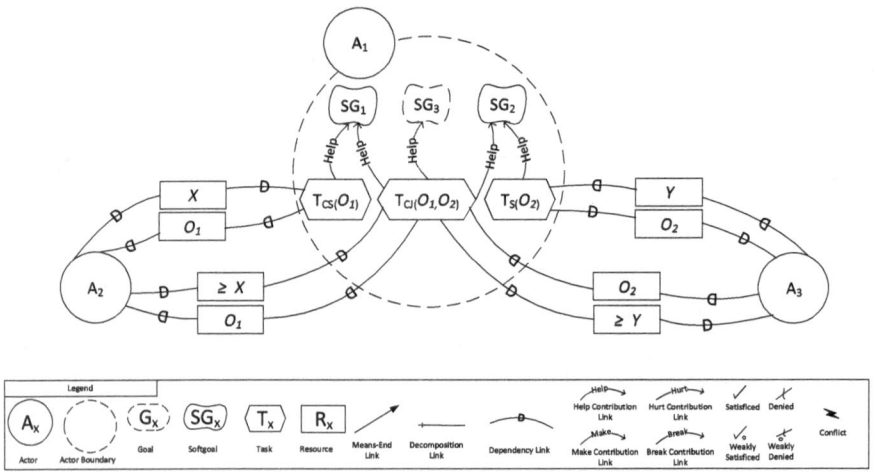

Fig. 4a. i* SR diagram of A_1 with complementarity between A_2 and A_3.

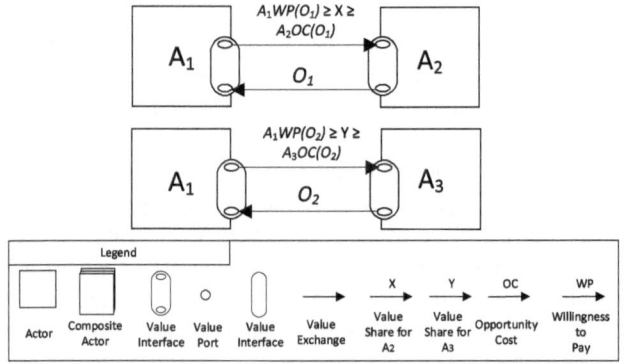

Fig. 4b. e3value diagram of A_1's value constellation with separate usage of O_1 and O_2.

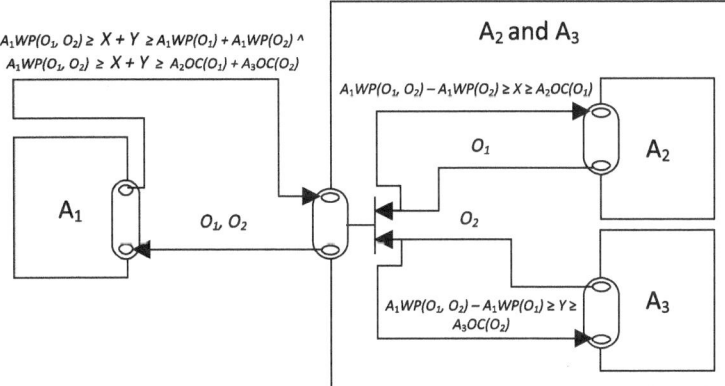

Fig. 4c. e3value diagram of A_1's value constellation with complementarity between A_2 and A_3.

Figure 4b shows a situation in which A_1 consumes O_1 and O_2 separately while Fig. 4c shows a situation in which A_1 consumes O_1 and O_2 jointly. Figure 4a shows both situations. Figure 4a shows the presence of complementarity between O_1/A_2 and O_2/A_3, which is an incentive for A_1 to use O_1 and O_2 jointly rather than separately. In Fig. 4a, A_1 is able to satisfy more objectives by using O_1 and O_2 together than by using either O_1 or O_2 separately. In a situation of complementarity, as depicted in Fig. 4b, it is not feasible to use the WP of A_1 for O_1 or O_2 as the upper bound on the value that their respective firms (i.e., A_2 and A_3) can appropriate from this joint value constellation. Rather, the presence of a surplus from synergy necessitates the calculation of the added values of A_2 and A_3 to determine the maximum amount of value that each firm can appropriate from this joint value constellation.

Complementarity exists in the case of joint usage of O_1 and O_2 because by using these products together the home user can satisfy more of its objectives than it can by using either O_1 or O_2 separately. Therefore, this home user is willing to pay a greater amount for the relatively higher utility or benefit that it can obtain this combined offering than that from using either of these products without the other. This presence of complementarity is indicated via the greater outbound value flow from the home user for O_1, O_2 in Fig. 4c compared to the sum of the outbound value flows from that home user for O_1 and O_2 in Fig. 4a. The difference between these value flows can be regarded as the surplus from synergy because it refers to an amount that is only present when O_1 and O_2 are together but is absent when O_1 and O_2 are separate.

The amounts of value, X and Y, that can be appropriated by actors, A_2 and A_3, is specified as a range because X and Y are dependent on each other. Since the total value that can be appropriated by all the actors is fixed, $A_1WP(O_1, O_2)$, then the more/less amount of value that is appropriated by an actor, A_2/A_3, reduces/increases the amount of value that is remaining for appropriation by another actor, A_3/A_2. As discussed in Sect. 3, if an actor, A_2/A_3, appropriates a greater amount of value than their added value then another actor, A_3/A_2, will only be able to appropriate an amount of value less than their opportunity cost. The presence as well as the magnitude of complementarity can be expressed and explained by using i* and e3value together in this way.

5   Conclusions and Future Work

In this paper, we proposed a modeling technique and method for articulating and analyzing strategic complementarity to aid in the understanding of business models and strategies of software businesses. The modeling technique offered by this paper is useful for understanding the presence of complementarity as well as the magnitude of synergy effects. We used an industrial case study from the literature to test our modeling method as well as to elicit decontextualized patterns to explain strategic complementarity. To further test the technique, we are conducting case studies in enterprise settings as well as in ecosystems and startup-ups.

References

1. Valença, G., Alves, C., Heimann, V., Jansen, S., Brinkkemper, S.: Competition and collaboration in requirements engineering: a case study of an emerging software ecosystem. In: 2014 IEEE 22nd International Requirements Engineering Conference (RE), pp. 384–393. IEEE, August 2014
2. Teixeira, J., Robles, G., González-Barahona, J.M.: Lessons learned from applying social network analysis on an industrial Free/Libre/Open Source Software ecosystem. J. Internet Serv. Appl. 6(1), 14 (2015)
3. Rajala, R., Rossi, M., Tuunainen, V.K.: A framework for analyzing software business models. In: European Conference on Information Systems, pp. 1614–1627, June 2003
4. Väyrynen, K.: Software business in industrial companies: identifying capabilities for three types of software business. In: Proceedings of the 31st International Conference on Information Systems (ICIS), Saint Louis, MO (2010)
5. Vanhala, E., Smolander, K.: What do we know about business models in software companies?-systematic mapping study. Int. J. IADIS 11(3), 89–102 (2013)
6. Pant, V., Yu, E.: Coopetition with frenemies: towards modeling of simultaneous cooperation and competition among enterprises. In: Horkoff, J., Jeusfeld, M.A., Persson, A. (eds.) PoEM 2016. LNBIP, vol. 267, pp. 164–178. Springer, Cham (2016). doi:10.1007/978-3-319-48393-1_12
7. Gordijn, J., Osterwalder, A., Pigneur, Y.: Comparing two business model ontologies for designing e-business models and value constellations. In: Proceedings of BLED 2005, 15 (2005)
8. Brandenburger, A.M., Nalebuff, B.J.: The right game: use game theory to shape strategy. Harvard Bus. Rev. 73(4), 57–71 (1995)
9. Tee, R., Gawer, A.: Industry architecture as a determinant of successful platform strategies: a case study of the i-mode mobile Internet service. Europ. Manag. Rev. 6(4), 217–232 (2009)
10. Kyriakopoulos, K., Moorman, C.: Tradeoffs in marketing exploitation and exploration strategies: the overlooked role of market orientation. Int. J. Res. Mark. 21(3), 219–240 (2004)
11. Milgrom, P., Roberts, J.: Complementarities and fit strategy, structure, and organizational change in manufacturing. J. Account. Econ. 19(2), 179–208 (1995)
12. Milgrom, P., Roberts, J.: Complementarities and systems: Understanding Japanese economic organization. Estud. Economicos 17, 3–42 (1994)
13. Brandenburger, A.M., Nalebuff, B.J.: Co-opetition. Doubleday, New York (1996)

14. Barquera, S., Hernandez-Barrera, L., Tolentino, M.L., Espinosa, J., Ng, S.W., Rivera, J.A., Popkin, B.M.: Energy intake from beverages is increasing among Mexican adolescents and adults. J. Nutr. **138**(12), 2454–2461 (2008)

15. Ng, S.W., Mhurchu, C.N., Jebb, S.A., Popkin, B.M.: Patterns and trends of beverage consumption among children and adults in Great Britain, 1986–2009. Br. J. Nutr. **108**(03), 536–551 (2012)

16. Tsuji, M.: Envisioning the Japanese economic system in the 21st century in relation to economies of network. In: Schober, F., Kishida, T., Arayama, Y. (eds.) Restructuring the Economy of the 21st Century in Japan and Germany, pp. 15–36. Duncker & Humblot, Berlin (1999)

17. Gomes-Casseres, B.: How alliances shape competition. In: Shenkar, O., Reuer, J. (eds.) Handbook of Strategic Alliances, pp. 39–54. Sage, Newbury Park (2005)

18. Yoffie, D.B., Kwak, M.: With friends like these: the art of managing complementors. Harvard Bus. Rev. **84**(9), 88–98 (2006)

19. Gomes-Casseres, B.: Competitive advantage in alliance constellations. Strateg. Organ. **1**(3), 327–335 (2003)

20. Golnam, A., Sanchez, R., Ritala, P., Wegmann, A.: The why and the how of coopetition: modeling the in-centives and design of coopetitive value networks. In: A Focused Issue on Building New Competences in Dynamic Environments. Research in Competence-Based Management, 7. Emerald Group Publishing Limited, pp. 29–60 (2014)

21. Casadesus-Masanell, R., Yoffie, D.B.: Wintel: cooperation and conflict. Manage. Sci. **53**(4), 584–598 (2007)

22. Castaldo, S., Dagnino, G.B.: Trust and coopetition: the strategic role of trust in interfirm coopetitive dynam-ics. In: Dagnino, G.B., Rocco, E. (eds.) Coopetition Strategy: Theory, Experiments and Cases, pp. 74–100. Routledge, New York (2009)

23. Pijpers, V., Gordijn, J.: $e^3forces$: understanding strategies of networked e^3value constellations by analyzing environmental forces. In: Krogstie, J., Opdahl, A., Sindre, G. (eds.) CAiSE 2007. LNCS, vol. 4495, pp. 188–202. Springer, Heidelberg (2007). doi:10.1007/978-3-540-72988-4_14

24. Pijpers, V., Gordijn, J., Akkermans, H.: Business strategy-it alignment in a multi-actor setting: a mobile e-service case. In: Proceedings of the 10th International Conference on Electronic Commerce (2008)

25. Gordijn, J., Yu, E., van der Raadt, B.: E-service design using i* and e3value modeling. IEEE Softw. **23**(3), 26–33 (2006)

26. Ouyang, F., Zhao, H.: Business models optimization using e3value and i* modeling: taking knowledge resource website as an example. Manage. Sci. Res. **3**(2) (2014)

27. Lucena, M., Santos, E., Silva, C., Alencar, F., Silva, M.J., Castro, J.: Towards a unified metamodel for i*. In: Second International Conference on Research Challenges in Information Science, RCIS 2008, pp. 237–246. IEEE, June 2008

28. Souza, E., Abrahão, S., Moreira, A., Araújo, J., Insfran, E.: Comparing Value-Driven Methods: an experiment design. In: Second International Workshop on Human Factors in Modeling (HuFaMo 2016). CEUR-WS, pp. 19–26 (2016)

29. Brandenburger, A.M., Stuart, H.W.: Value-based business strategy. J. Econ. Manag. Strategy **5**(1), 5–24 (1996)

30. Lieberman, M.B., Garcia-Castro, R., Balasubramanian, N.: Measuring value creation and appropriation in firms: the VCA model. Strategic Manage. J. (2016)

31. López, L.C., Franch, X.G.: Applying business strategy models in organizations. In: Proceedings of the 7th International i* Workshop 2014, Thessaloniki, Greece, 16–17 June (2014)

32. Bleistein, S.J., Cox, K., Verner, J.: Modeling business strategy in E-business systems requirements engineering. In: Wang, S., Tanaka, K., Zhou, S., Ling, T.-W., Guan, J., Yang, D.-Q., Grandi, F., Mangina, E.E., Song, I.-Y., Mayr, H.C. (eds.) ER 2004. LNCS, vol. 3289, pp. 617–628. Springer, Heidelberg (2004). doi:10.1007/978-3-540-30466-1_57
33. Giannoulis, C., Zikra, I., Bergholtz, M., Zdravkovic, J., Stirna, J., Johannesson, P.: A comparative analysis of enterprise modeling approaches for modeling business strategy. In: 6th IFIP WG 8.1 Working Conference on the Practice of Enterprise Modeling (PoEM 2013), Riga, Latvia, 6–7 November 2013, pp. 193–204, (2013)
34. Santos, G.A.V.: A theory of power in software ecosystems formed by small-to-medium enterprises. Ph.D. Thesis (2016)

Business Model Exploration for Software Defined Networks

Yudi Xu[1]([⊠]), Slinger Jansen[1], Xuesong Gao[2], Sergio España[1], and Dong Zhang[2]

[1] Department of Information and Computer Science, Utrecht University, Princetonplein 5, 3508TB Utrecht, The Netherlands
xuyudi.nl@gmail.com, {Slinger.Jansen,S.Espana}@uu.nl
[2] Huawei Building No. 156 Beiqing Rd Z-Park, ShiChuang Keji Shifanyuan, Haidian, Beijing 100095, China
{Gxs54830,Zhangdong.zhang}@huawei.com

Abstract. Business modeling is becoming a foundational process in the information technology industry. Many ICT companies are constructing their business models to stay competitive on the cutting edge of the technology world. However, when comes to new technologies or emerging markets, it remains difficult for the decision maker to make an assertive choice. This paper aims to fill this gap by providing organizations with an overall approach to better design and develop business models in an innovative ICT market. The business model canvas is used to analyze existing players in the market. Moreover, a case study is made of Software Defined Networking (SDN): a business model template for SDN is proposed as a representation tool to bridge the business concept and the SDN functionalities. The models and methods are evaluated and enhanced by interviewing experts from key players in the SDN market. In addition, the method is applied to a case organization for further evaluation, which indicates that an average satisfaction score of 0.77 out of 1 to the model. Therefore, the approach of creating new business models in innovative ICT market in this paper is found to be appropriate and effective in analyzing existing SDN providers and reusing their business components of activities into a new SDN strategy.

Keywords: Software defined networking · Business model canvas · Software engineering · Quality attributes · Business model innovation

1 Introduction

Contemporarily, the software defined networking (SDN) concept has been becoming a buzz word in the networking industry. SDN subverts the traditional design of network device by decoupling the controller plane and data forwarding plane so that it enables an application - centric networking solution to replace the primitive all-in-one network device architecture [12]. The impact of SDN cannot be neglected. Foreseeing that SDN will play an essential role in the future networking industry, many networking providers have joined this emerging market. Without much experience in this new market,

© Springer International Publishing AG 2017
A. Ojala et al. (Eds.): ICSOB 2017, LNBIP 304, pp. 99–112, 2017.
https://doi.org/10.1007/978-3-319-69191-6_7

managers and decision makers are uncertain which part of SDN they should focus on and which direction is the best-fit for the companies.

Accordingly, a business model template in the SDN domain is required to solve these problems. However, there is no previous evidence that a certain business model can match this new IT market.

1.1   Problem Statement

There exists a significant amount of literature on business models, all of which intend to define explicitly how organizations fulfill their missions and commercial activities [3, 15, 20]. According to [11], these studies vary in several aspects. For instance, some of them provided a set of tools and visualization methods to design business models [3], whereas some studies provided definitions and classifications of the business models [15], such as Brokerage, Advertising, Infomediary, Merchant, Manufacturer and Affiliate. Moreover, some studies [19] proposed the evaluation metrics to assess the success of the business model. However, those definitions or approaches cannot be directly utilized to analyze the booming SDN industry, because either some of the models are too complicated for the non-technical manager to use, or some of the definitions are just out of date.

Nonetheless, on one hand, as stated by [1], albeit business model unlocks latent value from technology, the business logic restrains the subsequent investigations for new, alternative models for other technologies. Since most business models are statically depicting the business strategy of an organization, it is difficult to catch up with the pace of a growing technology (e.g., SDN). On the other hand, there is a desperate need in the market, and companies are struggling to choose the best match SDN provider to upgrade their latent networks. In turn, network vendors (new entrants) are hesitating on what SDN strategy to follow and invest.

Additionally, little research has been done to solve those problems, which remains a barrier for companies to better design and develop new business models in an innovative ICT market. As stated by [13], the rapidly changing, competitive, and uncertain economic environment makes business decisions difficult and challenging. Surprisingly, the business model or software tools that can be utilized for strategic decision making are still scarce, because such tools could help organizations to better design and develop their business models. [5] also claimed that many companies found business model innovation difficult, as managers do not understand their existing business models, so they are unable to create an effective and efficient new business model. Accordingly, we present the following problem statement:

"When entering a new innovative IT market, it is challenging for companies to design and develop new business models, which leads to many failures and sub-optimal business models for organizations."

1.2   Research Purpose

As a follow up for the problems we propose in the previous section, the research purpose, therefore, is set up to fill these gaps. The author believes that (1) by investigating the existing business models is an efficient way to establish new business models in the ICT market. Additionally, [16] stated in their book that architecture is an approach to design business process. It follows four stages, from business silos, standardized technology, optimized core to business modularity. Thus, (2) A unified business model and architecture is an appropriate way to create a model that can be understood both by business and technical users. Therefore, to validate the above hypothesis, one case study was conducted to apply our SDN business model in practice, it validated the existing business model and further evaluated the unified business model for the SDN market.

The research method, including the BMC (business model canvas), unified quality model, and the SDN architecture are discussed in Sect. 2. A case study is introduced in Sect. 3, where we applied our SDN business model to a real business case to evaluate the theory. In Sect. 4, the contribution, as well as the limitation of this paper are discussed and in Sect. 5, we provided an overall summary and some recommendations for related future works.

2 Research Background

The business model canvas introduced in Sect. 2.1 provides a thorough business viewpoint to assist the business analyst alike people to gather business requirements, while the SDN architecture (Sect. 2.2) can lead the architecture people to map the business requirements to certain developing areas. In addition, the quality mapping (Sect. 2.3) in between helps to bridge this two viewpoints, and provides a quality attributes break down to help people understand the products deeper.

2.1 Business Model Canvas

The business model canvas has shown to be one of the most widely cited representation in the academic literature and was broadly applied in practice [21]. The concept has been used and tested around the world and is already used in organizations such as IBM, Ericsson, Deloitte, the Public Works and Government Services of Canada, etc.[1] It changes the way of the companies thinking from a product perspective to a business model perspective [11]. The canvas enables a shared language that allows us to easily describe and operate business models to build new strategies or improve the existing business models [14].

The business model canvas contains nine blocks that show the logic of how an organization makes profits (Fig. 1). These nine blocks cover four main areas of a successful business, which are customers, offer, infrastructure, and financial viability. It complies most of the components from the paper that Shafer, [18] have concluded. Furthermore, the business model canvas has been successfully applied in an innovative IT market. [11] summarize and share their findings regarding the business models canvas deployed in big data applications. They analyzed the existing big data application using business model canvas and taking into consideration of the fundamental

---

[1] http://www.businessmodelgeneration.com/canvas/bmc.

elements of business and illustrate how these applications make the profits by applying big data in their business. Moreover, [21] proposed a service business model canvas in their paper, which is established based on the business model canvas. They successfully applied the service business model canvas into the mobile payment service in the German retail industry.

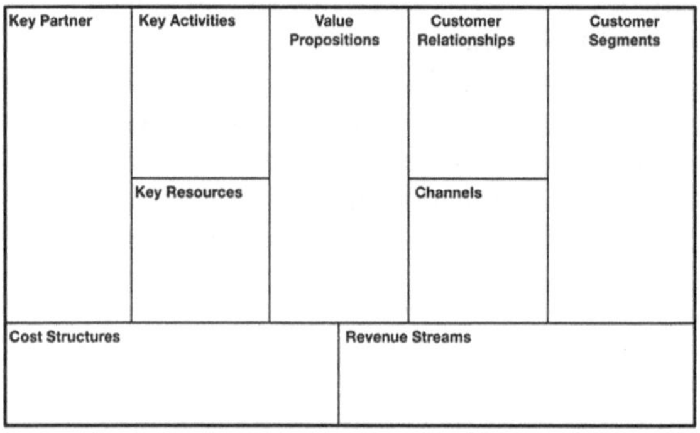

Key Partner	Key Activities	Value Propositions	Customer Relationships	Customer Segments
	Key Resources		Channels	
Cost Structures		Revenue Streams		

Fig. 1. Business model canvas

However, we could not find as many research papers of applying BMC in the IT fields as we found in other fields. Though some cases have shown its significant effects, we decided to apply it specifically in the SDN field to evaluate its effectiveness. Moreover, according to the study by [2], the ability of a firm to realize the benefits of new, external knowledge, assimilate it, and apply it to commercial ends is essential to its capabilities. Such capabilities are the absorptive capacity of the firm, which was suggested by the authors that it was a function of the organization's level of prior pertinent knowledge. In other words, analyzing the current knowledge in a market is considered as an effective way to stay innovative. Therefore, the author investigated the existing SDN providers and model them with the business model canvas to create reusable business components. Those reusable business components were utilized later to cover the missing parts of the case organization's business model canvas.

2.2 SDN Architecture

SDN is a business concept; its primary function is to decouple the data plane and the controller plane, and provide a network operating system to support various applications. However, the technical knowledge behind it is complicated. In this section, SDN is explained and simplified so that we can depict it from a business perspective. The SDN architecture (Reference Layer Model) was utilized to illustrate the essential SDN structures.

Researches have shown different designs of SDN architectures [7–9], but they all follow the three-layer model, i.e. data plane layer, controller layer and application layer. In the paper of [4], the SDN architecture is divided into three principal parts, the Application Plane, the Controller & Management Plane, and the Network Device.

There are four layers (Network Services Abstraction Layer, Control Abstraction Layer, Management Abstraction Layer and Device and Resource Abstraction Layer) that exist between those three parts and connect them as a whole SDN architecture (Fig. 2).

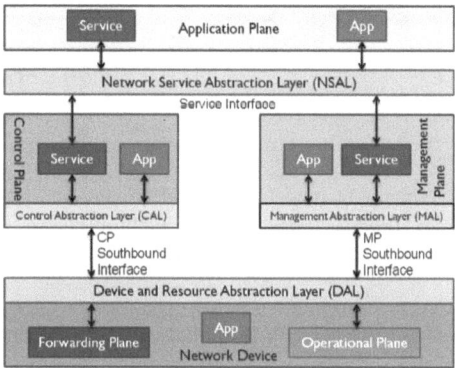

Fig. 2. SDN architecture [4]

In this paper, we will use this SDN architecture, together with other models to demonstrate the whole SDN business model. Although the SDN architecture is seen as a very technical model that is being used in representing the network, we are utilizing this model only to illustrate the SDN product (both software and hardware) within our SDN business model.

2.3 Unified Quality Model

Software engineering is a multi-discipline and complex field that connects a variety of processes and activities. All different phases in software engineering have developed their solutions to ensure the quality of the software products; however, those approaches are not well connected or integrated. Hence, [10] have proposed a unifying quality model to help software developers and managers to integrate all the processes and activities into one common foundation to assure consistency and continuity.

Our SDN business model is largely based on the unified quality model [10]. A high-level quality mapping model was built to interpret the unified quality model and modified it to fit our SDN case (Fig. 3).

The high-level SDN business model contains three parts. From left to right, there is requirement management, which is seen as the front end, the business part of the product.

As discussed in the previous section, the business model canvas can be utilized to analyze and present the business requirement, product value proposition, and other key blocks. However, in the SDN business model, we merely focus on the value proposition and customer segment due to the reason that we scoped the model from a software engineering perspective.

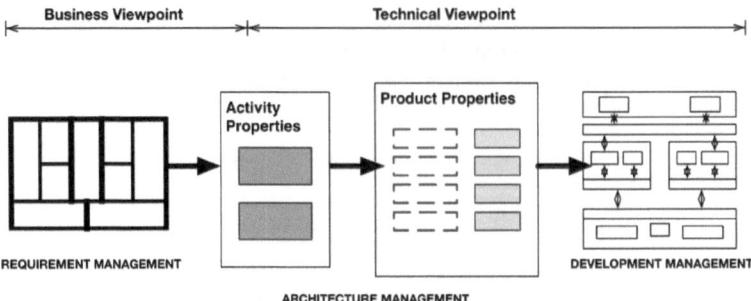

Fig. 3. High-level quality mapping model. This model represents from the business require-ments to Activity Properties, Product Properties and finally reaches to the SDN architecture for Apps and service development.

In the middle part, stand the activity properties and the product properties segment. The former one lists all the activities based on the business requirements, and the latter one consists of two sub-segments: the product functionalities and the product quality attributes (QA). Product functionalities illustrate the functionalities of the software, e.g., network monitoring or security. The product properties play as an extension or an add-on between the business model canvas and the product functionalities. Although the business model canvas can be linked to the functionalities based on the require-ments and propositions, however, it lacks the attributes of software behind the sense. In other words, the product attributes (QA) can contribute to helping the business analysts and software architect to better understand the requirements and software attributes.

On the right side, a product architecture is shown to connect the product attribute part to lead the business viewpoint to the technical viewpoint. In this paper, the SDN architecture is utilized as an "Appstore" to display the existing or "plan to develop" software for the SDN solution. Moreover, this "Appstore" can be further developed as a tool to exhibit the SDN eco-system to the customers. In Sect. 3.3, the "Appstore" concept will be further elaborated in the case of service chain example.

3 Case Study

According to [17], the structure and description of the case study is formed in Table 1.

Table 1. Case study research process is divided into 5 parts according to [17].

Name	Description
Case study design & objective	To understand the effective of using SDN model in practical use cases. The details of case study design are introduced in Sect. 3.2
Data collection preparation	Procedure: (1) question design, (2) plan meetings, (3) collect data, (4) Analyze data Protocols: Face to face meeting, calls and emails

(continued)

Table 1. (*continued*)

Name	Description
Data collection	4 separate face to face meeting with 4 interviewees in their company, 1 meeting with another employee via call and follow up emails
Data analysis	For SDN BMC model, we design and calculate the scores according to [14]. For the SDN business model, each question is given a range of score, and we calculate the weight of each question to reflect the effectiveness of how our interviewees thought of the model. Section 3.2 will provide a more explicit view
Reporting	The results of SDN BMC are shown in a BMC model (Fig. 4) with marked score in each block. The results of SDN business model are shown in Table 2

3.1 Background of the Case Organization

The case organization is a multinational ICT service and equipment provider, which has already proposed their own agile network solution and a high standard SDN controller. However, they do not possess a complete and perfect ecosystem to sustain and improve their SDN service on a long term. For example, they cannot make a decision whether they should develop their Cloud orchestration platform or should go completely for an existing popular open source platform (e.g., OpenStack). In the meantime, their competitors, for instance, HP, have already built up their SDN products and the first industry SDN AppStore ecosystem. Thus, our case organization remains an immature status in developing the business in the SDN market. The main reason, according to the people from the case organization, is the lack of a business model that can capture the entire ecosystem of the SDN.

Scholars claimed that technological change can become market revolutions that incumbent firms must master if they want to survive [6]. Besides, [6] indicated that the experiences of an enterprise to respond to a new market are imperfectly understood, i.e., the managers do not have a mature way to tackle with the new technological wave. Similarly, the case organization was eager to build this capability to develop their business model for SDN.

3.2 Case Study Design

The case study was divided primarily into two parts, (1) the expert interviews for the business model canvas and (2) the expert interviews for the unified quality model on the service chain example.

The business model canvas of our case organization is based on two experts' reviews within the case organization. In addition, some existing SDN organizations' data were utilized to improve and polish the business model canvas of our case organization.

According to the book of "business model generation" [14], we interviewed the interviewees by using the SWOT evaluation method. Four criteria were evaluated,

(1) Strength, (2) Weakness, (3) Opportunity, (4) Threats. Based on the book "business model generation" [14], in Strength/Weakness, 78 relevant questions were proposed[2]. Half of the questions are to evaluate strength, and half are designed to assess the weakness, e.g., the question to evaluate the strength: "Our value propositions are well aligned with customer needs", the question to evaluate the weakness: "Our value propositions and customer needs are misaligned." In the category of opportunity, 37 questions were created, and there were 21 questions in the category of threat. Each question has a score range of ±1 to ±5, 4 and 5 represented the high impact, 1 and 2 stood for the low impact, and 3 was the normal impact. Exception for the combination table of Strength/Weakness, because it merely showed the 39 questions, which had been calculated (The score of Strength plus the score of Weakness). Thus, the positive number was a strength, the negative number was a weakness, zero meant no strength or weakness. Questions of strength and opportunity were set to positive and questions of weakness and threat were set to negative. Furthermore, each category was divided into four sub-categories, which were offer, finance, Infrastructure and customer. The nine blocks in business model canvas were subsumed in each group.

Regarding the SDN business model (unified quality model), which is mentioned in Sect. 2.3, we applied it to a real service provided by the case organization – the service chain product. The service chain model is a concept that connects all the network service (e.g., firewall, load balancing and routing) so that those services can collaborate more efficiently. Figure 5 displays the service chain model via the SDN business model we proposed in Sect. 3.3.

The interviews of the unified quality model were based on some specific SDN examples. The blocks of value proposition and customer segments of the business model canvas were focused and represented, because the authors only investigated the unified model from a software engineering perspective. Thus, blocks such as cost structure, key partners and customer segments are not suitable. Accordingly, the unified quality model was modified based on the business requirements and case organization's circumstances.

3.3   Results

According to Sect. 3.2, the results of the case study are divided into two parts, (1) business model canvas, and (2) the SDN business model. Both of the results will be discussed below.

Figure 4 illustrates the results of the SWOT evaluation of the business model canvas. It concluded three main results in each block, (1) the strength/weakness assessment, (2) the opportunity assessment, (3) the threats assessment. For example, in the customer relationship block, the final score of the strength/weakness is 15, opportunity score is 22.5. Received a low treat score of −2.5, it accomplished total score of 35, which indicate that the case organization has performed relatively well in the value proposition filed. However, in the cost structure block, the treat score is as high as −7, which is close to the strength/weakness and even higher than the

---

[2] goo.gl/DTLS1h.

Key Partner (KP)		Key Activities (KA)		Value Propositions (VP)		Customer Relationships (CR)		Customer Segments (CS)	
KP strength/weakness assessment	4.5	KA strength/weakness assessment	6	VP strength/weakness assessment	10	CR strength/weakness assessment	15	CS strength/weakness assessment	10
KP opportunity assessment	23	KA opportunity assessment	12.5	VP opportunity assessment	23	CR opportunity assessment	22.5	CS opportunity assessment	13
KP threats assessment	-9	KA threats assessment	-2	VP threats assessment	-7	CR threats assessment	-2.5	CS threats assessment	-10.5
KP Total	18.5	KA Total	16.5	VP Total	26	CR Total	35	CS Total	12.5
		Key Resources (KR)				**Channels (CH)**			
		KR strength/weakness assessment	7.5			CH strength/weakness assessment	24		
		KR opportunity assessment	14.5			CH opportunity assessment	19.5		
		KR threats assessment	-5.5			CH threats assessment	-6		
		KR Total	16.5			CH Total	37.5		

Cost Structures (C$)				Revenue Streams (R$)			
C$ strength/weakness assessment	8.5	C$ threats assessment	-7	R$ strength/weakness assessment	21	R$ threats assessment	-11.5
C$ opportunity assessment	3.5	C$ Total	5	R$ opportunity assessment	20	KP Total	29.5

Total: 197

Fig. 4. SWOT evaluation results of the business model canvas from the case organization, which calculated the critical scores for each business model canvas block and exert a total score for future comparisons. The score does not necessarily indicate how well the case company has done, but is more considered as a benchmark to reflect and compare with the future evaluations.

opportunity score. Hence, it should raise more attention for the case organization. Moreover, a total score was given for the entire business model canvas. In our case organization's case, it achieved a total score of 197. This score does not indicate the performance of the organization directly, but as a benchmark for the future evaluation.

To summarize, on one hand, the business model canvas was suggested as an effective and efficient way to analyze the existing SDN providers in the market, and then compare and reuse the business model components when creating a new business model canvas. On the other hand, the SWOT analysis was backed by data and provided a quick understanding of the status of each business model canvas block and indicated several critical parts that the case organization should pay more attentions. Both results provided strong evidence that our research approach and the business model canvas was of great benefit to the case organization.

In the SDN business model below (Fig. 5), it contains three primary parts. On the left side, the business model canvas illustrates the business requirements of the flexibility of arranging different network services and the value proposition of service chain model. In the activity properties, the author provided two examples, (1) Networking Service, and (2) Service Orchestration. These two activities connect to the several product functionalities of Traffic Acceleration, Security Service, Load Balance and Central Management on a business requirement perspective and are also extended into several quality attributes to reflect the product functionalities on the software engineering view. Additionally, the activities are linked with the OpenFlow environment, where the networking is based on. On the right side of the model, the author listed all the correspond SDN software from the case organization, which are listed in the SDN architecture to present the exact solutions from the organization. Those solutions are mostly networking apps that are built on the SDN controller, and the SDN controller itself. Thus, we consider and expect this part of the model becoming an Appstore - like platform.

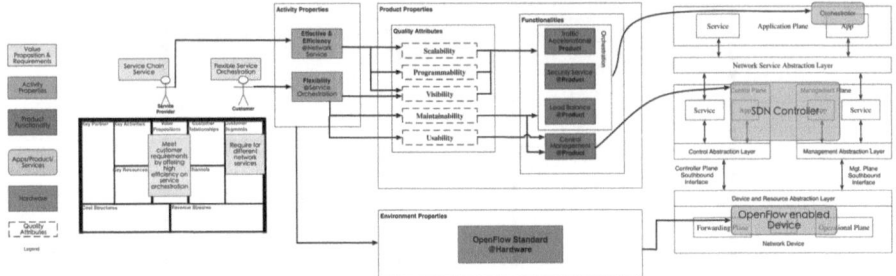

Fig. 5. Unified model of Service chain example - SDN business model as a whole representation of our proposal for the use case. It explains how we model the SDN use case from the business model canvas on the left for business requirements gathering to the middle part of activity property, product property and environment property of the product, and finally a software solution/proposition on the right side of the SDN architecture.

The above SDN business model was constructed and evaluated with five experts, who were from networking or marketing field in the case organization. The interview followed a time glass[3] way of asking questions, i.e., the author started with general questions (e.g., "What do you think of this model?", "Do you have similar model to handle these tasks in your daily work?") to have a high level overview of the situation of the case organization. After that, some detailed questions were asked and evaluated. For instance, "Does the BMC well reflect the business requirements from the customers?", "Do you think it is important to combine the business side with the technical side?". Such questions were scored from 1 to 5, and was listed in the following table (Table 1). On one side, the table indicates that except interviewee C, interviewee A, B, D and E all provided a very positive view of the SDN business model. On the other side, each scored question has shown a score from 64% to 80%, which is seen as a positive view as well. Therefore, the SDN business model we proposed should be seen as an appropriate solution for SDN.

3.3.1   Summary of the Results
The former one provided a benchmark score for SDN organization's self-evaluation, and the latter one illustrated an example to show how the unified quality model had been used to help the SDN organization to bridge the business and architecture part. In general, both the business model canvas and SDN business model have shown their effectiveness in tackling with the difficulties to establish the business model in the SDN field. Table 2, shows the interview results of the SDN business model.

Though the SDN business model was evaluated and proved to be beneficial to the SDN business, it remains immature in many areas. This section concludes the contributions in Sect. 4.1 as well as the limitations of the SDN business model in Sect. 4.2.

---

[3] http://www.cse.chalmers.se/~feldt/advice/runeson_2009_emse_case_study_guidelines.pdf.

Table 2. Interview results of the SDN business model

Question score								
Interviewee	Q1	Q2	Q3	Q4	Q5	Q6	Avg. (Interviewee)	Percentage
A	4	4	5	4	5	4	4.33	0.87
B	4	5	4	4	5	4	4.33	0.87
C	3	3	2	3	4	2	2.83	0.57
D	4	5	4	3	4	3	3.83	0.77
E	4	5	4	3	4	3	3.83	0.77
Avg. (Question)	3.8	4.4	3.8	3.4	4.4	3.2		
Percentage	0.7	0.8	0.7	0.6	0.8	0.6		
	6	8	6	8	8	4		

Interview questions	
Q1	Does the BMC well reflect the business requirements from the customers? (1-5)
Q2	Is the BMC a good tool to brainstorm with the customers and the colleagues? (1-5)
Q3	Does the unified quality model well represent the customer activities, the product and the environment and the functionalities of the service and applications? (1-5)
Q4	Does the SDN architecture illustrate a clear image to you the overall SDN service and apps from in your company? (1-5)
Q5	Do you think it is important to combine the business side with the technical side? (1-5)
Q6	Does the SDN solution model solve the problems in your current work? (1-5)

4   Discussion

4.1   Contribution

In regard to the research results, the most noteworthy discovery is the use of the combination of the business model canvas, unified quality model [10], and SDN architecture on modeling and designing a business model for the SDN market. (1) The business model canvas was applied in a new way, and we proved that this modular tool was effective and efficient in modeling and designing business models in an innovative ICT market. Although the new model does not cover the full set of SDN features and SDN quality attributes due to research limitations, (2) it proposed an industry-first theoretical concept to combine the business model with the technical architecture for SDN solution/product's design and development. As such, (3) this paper can also be seen as a validation for application of the BMC in a certain domain. Last but not least, (4) the overall research approach also delineated an appropriate way of conducting similar research for the future.

4.2   Limitation

Due to the fast growing nature of the SDN market, every organization is proposing new products, new services in every single day. Thus, (1) the data we have retrieved we used in this paper may not be suitable in the future due to its rapidly change nature. (2) Another limitation of the SDN business model is its applicability in different enterprises. As the validation was conducted only in one case organization, the generosity of the model is limited. (3) The quality model did not use the full blocks of the business model canvas, it only analyzes the model from a software engineering perspective, which may lead to the incompleteness of the model.

5   Conclusion

The following sections summarize the final conclusion and the indications for the future research. Specifically, this chapter introduces a research summary that concludes an overview of the entire research story, and lastly, puts forward some opportunities for future researches and authors' vision for SDN business model.

5.1   Research Summary

In this paper, we propose to utilize the business model canvas as a method to model existing SDN providers in the market and summed up an SDN quality model to capture essential SDN features. The business model canvases of the selected organizations were compared and validated by interviewing experts, and their business components were stored in a dictionary for reusing in creating a new business model for the case organization. Moreover, based on the SDN quality model and business model canvas, we proposed an industry-first SDN business model that combines the business model with the technical architecture via a unified quality model.

Both the business model canvas and the quality model were evaluated through case studies. As a consequence, the business model canvas was proved to be efficient on analyzing an innovative IT market, which, in our case is SDN. Meanwhile, by connecting the business viewpoints and the technical viewpoints, the quality model provided a holistic view on the entire SDN business ecosystem, which was evaluated to reach a 77% satisfaction rate in the case organization.

5.2   Future Work

Throughout the method design, data collection, modeling and interviewing phases, it revealed many potential opportunities for future research. The recommendations listed in this section are divided into two parts. One is the business model canvas, from a business model perspective, and the other focuses on the SDN side. Both parts of opportunities are based on the limitations we have confronted, and the suggestions from the expert reviews.

5.2.1   Business Model Future Work

Regarding the business model, especially for the business model canvas methodology, there are tons of opportunities for future studies. Literature revealed that there was relatively a small number of researches have been done on the business model canvas in an IT field. Thus, (1) more researches and case studies need to be conducted to further validate the efficiency and effectiveness of business model canvas. Those results can strengthen the theory of applying business model canvas into innovative ICT studies. Moreover, (2) the evaluation methods could be enhanced by future research to improve the accuracy of the evaluation process.

Furthermore, there is a sister model of business model canvas called value proposition canvas. It expands the value proposition and customer segment blocks of the original business model canvas. Thus, it can zoom in the critical needs of its customers as well as the values and products that a company can serve its customers. From a value proposition perspective, (3) further research can provide a holistic analysis of the business requirements and map them to the quality attributes to enrich the applicability of the model.

5.2.2   SDN Future Work

Focusing on a business model scope, this paper provided an in-depth view of how to design and develop business models for SDN. However, a fast growing market like SDN deserves wider attention. Suggested by the business model canvas experts, the business model analysis should not only focus on the quality model or SDN architecture part but also needs to cover the whole SDN eco-system to make the deliverables valuable to the commercial ends. (1) A full SDN eco-system may inspire research on the topics of SDN revenue chain, SDN provider network analysis, Open SDN system collaboration, innovation, etc. Moreover, the SDN architecture part of the SDN business 3-layers model generates future opportunities to create a holistic Appstore solution to help customers to choose the right networking apps and services.

In addition, from a technical point of view, (2) future research can dive to analyze the SDN features to provide an explicit list of critical features or functions an SDN product must have. For example, suggested by one of our interviewees, it is worth doing a research on how to rank the capabilities of the SDN features, such as malicious activities detection & mitigation, i.e., to what extent or level can an SDN product fulfill that function. In other words, SDN network capability testing may become another fruitful business in the future.

References

1. Chesbrough, H., Rosenbloom, R.S.: The role of the business model in capturing value from innovation: evidence from xerox corporation's technology spin-off companies. Industr. Corp. Change 11(3), 529–555 (2002)
2. Cohen, W.M., Levinthal, D.A.: Absorptive capacity: a new perspective on learning and innovation. Admin. Sci. Q. 35(1), 128–152 (1990)
3. Gordijn, J., Akkermans, H.: Designing and evaluating e-business models. IEEE Intell. Syst. 4, 11–17 (2001)
4. Haleplidis, E., Denazis, S., Pentikousis, K., Salim, J.H., Meyer, D., Koufopavlou, O.: SDN layers and architecture terminology. Internet Engineering Task Force, Internet Draft (2014)
5. Johnson, M.W., Christensen, C.M., Kagermann, H.: Reinventing your business model. Harv. Bus. Rev. 86(12), 57–68 (2008)
6. King, A.A., Tucci, C.L.: Incumbent entry into new market niches: the role of experience and managerial choice in the creation of dynamic capabilities. Manage. Sci. 48(2), 171–186 (2002)

7. Kim, H., Feamster, N.: Improving network management with software defined networking. IEEE Commun. Magaz. **51**(2), 114–119 (2013)
8. Kreutz, D., Ramos, F.M., Verissimo, P.E., Rothenberg, C.E., Azodolmolky, S., Uhlig, S.: Software-defined networking: a comprehensive survey. Proc. IEEE **103**(1), 14–76 (2015)
9. Kirkpatrick, K.: Software-defined networking. Commun. ACM **56**(9), 16–19 (2013)
10. Lochmann, K., Goeb, A.: A unifying model for software quality. In: Proceedings of the 8th International Workshop on Software Quality, pp. 3–10. ACM, September 2011
11. Muhtaroglu, F., Demir, S., Obali, M., Girgin, C.: Business model canvas perspective on big data applications. In: 2013 IEEE International Conference on Big Data, pp. 32–37. IEEE, October 2013
12. Nunes, B.A.A., Mendonca, M., Nguyen, X.N., Obraczka, K., Turletti, T.: A survey of software-defined networking: past, present, and future of programmable networks. IEEE Commun. Surv. Tutor. **16**(3), 1617–1634 (2014)
13. Osterwalder, A.: The business model ontology: a proposition in a design science approach (2004)
14. Osterwalder, A., Pigneur, Y.: Business Model Generation: A Handbook for Visionaries, Game Changers, and Challengers. Wiley, Hoboken (2010)
15. Rappa, M.: Managing the digital enterprise-business models on the Web (2001)
16. Ross, J.W., Weill, P., Robertson, D.: Enterprise Architecture as Strategy: Creating a Foundation for Business Execution. Harvard Business Press, Boston (2006)
17. Runeson, P., Höst, M.: Guidelines for conducting and reporting case study research in software engineering. Empir. Softw. Eng. **14**(2), 131 (2009)
18. Shafer, S.M., Smith, H.J., Linder, J.C.: The power of business models. Bus. Horizons **48**(3), 199–207 (2005)
19. Van Belle, J.P.: A framework for the evaluation of business models and its empirical validation. Electron. J. Inf. Syst. Eval. **9**(1), 31–44 (2006)
20. Weill, P., Vitale, M.: What IT infrastructure capabilities are needed to implement e-business models. MIS Q. Exec. **1**(1), 17–34 (2002)
21. Zolnowski, A., Weiß, C., Bohmann, T.: Representing service business models with the service business model canvas–the case of a mobile payment service in the retail industry. In: 2014 47th Hawaii International Conference on System Sciences (HICSS), pp. 718–727. IEEE (2014)

Software Ecosystems and App Stores

How Do Software Ecosystems Co-Evolve?
A View from OpenStack and Beyond

Jose Teixeira[1] and Sami Hyrynsalmi[2]([⊠])

[1] Åbo Akademi University, Turku, Finland
jose.teixeira@abo.fi
[2] TTY Pori, Tampere University of Technology, Pori, Finland
sami.hyrynsalmi@tut.fi
http://www.jteixeira.eu

Abstract. Much research that analyzes the evolution of a software ecosystem is confined to its own boundaries. Evidence shows, however, that software ecosystems co-evolve independently with other software ecosystems. In other words, understanding the evolution of a software ecosystem requires an especially astute awareness of its competitive landscape and much consideration for other software ecosystems in related markets. A software ecosystem does not evolve in insulation but with other software ecosystems. In this research, we analyzed the OpenStack software ecosystem with a focal perspective that attempted to understand its evolution as a function of other software ecosystems. We attempted to understand and explain the evolution of OpenStack in relation to other software ecosystems in the cloud computing market. Our findings add to theoretical knowledge in software ecosystems by identifying and discussing seven different mechanisms by which software ecosystems mutually influence each other: sedimentation and embeddedness of business relationships, strategic management of the portfolio of business relationships, firms values and reputation as a partner, core technological architecture, design of the APIs, competitive replication of functionality and multi-homing. Research addressing the evolution of software ecosystem should, therefore, acknowledge that software ecosystems entangle with other software ecosystems in multiple ways, even with competing ones. A rigorous analysis of the evolution of a software ecosystem should not be solely confined to its inner boundaries.

Keywords: Business ecosystem · Software ecosystem · Evolution · Open-source · Openstack

1 Introduction

In the so-called 'Information Age' companies and organizations do not live in isolation; instead, business activities of modern companies are highly interwoven with other companies. Furthermore, the fate of a company nowadays depends on its connections and environment where they are working — not anymore solely

© Springer International Publishing AG 2017
A. Ojala et al. (Eds.): ICSOB 2017, LNBIP 304, pp. 115–130, 2017.
https://doi.org/10.1007/978-3-319-69191-6_8

on the company itself. From these observations, James F. Moore [19] built his theory and concept of 'business ecosystem'. According to Moore [20], a business ecosystem consists of a set of companies working on a shared innovation. The companies work together, cooperatively and competitively, for creating value for customers; the ecosystem advances as companies and the innovation co-evolve together.

Since Moore's seminal article, a plethora of different kinds of artificial ecosystems has been defined and used [24]. One of the most important is 'software ecosystem' as software is pervasive and ubiquitous by its nature — there hardly is any industrial domain where software would not be a part of. That is, software is available nowadays everywhere and it is rarely built on isolation. Software ecosystems have become also an important research field and there are hundreds of studies addressing different kinds of software ecosystems (c.f. [17,18]).

As proposed by Jansen et al. [15], a software ecosystem consists of *"the set of businesses functioning as a unit and interacting with a shared market for software and services, together with the relationships among them. These relationships are frequently underpinned by a common technological platform or market and operate through the exchange of information, resources and artefacts."* From the definition, it seems clear that there are a relationship between software ecosystem and business ecosystem conceptualizations. However, there is one major caveat: Whereas Moore's view on business ecosystems focused on co-evolution, the definition of software ecosystem does not cover this aspect.

Since the ecosystem concept has been accepted as a perspective for business development, management and governance, it is also necessary to discuss the interactions between ecosystems. Whether and how ecosystems influence each other and to what degree, are intriguing questions. That is, it is essential for both scholars and practitioners to analyze the competitive landscape, in order to better understand software ecosystem evolution. This study focuses on the relatively uncovered area in the field of software ecosystems: the *co-evolution* of them. Specifically, we focus on how ecosystems influence each other evolution (i.e. co-evolution of ecosystems). The starting research hypothesis is that an ecosystem does not evolve in isolation; instead, the ecosystems are interwoven with each other (e.g., characteristics of one can affect the other or change in one can also affect the other). That is, this study seeks to answer a question

RQ *How do software ecosystems co-evolve?*

To answer the presented research question, we performed a case study by taking the OpenStack software ecosystem as our focal unit of analysis. By analyzing OpenStack in relation to other software ecosystems in the industry (e.g., CloudStack) we identified and explored seven different ways in which software ecosystems are interwoven with other software ecosystems: 1. *Sedimentation and embeddedness of business relationships*, 2. *Strategic management of the portfolio of business relationships*, 3. *Firm's values and reputation as a partner*, 4. *Core technological architecture*, 5. *Design of external APIs*, 6. *Technological replication of new functionalities*, and 7. *Complementors' multi-homing*.

The remaining of this paper is structured as follow. The next section will briefly present the related work whereas Sect. 3 views on the empirical background of our study subject. Section 4 presents the research approach used, Sect. 5 results and Sect. 6 their implications and limitations. The final section concludes the study.

2   Related Literature

Moore [19], in his seminal essay on the new ecology of competition, defined that business ecosystems evolve through distinct phases. He identified and named four stages which are: 1. *Birth* where companies define value propositions of a seed innovation. 2. *Expansion* where the ecosystem seeks to expand to new territories. 3. *Leadership* where participating companies start to struggle for a leadership. As an example, Moore used Microsoft's and Intel campaign against IBM during the "clone wars" of personal computers. 4. *Self-Renewal* or *Death* where an ecosystem faces an external threat and it is forced to either renew itself or cease to exist.

As software ecosystem share distinct similarity with the older ecosystem concept, it is surprisingly how little have been written on the evolution of different kinds of ecosystems. However, there are a few prior studies existing. Similarly, as have entire software ecosystem literature diverged into communities [24], also existing studies can be categorized into two groups with a remarkable different basis.

In the first group, there are studies addressing software ecosystem as a business network and previous studies have addressed how the relationships between the firms have developed. For example, Basole [2] studied the convergence of entire mobile ecosystem— including software and hardware vendors as well as network operators— however, it focused on the interfirm relationships and visualization of cooperative networks. Basole and Karla [3] studied the evolution of mobile platform ecosystems. However, also their focus was on the visualization and on the interfirm relationships inside an ecosystem. Hanssen [9] followed a transformation of a product line organization to an emerging software ecosystem and focused on why and how the transformation was done.

In the second group, there are studies addressing software ecosystems as a collection of interdependent projects and these studies on the evolution of software ecosystem's codebase over time (e.g. [5,7]). Already 2007, Yu and Bush [31] noted that software projects evolve and there are certain types of relationships between the actors. Later, Yu et al. [32] adapted different symbiosis types, that might affect the evolution of projects, from biology and applied them to relationships between software projects. Furthermore, Scacchi and Alspaugh [23] studied how different licenses affect on the ecosystem evolution.

To summarize, while there are few studies addressing the evolution of software ecosystems, they represent different ends of the spectrum: On one corner, there are studies on the relationships and evolution of software code base; and on the other corner, studies have focused on visualizing interfirm relationships of companies with Social Network Analysis. To the best of the authors' knowledge, this study is unprecedented as it combines both of the existing schools of thought in the study of ecosystem evolution: We study software ecosystems as a business network construction but acknowledge the importance of source code and address the evolution of the ecosystem and interfirm relationships through the developments in the shared codebase. In addition, we specifically focus on the co-evolution of competing software ecosystems. Generally, *co-evolution* refers to cases where two entities affects to each others' evolution. Here, the entities are ecosystems and their actors.

3   Empirical Background

The cloud computing business is dominated by a relatively small number of players, including (1) Amazon, a pioneer in cloud computing services selling the Amazon EC2; (2) Google, selling services around its Compute Engine (Google Compute); and (3) Microsoft, heavily marketing cloud strategies based on its Azure cloud computing infrastructure (Microsoft Azure). The entrance costs for building and providing a public cloud computing infrastructure are very high as they often require global-distributed data-centers, fast and large accesses to the Internet backbone, much computing and storage power. Public cloud providers must provide very low latency – after all, they are convincing its enterprise customer to move from self-managed in-house computing infrastructures to vendor-managed computing infrastructures out there.

The leader of the cloud computing industry (i.e., Amazon, Google, and Microsoft) do not provide cloud infrastructure products, merely computing services. In practice and if there were no alternatives, all cloud computation would run in hardware and software infrastructures controlled by very few players. Such control from the cloud computing service provider locks-in its customers [1]. Surprisingly, the leading product alternatives to Amazon EC2, Google Compute and Microsoft Azure are not commercial but rather four open-source projects. They include: (1) OpenStack, our unit of analysis; (2) CloudStack, backed by Citrix and the Apache Software Foundation; (3) Eucalyptus, a system that is compatible with Amazon EC2 services and backed by many IT consulting firms; and (4) OpenNebula, more present in the European markets and backed by C12G, a Spanish company. During our research, we perceived that many cloud computing vendors associated with the leading open-source cloud computing ecosystems to ease the pain of "selling cloud computing services that are famous and infamous for their single-vendor locking mechanisms".

OpenStack is a software cloud computing infrastructure capable of handling big data. It is often offered as an IaaS (Infrastructure-as-a-Service) solution. The development of this open-source software involves private companies (such as AT&T, Canonical, Ericsson, IBM, Intel *etc.*), public organizations (such as NASA, CERN, Johns Hopkins University *etc.*) as well as independent, non-affiliated individuals.

We selected OpenStack as our case study subject due to four main factors. First, it is truly heterogeneous software ecosystem including start ups, high-tech corporate giants, non-profit and public organizations as well as individual software developers. Second, it is highly inter-networked. That is, there are several companies and individual contributors working together. Thus, there is a rich data available for co-evolution. Third, its size is large enough for a meaningful study (more than 70.000 individual contributors and more than 600 supporting companies from 185 countries that have contributed with more than 20 million lines of source-code[1]). Finally, it is well-studied (see e.g. [26]) and, therefore, there is a good amount of scholarly information published.

4   Method

In this section, we present our research design. Given the multidisciplinary nature of our research approach which borrowed significantly across disciplines, many interwoven methodological issues are disclosed. We employed a case study research strategy [30] that relied on naturally occurring data which emerged *per se* on the Internet. Such data (e.g., web pages, wikis, blogs, public announcements, market-research reports, technical documentation, the software, source code repositories, videos broadcasted from the OpenStack summits, among many others data sources) are not a consequence of researchers' own actions, but rather are developed by the OpenStack community in their own pursuits of developing an open-source infrastructure for handling and storing big amount of data.

Given the open-source nature of our focal unit of analysis, many but heterogeneous data regarding OpenStack is available. Therefore we have selected a novel approach by combining three well-known technique: mining software repositories (MSR) of OpenStack repository, Social Network Analysis (SNA) of the contributing developers, and qualitative analysis of archival data (QA). All within a mixed methods design, that reconstruct as well as visualize the evolution of the software ecosystem as a sequence of networks connectiong firms and individuals that jointly develop the OpenStack ecosystem.

We started our efforts qualitatively by searching publicly available data sources such as news articles, public announcements by companies, financial figures as well as press reports. Those helped us to create a picture of the cloud computing industry where OpenStack is a part of. In addition, we went through OpenStack documentation regarding how the software ecosystem is developed (i.e. the technical information) and governed (e.g., structures, policies, and procedures). While keeping in mind the limitations on the use of archival data [30], we gained valuable insights from OpenStack community and its surrounding industrial environment. After gaining an understanding of the surrounding industrial dynamics and understanding of how OpenStack software is developed, we extracted the developer and affiliation information from the publicly-available OpenStack Nova repository. Then, we created and analyzed the social network of the project by using the SNA guidelines given in [28].

As in [26], we took advantage of naturally occurring digital trace data (i.e., the OpenStack Nova project repository and its *changelog*) and built cooperative

---

[1] See https://www.openstack.org/community/.

social networks that were analyzed using a variety of tools: *Gephi*, *Visone*, and the *sna* and *statnet* statistical modules for *R*. To better explore cooperation at the ecosystems level, we also modeled cooperative relationships in the tridimensional (3D) space using *Blender*. We mined evidence of cooperation from the source code and by visualized the social structures with SNA. This revealed the cooperation in the OpenStack ecosystem and we later enrichment this data with qualitative information from the public sources used in QA. The use of all these methods were helpful in terms that they both showed the social structures as well as helped to explain them.

We highlight the visualization of the collaboration network. The changes in this network, over time, show the dynamics among the OpenStack ecosystem. We aim to understand the visualized networks with the information gathered from the industry in previous steps. In this, we follow prior work (e.g. [2,26]) done in multi-disciplinary settings.

5   Results

We present our results in a chronological narrative format. The textual narrative is complemented with visualizations that capture the evolution of the OpenStack ecosystem. Besides richly describing the evolution of the OpenStack ecosystem, we also attempt to interpret such evolution and explain it by employing multiple theoretical lenses. Our analysis aggregates both empirical and theoretical issues that are later addressed in the discussion section.

We start with the words of, at that time Senior Vice President and General Manager of Rackspace, *Jim Curry*. In this, the first public disclosure of the OpenStack project, Curry emphasizes the roles of NASA's and Rackspace's roles as initial contributors to the project – that is, it is built with experienced partners and the project did not start from scratch.

> "Our mission statement says this: *To produce the ubiquitous Open Source Cloud Computing platform that will meet the needs of public and private clouds regardless of size, by being simple to implement and massively scalable.*
>
> That is a big ambition. The good news is that OpenStack is starting with code contributions from two organizations that know how to build and run massively scalable clouds – Rackspace and NASA." — Jim Curry, founder of OpenStack on behalf of Rackspace, 19 July 2010[2]

The footsteps of Rackspace in NASA started as a supplier of Anso Labs. A startup company which was later acquired by Rackspace on February 9, 2011[3]. Before OpenStack, Anso Labs and Rackspace have been working in Nebula – a Federal cloud computing platform. Nebula emerged at NASA Ames Research Center at Moffett Field, California in 2008. It allowed NASA researchers to

---

[2] See https://www.openstack.org/blog/2010/07/introducing-openstack/.

[3] See https://gigaom.com/2012/05/24/nasa-backs-off-openstack-development/.

manage the computation of data-intensive research projects in a cloud computing way. The design of Nebula reflected the growing popularity of the Amazon Web Services (AWS) cloud computing environments.

"Nebula's architecture is designed from the ground up for interoperability with commercial cloud service providers such as Amazon Web Services, offering NASA researchers the ability to easily port data sets and code to run on commercial clouds." — NASA under the Open Government Initiative, 7 April 2010[4]

The NASA Nebula team started by adopting the Eucalyptus open-source cloud computing infrastructure (now a competitor of OpenStack), as it resembled the EC2 compute cloud and S3 storage cloud technologies from Amazon. However, NASA faced scalability issues. After all, NASA demands computing and storage were very high. Nebula could accommodate files as large as eight terabytes. Furthermore, Nebula could support only an individual file system of 100 TB. As an example, the maximum for Amazon EC2 file size was just one terabyte and and for file system size was also one terabyte[5].

In addition of scaling requirements to handle big data, NASA engineers were not happy with the 'open-core' business model strategy of Eucalyptus Systems Inc to monetize its cloud computing software ecosystem. According to NASA, Eucalyptus-based clouds were not entirely open-source.

"NASA engineers attempted to contribute additional Eucalyptus code to improve its ability to scale, they were unable to do so because some of the platform's code is open and some isn't. Their attempted contributions conflicted with code that was only available in a partially closed version of platform maintained by Eucalyptus Systems Inc., the commercial outfit run by the project's founders." — Chris Kemp, NASA chief technology officer, 20 July 2010[6].

As argued in prior related research (see [25,26]), the visualizations in Figs. 1, 2 and 3[7] helps us to understand how the cloud industry's actors cooperate in OpenStack. Such visualizations, obtained with combining MSR and SNA, helps us to visualize the evolution of the software ecosystem as an evolving complex network of companies and individuals interacting with each other to develop complex[8] software. The diameter of a node reflects its *degree-centrality* – in other

---

[4] See https://www.nasa.gov/pdf/440932main_Nebula.pdf.

[5] See https://www.nasa.gov/open/nebula.html.

[6] See https://www.theregister.co.uk/2010/07/20/why_nasa_is_dropping_Eucalyptus_from_its_nebula_cloud/.

[7] Please note that all figures are encoded as Scalable Vector Graphics, therefore readers can freely zoom in and zoom out for a better visualization of the networks.

[8] Complex as it involves different programming languages, different operating systems, dozens of different hardware configurations, hundreds of firms, thousands of software developers, and over one million of lines of code.

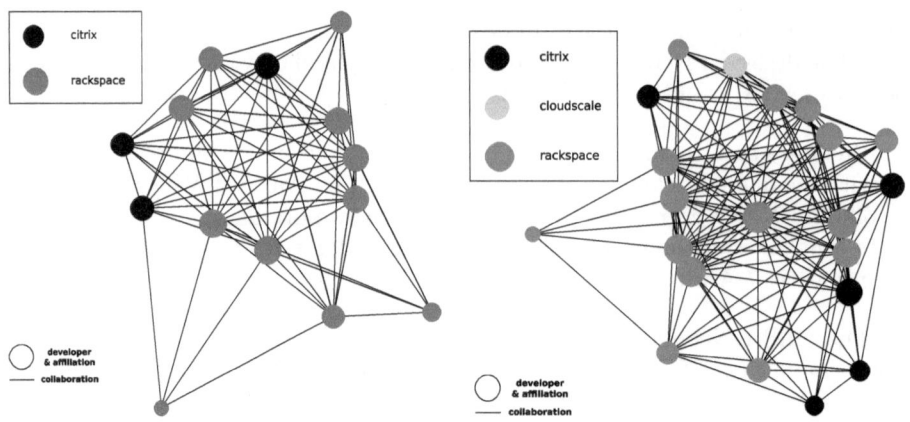

Fig. 1. Austin → Bexar [26].   **Fig. 2.** Bexar → Cactus [26].

words, a large node depicts a well-connected developer. The value of degree-centrality is a sum of the number of adjacent nodes with which a focus node is connected to. Thus, a high degree-centrality value, the more likely the developer is to be cooperating with other developers.

To start with, Fig. 1 captures the cooperation in the OpenStack Nova project from the Austin (October 21st 2010) to the Bexar (February 3rd 2011) release. The figure illustrates the cooperation between individual software engineers and their affiliated companies. For example, as shown by the figure, Citrix had three developers working on the project together with Rackspace.

Citrix's, who had worked before with Rackspace in Desktop visualization technologies[9], aim was to ensure that their XenServer platform would be included in OpenStack's future plans.

> "As a longtime technology partner with Rackspace, Citrix will cooperate closely with the community to provide full support for the XenServer plat-form and our other cloud-enabling products." — Peter Levine, SVP and GM, Citrix, 19 July 2010[10].

Our second visualization, in Fig. 2, captures the cooperation from the Bexar (February 3rd 2011) to the Cactus (April 15th 2011) release. The figure illustrates the entrance of a new actor, a developer from the company Cloudscaling.

The company started in 2006 with personnel previously working for Amazon and VMWare. It started by selling customized cloud infrastructures for large service providers. For example, Cloudscaling had Korea Telecom as an early customer. In 2010, the company shipped an OpenStack-based storage cloud to

---

[9] See https://ir.rackspace.com/phoenix.zhtml?c=221673\&p=irol-newsArticle\&ID=1608440.

[10] See https://www.rackspace.com/blog/newsarticles/rackspace-open-sources-cloud-platform.

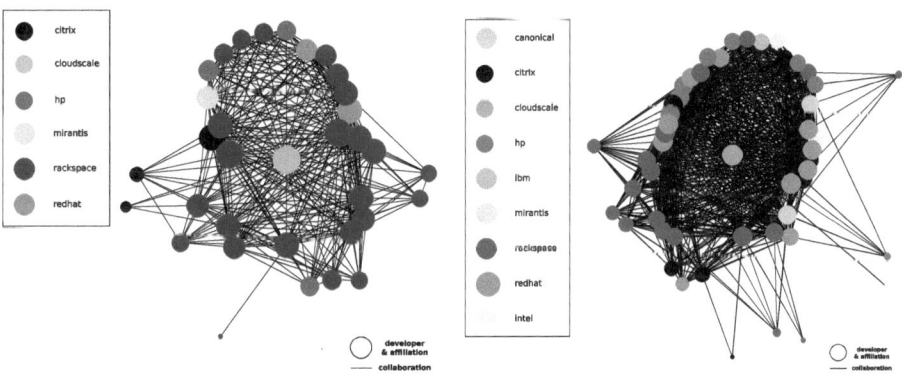

Fig. 3. `Cactus → Diablo` [26].   **Fig. 4.** `Diablo → Essex` [26].

Korea Telecom. It was first OpenStack delivery without Rackspace. Together with Mirantis, they were among the first pure-play OpenStack firms deploying OpenStack-based in-premise private clouds (e.g. Korea Telecom and PayPal). While CloudScaling kept a strategy of compatibility with Amazon EC2 APIs, Mirantis was more on the position that OpenStack should not follow the designs of its competitor but challenge it[11].

> "We are introducing a cloud infrastructure suite of products that essentially delivers an Amazon Web Services-like cloud, but on a customer's premise." — Michael Grant, Cloudscaling's CEO, 9 February 2012[12].

Our visualizations in Figs. 3 and 4 capture cooperation from the `Cactus` (April 15th 2011) to the `Diablo` (September 22nd 2011) release and cooperation from the `Diablo` (September 22nd 2011) to the `Essex` (April 5th 2012) release. HP and IBM (large IT companies), Mirantis (an OpenStack pure-play startup), Red Hat (a Linux operating system distribution's vendor), Canonical (company behind the Ubuntu Linux distribution), VMware (an expert on the virtualization software and services) and Intel (selling CPUs that powered cloud infrastructures) got involved in the coopetitive[13] software project.

Mirantis, founded in 2011, marketed itself as a "pure-play" OpenStack company. The startup started collaboration early with Red Hat. Besides cooperating in the development of OpenStack, both firms partnered in implementation and integration services at common customers[14]. Mirantis was involved in the early

---

[11] See presentation entitled "OpenStack Co-Opetition: A View from Within" from Boris Renski (co-founder and chief marketing officer of Mirantis) presented on 04 Nov 2013 at the OpenStack summit, Hong Kong. Available on youtube at https://www.youtube.com/watch?v=i7HXu2abNj0.

[12] See Nancy Gohring news article at http://www.infoworld.com/article/2619192/.

[13] Coopetitive as firms within OpenStack cooperate and compete simultaneously. See [26, p. 6] for a relational map of competition among OpenStack firms.

[14] See https://www.redhat.com/en/about/press-releases/red-hat-and-mirantis-partner-across-products-and-services.

deployments of OpenStack at large enterprises such as Paypal, AT&T, Comcast, and Wells Fargo among others.

In the meantime, HP launched an OpenStack-based cloud computing services. The company started marketing itself as the leading organization behind the project. In addition, they marketed OpenStack as free of single-vendor locking as there were a full ecosystem behind the project[15]. At that time, it was the only cloud computing solution with a such promise. After all, cloud computing services are known by locking-in its customers [1].

With a very good track of contributions to open-source projects IBM (top contributor to the Eclipse IDE project), RedHat (top contributor to the Linux kernel) and Canonical (top contributor to the GNOME Linux Desktop project) also joined OpenStack. In common, all those companies had much expertise on Linux, the host operating system of OpenStack. RedHat and Canonical aimed at being the *defacto* host operating system for OpenStack-based clouds[16].

IBM entered with force in OpenStack and showed much commitment to the platform. Besides contributing with much source-code to the project, it helped many of its customers to deploy openStack. Moreover, it entered into the public cloud business with OpenStack as well. In the case of IBM, as well with HP and Intel, money could be made by selling complementary hardware optimized for OpenStack. On the space of virtualization technologies, VMware did not want to lose ground to Citrix, and its contributions to OpenStack ensured compatibility with its vSphere, NSX, vSOM and vCloud offering[17].

6   Discussion

In this section we discuss our most significant results. The structure of the discussion reflects our mixed-methods analytical approach where we attempted to maker sense of the retrieved social network visualizations capturing cooperative relationships within a complex software ecosystem. After all, "the fundamental quest of SNA is to understand the structure of the network" [6, p. 36].

6.1   A Theoretical and Empirical Evolutionary Approach
   to Software Ecosystems

In order to understand and explain why the retrieved social network visualizations took such topology and not other, much theoretical and empirical background knowledge was required. The use of certain theory to understand and explain our results was complemented with our understanding of the competitive cloud computing industry in which OpenStack is embedded, as well as with our understanding of how OpenStack is developed and governed. Besides literature directly adressing software ecosystems (c.f. [15], among many others),

---

[15] See   https://www.openstack.org/foundation/companies/profile/hewlett-packard-enterprise.

[16] See   https://www.openstack.org/blog/2013/11/openstack-user-survey-october-2013/.

[17] See http://www.vmware.com/products/openstack.html.

our explanation integrated as well with theory on the embeddedness of business relationships [27], management of the portfolio of business relationships [10], cooperation among competitors [21], materiality of technology [33], innovation and intelectual property [8] and multi-homing strategy [16]. Empirical and theoretical knowledge was complementary – we could not explain the complex evolution of the OpenStack ecosystem without much knowledge on the surrounding industrial background of OpenStack or knowledge on the internal socio-technical practices by key actors within the development of OpenStack. Furthermore, a theory was fundamental to derive why the cooperative relationships (captured with SNA from the source-code) within OpenStack evolved in one way and not other.

By tentatively explaining the retrieved networks, and by focusing on Open-Stack in relation to other software ecosystems in the industry, we identified seven mechanisms that shaped the evolution of OpenStack. Such mechanisms are not internal to OpenStack, but are rather enacted by other software ecosystems in the industry. In other words, we identified different ways on how do software ecosystems mutually co-evolve. We found seven mechanisms by which software ecosystems mutually influence each other — but we do not reject the existence of others. The mechanisms reported here can be seen as that drive the evolution of a software ecosystem in relation to others. Interesting enough, some of those identified causal mechanisms are enacted by competing software ecosystems.

6.2   Mechanisms of Co-Evolution Among Software Ecosystems

In the following, we will present the identified co-evolution mechanisms. The list is not complete and further work is needed to validate the mechanism. In addition, some of the mechanisms may overlap partially; however, we have decided to present them separately in order to validate or reject them in further studies.

(α) **Sedimentation and embeddedness of business relationships:** When analyzing the complex history of OpenStack, we quickly notice that prior business relationships had much impact on the evolution of OpenStack. For example, Rackspace entered in the NASA Nebula project (the precursor of OpenStack) as a supplier of Anso Labs (a company that it was later acquired by Rackspace). Another early contributor to OpenStack, Citrix, worked before with Rackspace in the development of Desktop visualization technologies before embracing Open-Stack. As pointed out by strategic management theory, business partnerships often accumulate in a process of sedimentation (c.f. [29]). Moreover, actors tend to cooperate with actors that they had previously worked with and tend to buy from existing suppliers (over new suppliers) — all in the so-called paradox of the embeddedness of business relationships (c.f. [27]).

(β) **Strategic management of the portfolio of business relationships:** Many of the firms contributing to OpenStack (e.g., IBM, HP, and RedHat) manage a vast portfolio of business partnerships. However, the value from a stand-alone partnership may not necessarily be value-creating from the overall portfolio perspective. Potential synergies between multiple alliances must be balanced to mitigate conflicts with other alliances (c.f [10]). Companies such as IBM and HP needed to show commitment to OpenStack as contributions to other cloud computing ecosystems could potentially damage cooperation. Firms that strategically engage with a software ecosystem might not be able to participate in competing others to not damage existing relationships. After all, the "friends of my enemies are my enemies" and the "enemies of my enemies are my friends".

(γ) **Firms values and reputation as a partner:** Another found mechanism with significant impact on the co-evolution of software ecosystems is each firm values and reputation as a good partner. Something especially important in cooperation among competitors (c.f. [21,25]). In the case of OpenStack, RedHat had a good reputation as a top contributor to Linux; IBM had a good reputation as a top contributor to Eclipse; Mirantis had a good reputation in deploying OpenStack to its customers while contributing back upstream to the community. On the other hand, Eucalyptus had lost some of its reputation of working in a truly open-source way by closing parts of the Eucalyptus cloud computing ecosystem. The evolution of software ecosystems is then a function of the values and reputation of existing and possible participants. With the loss of reputation, a player might disappear from an ecosystem while becoming unwelcome in others as well.

(δ) **Core technological architecture:** OpenStack is only functional with a "host OS". At the early days of OpenStack, Citrix and Rackspace welcomed much the expertise on Linux from RedHat and Canonical. In the cooperative side, they could optimize the "host OS" to better run OpenStack. On the other hand, on the competitive side, this two companies competed with others for customers with the sales argument that "we know Linux, we know OpenStack and we are the only ones that can support both". This reminded us that the stacking of architectural layers influences the software ecosystem evolution. The materiality of a software ecosystem (c.f. [33]) influences the materiality of other software ecosystems. In the case of OpenStack, the architecture of the OpenStack core was very much influenced by the architecture of Linux, the architecture of Eucalyptus (now a competitor) and consequently the architecture of Amazon EC2.

(ϵ) **Design of external APIs:** We also noted that not only the technological architecture of a software ecosystem influences its co-evolution with others, but also the design of its external APIs. At the early days of OpenStack, the design of the APIs from OpenStack, Eucalyptus, and Amazon EC2 converged. As the open-source cloud computing alternatives matured, Eucalyptus pursued compatibility with the established Amazon AWS APIs while OpenStack opted to diverge and provided interfaces to its computing and storage services in a distinct way. At that time, many decided to get away from OpenStack and move to Eucalyptus and CloudStack because its API was very different from the established Amazon AWS APIs. Many customers wanted to easily move applications from Amazon EC2 to their own private clouds and the other way around – Amazon AWS still remains the leader in public cloud services.

(ζ) **Competitive replication of new functionality:** Competition forces players to copy functionality from each other to keep the pace. Besides the existence of many intellectual property protection mechanisms, this happens quite often in the software industry (c.f. [8]). OpenStack started by implementing (and improving) many of the functionalities provided by Eucalyptus and Amazon E2C. Moreover, whenever firms tried to embed OpenStack within a proprietary product (e.g., a new cloud orchestrator that embedded OpenStack in it), OpenStack implemented a "new, official and open-source version" of it (i.e., OpenStack launched a new sub-project implementing the official orchestrator for OpenStack). In other words, OpenStack expanded its core by replicating complements. After all, copying an idea and making it open-source is often a more powerful tactic than copying open-source software and making it proprietary.

(η) **Complementors' multi-homing:** Due to the nature of software, the complements of ecosystems are often intangible. This means that these products and services (that add much value to the overall ecosystem) can be transferred or moved to a different ecosystem and setting with a relatively little effort. The phenomenon where a single complementing actor is offering his or her products or services to two or more ecosystems at the same time is called *multi-homing* (c.f. [12–14,22]); the opposite strategy is known as *single-homing*. For example, due to the success of the 'Flappy Bird' mobile game, it was quickly copied into all major mobile application ecosystems, and beyond [11]. Within OpenStack, Xen from Citrix and ESXi from VMWare are Hypervisors[18] that work both in the OpenStack and Eucalyptus software ecosystems. The contributions that shape the ecosystem evolution, are often due to the complementors interest in making their offering available across different ecosystems. Citrix and VMWare wanted to be sure that their hypervisors run on different cloud computing platforms. In the realm of CPUs, Intel and AMD, also contributors to the OpenStack, are also interested in making sure that their CPUs work across different cloud computing platforms — therefore they contribute to most open-source cloud computing software ecosystems. The same happens with Cisco, Juniper Networks, IBM and HP among other vendors of networking technology.

6.3 Implications and Limitations of the Study

Besides richly narrating the evolution of a software ecosystem, our focal perspective of attempting to understand the evolution of a software ecosystem as a function of other software ecosystem extends the literate on software ecosystems evolution [2,9,32].

Future research towards a deeper understanding of ecosystems' evolution should acknowledge that ecosystems do not evolve in insulation. Careful analysis of a software ecosystem evolution should take in consideration other software ecosystems as well, including competing ones. We argue then that, in order to understand the evolution of an ecosystem, we need to look way beyond it.

---

[18] A hypervisor is either a software or a hardware solution that creates, follows and runs virtual machine instances.

New methodologies, capable of capturing inter-ecosystem dependencies, are needed to addresses such findings (c.f. [4,25], for recent advancements in this direction).

Naturally, there are certain limitations for this study. First, this study uses a single case study research design to identify mechanisms of co-evolution. Therefore, it is likely our list of mechanisms is not full and further work is needed in order to validate the identified mechanism as well as to find new ones. In addition, we used one ecosystem as a focal point and studied co-evolution from its point-of-view. While we selected the case study ecosystem carefully, there are threats involved in the single case study research design. In future work, multiple ecosystem point-of-view should be used to validate our results.

Second, we selected an open-source software ecosystem as the case subject and generalizing the results to the other kinds of ecosystems should be done with care. There are some previous discussion on the limits on generalizing results from different kinds of software ecosystems to another kinds (c.f. [11,24]); however, the results of this study does not heavily rely on a certain ecosystem type. Therefore, they should be generalizable to, at least, open-source software ecosystem and, with some limitations, to general type of software ecosystems.

Third, we used developers' point-of-view in studying co-evolution of software ecosystems. Another option could be study the business connections between the participating companies (c.f. [3,4]). However, as software ecosystem are built from the developers' point-of-view [17], our decision seem to justifiable. Nevertheless, the further studies should pay attention also on other perspectives of ecosystems' co-evolution.

7 Conclusion

Our findings contribute to a deeper understating of the evolution of software ecosystem. We found that a software ecosystem co-evolve with other software ecosystems in at least seven different ways. Understanding the evolution of a software ecosystem requires an especially astute awareness of its competitive landscape as well as knowledge on its internal socio-technical practices. Research addressing the evolution of software ecosystem should, therefore, acknowledge that software ecosystems entangle with other software ecosystems in multiple ways, even with competing ones.

References

1. Armbrust, M., Fox, A., Griffith, R., Joseph, A.D., Katz, R., Konwinski, A., Lee, G., Patterson, D., Rabkin, A., Stoica, I., et al.: A view of cloud computing. Commun. ACM **53**(4), 50–58 (2010)
2. Basole, R.C.: Visualization of interfirm relations in a converging mobile ecosystem. J. Inf. Technol. **24**(2), 144–159 (2009)
3. Basole, R.C., Karla, J.: On the evolution of mobile platform ecosystem structure and strategy. Bus. Inf. Syst. Eng. **3**, 313–322 (2011)

4. Basole, R.C., Russell, M.G., Huhtamäki, J., Rubens, N., Still, K., Park, H.: Understanding business ecosystem dynamics: a data-driven approach. ACM Trans. Manag. Inf. Syst. (TMIS) **6**(2), 6 (2015)

5. Bavota, G., Canfora, G., Penta, M.D., Oliveto, R., Panichella, S.: The evolution of project inter-dependencies in a software ecosystem: the case of apache. In: 2013 IEEE International Conference on Software Maintenance, pp. 280–289 (2013)

6. Carrington, P.J.: Social network research. In: Mixed Methods Social Networks Research: Design and Applications, vol. 36. Cambridge University Press (2014). Chap. 2

7. German, D., Adams, B., Hassan, A.: The evolution of the R software ecosystem. In: 17th European Conference on Software Maintenance and Reengineering, pp. 243–252 (2013)

8. Guildea, B.: App stores: a digital no man's land or innovation's bane? J. Intellect. Property Law Pract. **11**(6), 445–449 (2016)

9. Hanssen, G.K.: A longitudinal case study of an emerging software ecosystem: implications for practice and theory. J. Syst. Softw. **85**(7), 1455–1466 (2012)

10. Hoffmann, W.H.: How to manage a portfolio of alliances. Long Range Plan. **38**(2), 121–143 (2005)

11. Hyrynsalmi, S.: Letters from the War of Ecosystems – An Analysis of Independent Software Vendors in Mobile Application Marketplaces. Doctoral dissertation, University of Turku, Turku, Finland , TUCS Dissertations No 188 (2014)

12. Hyrynsalmi, S., Mäkilä, T., Järvi, A., Suominen, A., Seppänen, M., Knuutila, T.: App store, marketplace, play! an analysis of multi-homing in mobile software ecosystems. In: Proceedings of the Fourth International Workshop on Software Ecosystems. CEUR Workshop Proceedings, vol. 879, pp. 55–68. MIT Sloan School of Management, Cambridge. CEUR-WS (2012)

13. Hyrynsalmi, S., Suominen, A., Mäntymäki, M.: The influence of developer multi-homing on competition between software ecosystems. J. Syst. Softw. **111**, 119–127 (2016)

14. Hyrynsalmi, S., Suominen, A., Jansen, S., Yrjönkoski, K.: Multi-homing in ecosystems and firm performance: does it improve software companies' ROA?. In: Proceedings of the International Workshop on Software Ecosystems Co-located with 10th International Conference on Information Systems (ICIS 2016). CEUR Workshop Proceedings, vol. 1808, pp. 56–69, Dublin. CEUR-WS (2016)

15. Jansen, S., Finkelstein, A., Brinkkemper, S.: A sense of community: a research agenda for software ecosystems. In: 31st International Conference on Software Engineering – Companion Volume, ICSE-Companion 2009, pp. 187–190. IEEE (2009)

16. Landsman, V., Stremersch, S.: Multi-homing in two-sided markets: an empirical inquiry in the video game console industry. J. Mark. **75**(6), 39–54 (2011)

17. Manikas, K.: Revisiting software ecosystems research: a longitudinal literature study. J. Syst. Softw. **117**, 84–103 (2016)

18. Manikas, K., Hansen, K.M.: Software ecosystems – a systematic literature review. J. Syst. Softw. **86**(5), 1294–1306 (2013)

19. Moore, J.F.: Predators and prey: a new ecology of competition. Harvard Bus. Rev. **71**(3), 75–86 (1993)

20. Moore, J.F.: The Death of Competition: Leadership and Strategy in the Age of Business Ecosystems. Harper Business, New York (1996)

21. Rochet, J.C., Tirole, J.: Cooperation among competitors: Some economics of payment card associations. Rand Journal of economics pp. 549–570 (2002)

22. Rochet, J.C., Tirole, J.: Platform competition in two-sided markets. J. Eur. Econ. Assoc. **1**(4), 990–1029 (2003)
23. Scacchi, W., Alspaugh, T.A.: Understanding the role of licenses and evolution in open architecture software ecosystems. J. Syst. Softw. **85**(7), 1479–1494 (2012)
24. Suominen, A., Hyrynsalmi, S., Seppänen, M.: Ecosystems here, there, and everywhere. In: Maglyas, A., Lamprecht, A.-L. (eds.) Software Business. LNBIP, vol. 240, pp. 32–46. Springer, Cham (2016). doi:10.1007/978-3-319-40515-5_3
25. Teixeira, J., Mian, S., Hytti, U.: Cooperation among competitors in the open-source arena: the case of openstack. In: Proceedings of the International Conference on Information Systems (ICIS 2016). Association for Information Systems (2016)
26. Teixeira, J., Robles, G., González-Barahona, J.M.: Lessons learned from applying social network analysis on an industrial free/libre/open source software ecosystem. J. Internet Serv. Appl. **6**(1), 14 (2015)
27. Uzzi, B.: Social structure and competition in interfirm networks: the paradox of embeddedness. Adm. Sci. Q. **42**(1), 35–67 (1997)
28. Wasserman, S., Faust, K.: Social Network Analysis: Methods and Applications, vol. 8. Cambridge University Press, Cambridge (1994)
29. Wassmer, U., Dussauge, P., Planellas, M.: How to manage alliances better than one at a time. MIT Sloan Manag. Rev. **51**(3), 77 (2010)
30. Yin, R.K.: Applications of Case Study Research. Sage, UK (2011)
31. Yu, L., Ramaswamy, S., Bush, J.: Software evolvability: an ecosystem point of view. In: Third International IEEE Workshop on Software Evolvability, pp. 75–80. IEEE (2007)
32. Yu, L., Ramaswamy, S., Bush, J.: Symbiosis and software evolvability. IT Professional **10**(4), 56–62 (2008)
33. Zammuto, R.F., Griffith, T.L., Majchrzak, A., Dougherty, D.J., Faraj, S.: Information technology and the changing fabric of organization. Organ. Sci. **18**(5), 749–762 (2007)

Health Measurement of Data-Scarce Software Ecosystems: A Case Study of Apple's ResearchKit

Paul van Vulpen$^{(\boxtimes)}$, Abel Menkveld, and Slinger Jansen

Utrecht University, Utrecht, The Netherlands
{p.n.vanvulpen,a.a.menkveld}@students.uu.nl,
slinger.jansen@uu.nl

Abstract. Current methods for measuring open source software ecosystem health are unable to measure the health of young software ecosystems, due to a lack of data. This paper proposes a new method for measuring software ecosystem health. By using a mixed method design with interviews as the primary data source, a health measurement can be performed on data scarce ecosystems. This is applied to ResearchKit, Apple's SDK to create applications for medical research. The case study shows that the ResearchKit ecosystem is threatened by the outbound links of the third-party software developers. These developers intend to create web-based applications as ResearchKit suffers from a selection bias that makes it unsuitable for most medical research. The interviews exposed an inherent problem that is unrelated to ecosystem size and may not have been found in a traditional health measurement.

Keywords: Software ecosystems · Ecosystem health · Open source

1 Introduction

The rising collaboration of software companies with third-party developers allows software ecosystems to form. A software ecosystem is defined as "a set of actors functioning as a unit and interacting with a shared market for software and services, together with the relationships among them. These relationships are frequently underpinned by a common technological platform or market and operate through the exchange of information, resources and artifacts" [1].

Software vendors that have created a software ecosystem around their product have to rely on the software ecosystem to be successful. In order to ensure the success of a product, the ecosystem needs to be healthy, as ineffective use of a software ecosystem will lead to the demise of software vendors, as stated by Jansen et al. [2]. Therefore, to evaluate future success of an ecosystem orchestrator, a health measurement of the software ecosystem is essential.

The Open Source Ecosystem Health Operationalization (OSEHO) is a framework that provides a health measurement based on a list of metrics that differ for each software ecosystem [1]. However, to perform a health measurement based

© Springer International Publishing AG 2017
A. Ojala et al. (Eds.): ICSOB 2017, LNBIP 304, pp. 131–145, 2017.
https://doi.org/10.1007/978-3-319-69191-6_9

on OSEHO, there currently is a focus on quantitative research methods. The quality of this analysis is highly dependent on the data and several challenges concerning unavailable, missing or incorrect data are reported [1].

Therefore, this paper proposes a new method of ecosystem health measurement. By interviewing developers, more in-depth information is to be found, which may predict the rise of an ecosystem. This way, not only well-established ecosystems can be assessed, but young and small ecosystems that are still data-scarce can be analyzed. In other domains, a mixed methods design has proven to provide both a "richer, contextual basis for interpreting and validating results" and "an increase of the robustness of results because findings can be strengthened through triangulation" as stated by Kaplan and Duchon [3]. This leads to the following research question:

Research question: *H*ow can qualitative research methods be used to measure the health of open source software ecosystems?

This paper is written in the following structure. Section 2 reviews previous work and describes the framework for measuring ecosystem health. Section 3 describes the case study, research methodology and metrics. Section 4 covers the results of this research. In Sect. 5, the results are analyzed. Finally, Sect. 6 provides the discussion of the research, and in Sect. 7 the conclusion about software ecosystem health is made.

2   Previous Work

Software ecosystem health is a new research domain within software ecosystems. Few researchers discuss the specific topic within their work. A compact definition of software ecosystem health is given by Lucassen et al. [4] as "longevity and a propensity for growth." Some theories link software ecosystem health to biological ecosystem health, such as Dhungana et al. [5] and Wynn [6]. Newer research mainly focuses on extending the models of den Hartig [7] and Iansiti and Levien [8]. Den Hartig and Iansiti & Levien cover business ecosystems and recognize three determinants of ecosystem health. These are productivity, robustness and niche creation. The determinants are defined by den Hartig [7] as:

- robustness, the capability of an ecosystem to face and survive disruptions
- productivity, the efficiency with which an ecosystem converts inputs into outputs
- niche creation, the capacity to create meaningful diversity and thereby novel capabilities

Jansen [1] extends the model of Den Hartig by providing indicators for each of the determinants of open source software ecosystem health. Furthermore, the model is extended by adding two scopes, network level and project level. At network level, the determinants of ecosystem health are operationalized for the ecosystem domain. The project level covers determinants that investigate ecosystem health by analyzing projects within the software ecosystem. OSEHO has been used to measure the health of other software ecosystems such as e-commerce ecosystems by Alami et al. [9] and content management systems by van Lingen et al. [10]. The indicators are diverse as the availability of data for open source ecosystems is limited and different for each ecosystem [1]. Therefore, a refit of OSEHO to the analyzed framework is required.

3 Research Method

3.1 Case Study

The method for measuring ecosystem health of young software ecosystems is exemplified in a case study of the ResearchKit software ecosystem. ResearchKit[1] is an open source framework introduced and developed by Apple[2] that allows medical researchers and app developers to create applications for medical research. The goal of ResearchKit is to revolutionize the medical sector by having a software ecosystem that entails applications that give new medical insights on a faster scale than traditional medical research. The cooperation of Apple, third-party developers and medical researchers leads to a product that serves the market. Therefore, the environment of ResearchKit is defined as a software ecosystem. The open source code of ResearchKit has been released on GitHub in March 2015. However, the amount of data in this ecosystem is not sufficient to perform a traditional ecosystem health measurement. Therefore, the ResearchKit software ecosystem health should be measured by combining interviews and quantitative methods.

3.2 Ecosystem Health Metrics

The metrics used to measure the ecosystem health determinants in the interviews and GHTorrent search are discussed in this section. Because ecosystems and possible metrics differ, the metrics that should be used to measure the ResearchKit have to fit the ecosystem. The selected metrics are based on the 41 metrics of ecosystem health distinguished in the OSEHO framework [1]. For each metric included, the reason why it was added and a definition are shown below. Other metrics of OSEHO are not included due to a lack of data (such as new downloads), or because they are not practicable in this context (such as market share). The overview of the metric selection is shown in Table 1.

Some of the metrics are selected because of a pilot interview at C tracker. C tracker is an application within the ResearchKit ecosystem that is being used to gather medical data from Hepatitis C patients through the use of their smartphone. The pilot interview aimed to shed light on metrics of ecosystem health that are related to the third-party developers. Therefore, the metric **knowledge creation (1)** was added. Third-party developers should experience additional

---

[1] http://researchkit.org/.
[2] http://www.apple.com/researchkit/.

benefits of participating in the ResearchKit ecosystem in the form of easier subject collection, faster research paper development etc. This is an indication of the productivity of the ResearchKit ecosystem.

Usage (2) is defined as the number of end users of the released applications. Usage is added as a metric because the ecosystem can only exist when sufficient research subjects are available. The data about number of end users is an indicator of productivity and is only accessible through interviews, as Apple does not provide numbers of app downloads in its App Store.

The **growth of the software framework (3)** is measured by Van Lingen, Palomba and Lucassen [10] as the growth of the framework in modules. In the ResearchKit software ecosystem, this is measured as the number of commits to the software framework. The software framework is available on GitHub where Apple or other companies can edit and extend ResearchKit.

The total number of **active projects (4)** is measured based on the activity in the App Store. The total number of applications in the App Store is available, and it gives an indicator of the robustness of the ecosystem [1]. The number of active projects is a metric of ecosystem health, as it is a direct indicator of the size of the ecosystem. Lucassen et al., van Lingen et al., and Goeminne & Mens use this metric for ecosystem health measurement [4,10,11].

Contributor satisfaction (5) is the satisfaction of the developers of applications in the ecosystem. Developer satisfaction is supposed to be one of the most important metrics in project health as concluded by Lakhani and Wolf [12]. A high developer satisfaction binds developers to the ecosystem. Therefore, contributor satisfaction is an indicator of robustness.

The **end user rating (6)** is collected by scraping the App Store for ratings of end users. A high rating from end users is essential because they have to use the developed applications and participate in research to allow this ecosystem to function. Therefore, the end user rating is an indicator of the robustness of the ecosystem. Stoyanov et al. concluded that ratings can be used to measure the quality of mobile health applications [13], which is important for ecosystem health in this domain.

Outbound links to other SECOs (7) is defined as the other ecosystems where the contributors are active in. The pilot interview showed that the development team of C Tracker was also active with ResearchStack, the Android counterpart of ResearchKit. The multi-homing activities of developers may or may not be beneficial for the robustness of the ecosystem.

Interest (8) is measured both on developer and end user level. Search statistics using Google Trends are analyzed to measure the worldwide public interest in ResearchKit. This is done similarly to van Lingen et al. [10], who define the findability of Google Trends as an indicator of software ecosystem health when comparing several ecosystems. In this paper, the findability will be analyzed over time to measure the robustness in terms of public interest. Furthermore, developer interest is measured using the growth of the number of forks on GitHub. A fork is a separate repository where a third-party developer has full writing permissions. Forks may act as a first step to new projects [1]. Lucassen et al. [4] show that the number of forks is an indication of software ecosystem health.

Variety in projects (9) & **variety in developer type (10)** measure the niche creation of the ResearchKit ecosystem. Variety in projects measures what the goals and features are of the applications in this ecosystem. Variety in developer type discusses who the contributors to this ecosystem are. Their size and location may also influence ecosystem health. Iansiti & Levien state that a healthy ecosystem possesses the capabilities to increase meaningful diversity over time through the creation of new valuable functions [8]. In this article, it is argued that both variety in projects and developer type lead to an increased capability to create meaningful diversity in the software ecosystem.

Table 1. Overview of the selected software ecosystem health metrics

Determinant	Metric (number)	Source
Productivity	Knowledge creation (1)	Interviews
	Usage (2)	Interviews
	Growth of the software framework (3)	GitHub
Robustness	Active projects (4)	App Store
	Contributor satisfaction (5)	Interviews
	End user rating (6)	App Store
	Outbound links to other SECOs (7)	Interviews
	Interest (8)	Google Trends, Github
Niche creation	Variety in projects (9)	Interviews, Online search, App Store
	Variety in developer type (10)	Interviews, Online search, App Store

3.3   Data Collection

GHTorrent is used to obtain the historical evolution of the ResearchKit open source project. The GHTorrent project [14] provides queryable data offered through the GitHub REST API, created by the Software Engineering Research Group of TU Delft. The MySQL database is queried using the DBLite web-based client. For every GitHub commit to the ResearchKit project, the commit date, committer username and committer employer are retrieved. Next, all projects that were forked from the ResearchKit projects have been retrieved, together with their creation date, username and the user's employer. The data used in this work is dated 28 September 2016.

The **interviews** were conducted with key developers of ResearchKit applications. To find the developers of ResearchKit applications, the App Store was searched for these applications. In the App Store, 15 applications that used ResearchKit were found. The developers of these applications were sent an email request for an interview. A reply was received from eight developers (response rate $8/15 = 53\%$). Two of these developers did not have a final interview, as one of the developer teams replied that their application was used so rarely that they did not have enough information to give an interview and the other team did not reply to email response after the initial contact. Out of the remaining six developers, three developers were interviewed using Skype or Join.me. The other three developers answered the questions by email. The interviews had a semi-structured design and the interview questions were based on the metrics.

4   Results

In performing a qualitative ecosystem health measurement, the selection of ecosystem health metrics is the first step. An indicator should be selected when literature about the research topic states that the indicator is relevant for ecosystem health measurement. Then, data availability for each indicator has to be reviewed. Indicators that are not sufficiently covered by quantitative data sources are then selected to be measured in interviews. The interviews should be held at third party developers to measure the selected ecosystem health metrics. This can overcome the aforementioned problem of data scarcity when performing a software ecosystem health measurement. An operationalization of the measurement is shown below for ResearchKit.

4.1   Productivity

The interviews made clear that **knowledge creation** by developing an application with ResearchKit is significantly better than previous methods, such as paper questionnaires. The first advantage mentioned is that an application can provide validation steps and therefore reduce the occurrence of invalid data. The ResearchKit framework also allows for easy collection of sensory data. This is possible by manual coding but is easier when using ResearchKit. The lead software developer of C Tracker states:

> *You need to show surveys nicely on the screen and alternative solutions have not been nicely done; but ResearchKit is great. (...) So ResearchKit gives access to sensory data, you can do this yourself, but since ResearchKit provides it, you can more easily build an app around it.* - Lead Software Developer of C Tracker

Medical research using an application developed with ResearchKit is more effective than conventional methods, but also more effective than developing an application without ResearchKit. Furthermore, the research team that has developed the Mole Mapper application stated that "the first publication in a major journal was accepted," with data acquired through the Mole Mapper application.

Knowledge is not only created by the implementation of the ResearchKit framework itself, contributors are also adding knowledge to the ecosystem framework. This can be done by adding code extensions to the open source GitHub project, or sharing developer experiences, as explained by two interviewees:

We have sent pull requests that they accepted. It seems to work. (...) ResearchKit has a lot of contributors who have added back the active tasks modules. - Lead Software Developer of C Tracker

We did contribute some of the forms to the community and did relate to Apple what we were doing and how we approach challenges that we faced. Other community members who were facing similar experiences now have a guide on how we solved that problem. - Chief Information Officer of StopCOPD

The **usage** of the medical research applications varies. C Tracker mentioned 700 end users and Mole Mapper mentioned 3000 subjects in their first study. Bigger studies in terms of participants are mPower and PRIDE Study. mPower has reported more than 10,000 participants and PRIDE Study over 16,000. Another developer reveals that their application has not been used very much, as the developer was unable to get the application out to patients to try. The development team of StopCOPD already had a web-based platform and the release of an application developed with ResearchKit did not significantly impact usage.

Figure 1 shows the **growth of the software framework** in the green area that is expanding over time. Figure 2 shows the contribution of Apple to ResearchKit in comparison with other software companies.

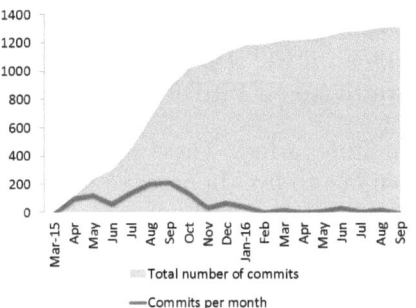

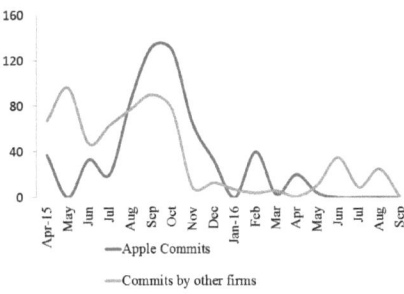

Fig. 1. Number of commits per month and cumulative number of commits to ResearchKit (Color figure online)

Fig. 2. Commit comparison of Apple and other firms over time

4.2 Robustness

Out of the 15 **active projects** listed in the U.S. App Store's ResearchKit page, four apps have been updated in the last six months. Out of the other applications, nine have been updated in the last year and two apps have not been updated for more than a year. In addition to this, two applications that have been launched in the first wave of ResearchKit apps have been retracted from the App Store.

The **contributor satisfaction** of interviewed developers with the use of ResearchKit was overall high. Using this framework speeds up the development process and ensures consistency throughout the ecosystem.

So you have a nice app and a really nice package that looks good and works well. But it's not something that you are unable to do without ResearchKit. It's just nicer and more quickly done. - Lead Software Developer of C Tracker

Another aspect of ResearchKit that positively impacted contributor satisfaction is the fast collection of research subjects. The development and publication of a mobile application proves to be a fast way of collecting subjects and consenting them to participate in research. The principal investigator of PRIDE Study was satisfied with the faster development of a medical research application and the digital consent.

It allowed us to recruit people quickly by having an app. People have to consent to participate in research. That is done through the app which is relatively new in this whole process. - Co-Director and Principal Investigator of PRIDE Study

ResearchKit does have aspects that negatively impact contributor satisfaction. Bugs were found by developers that would not occur when an application is developed without ResearchKit.

We ran into this issue with ResearchKit which is a bug in the branching logic of surveys. The developers had to do coding of the correct order both forwards and backwards through the survey, which I think was just really annoying. As ResearchKit develops more, it will be hopefully less of a problem. - Co-Director and Principal Investigator of PRIDE Study

The **end user rating** is measured by App Store ratings. These are shown in Table 2. The score is measured on a scale from one to five. In order to measure an average rating of the developed applications, only applications with five or more ratings have been taken into account, to reduce the influence of individual ratings on infrequently rated applications. These applications received 60.67 (SD = 71.02) ratings on average. The users scored the applications with an average score of 3.21 (SD = 0.59).

The **outbound links to other SECOs** are present on a large scale in this ecosystem as all interviewees reported that their research team did some kind of multi-homing. The goal of the medical studies is to reach as many subjects as possible, and developing applications for multiple platforms is a way to reach more subjects. The Android counterpart of ResearchKit is ResearchStack[3], an upcoming development that also provides a framework for developing medical research applications. ResearchStack is used by several of the interviewed developers.

Our developers are also working with ResearchStack. We have worked with this system to port one study over to ResearchStack and are in the process of doing so for additional studies. - Principal Investigator (anonymized)

---

[3] http://researchstack.org/.

Table 2. Applications using the ResearchKit framework, listed on the ResearchKit overview page in the U.S. App Store

App name	Developed by	Launch	Last updated	Number of ratings	Score *****
MyHeart Counts	Stanford Medicine	Mar 2015	Dec 14 2016	225	2.91
PRIDE Study	University of California	Jun 2015	Jul 25 2016	99	2.86
GlucoSuccess	Massachusetts General Hospital	Mar 2015	May 13 2015	93	2.78
SleepHealth	American Sleep Apnea Association	Mar 2016	Jun 24 2016	46	2.78
Parkinson mPower Study	Sage Bionetworks	Mar 2015	Mar 21 2016	43	3.60
Mole Mapper Melanoma Study	Sage Bionetworks & Oregon Health & Science University Dermatology	Oct 2015	June 4 2016	13	3.62
EpiWatch	Johns Hopkins University	Oct 2015	Feb 19 2016	12	2.42
PPD ACT	Psychiatry and Genetics at the University of North Carolina	Mar 2016	Jun 27 2016	9	4.22
Autism & Beyond	Duke University Health System	Oct 2015	Nov 11 2015	6	3.67
VascTrac	Stanford Cardiovascular Institute	Sep 2016	Sep 22 2016	2	5.00
TeamStudy	Harvard & Sage Bionetworks	Mar 2016	Jan 4 2017	2	5.00
Concussion Tracker	NYU Langone Medical Center	Nov 2015	Feb 1 2016	1	5.00
C Tracker	Boston Children's Hospital	Oct 2015	Feb 15 2016	0	–
EPV	Yale University	Oct 2015	Jan 29 2016	0	–
StopCOPD	COPD Foundation	Nov 2015	Jun 29 2016	0	–

We find it critical to allow each ResearchKit study to be ported to Android phones using tools such as ResearchStack. The heterogeneity of Android devices makes Android much more challenging. We are outlining how to approach ResearchStack, and it is definitely in the works. - Principal Investigator of VascTrac

Another way to target more subjects is by eliminating the use of a smartphone by developing a web-based service. This service is accessible through multiple devices ranging from computers to phones. This also eliminates a selection bias. When using an application developed with ResearchKit for medical research, the subjects are automatically users of iPhones, and this will bias the sample. Using a web-service with multi-device access eliminates this bias.

In the United States iPhones are owned, by effectively well-to-do people and we don't have as much racial and ethnic diversity as we would like. (...) So we're moving to a web-based platform that will allow people on any device to participate. Co-Director and Principal Investigator of PRIDE Study

Figure 3 shows the number of forks created by developers on GitHub. The release of ResearchKit sparked the **interest** of developers and 484 forks were made in the first three months. After the initial three months, the number of created forks per month declined to an average of 10 forks per month.

The (end user) interest in ResearchKit, based on data from Google Trends[4], is visualized in Fig. 4. The numbers show that the search terms 'ResearchKit' and 'Research Kit' have a 2 till 3% popularity in the last quarter of 2016, in comparison with its peak popularity during the launch in March 2015.

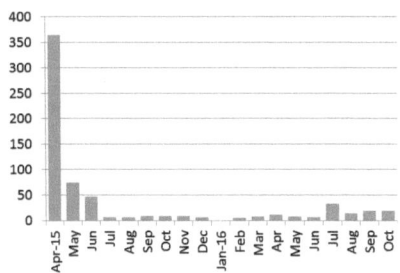

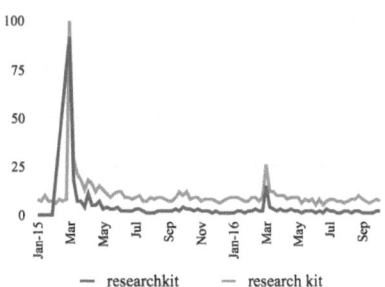

Fig. 3. Number of forks per month on the ResearchKit GitHub project

Fig. 4. Google search interest in ResearchKit

4.3 Niche Creation

The **variety in projects** developed with ResearchKit is high. Out of the apps mentioned in Fig. 2, 12 are developed for medical research dedicated to a disease. The other applications conduct research on related medical subjects, not specifically dedicated to a single disease. The interviews show different kinds of research conducted with ResearchKit. The first type of research aims to find a relation between people's perceptions or way of living and a disease. For example, C Tracker, GlucoSuccess and MyHeart Counts are applications that try to analyze a subject's behavior and link this to their disease. The second type of research tries to build up a community of like-minded and learn from their needs, of which PRIDE study is an example. These different types of research demand for as many subjects as possible, but also require an obtained sample to be representative of the population intended to be analyzed. A third study design is more exploratory in the sense that it tries to determine whether the iPhone's sensory data could be helpful as a research instrument. One example is the EpiWatch app, which gathers data to facilitate the creation of a seizure detection app. The Parkinson mPower Study is also using this study design. When developing an application with an exploratory goal, a large data set is still vital, but a non-random sample is not a requirement for this research.

Table 2 also shows the developers of the applications in the App Store, in order to analyze the **variety in developer type**. The developers are not new start-ups that wish to enter the medical research sector. Instead, the developers

---

[4] https://www.google.com/trends/.

consist of universities, hospitals, foundations and nonprofit organizations. The organizations only take part in the ecosystem with a single application, except for Sage Bionetworks, a nonprofit organization that has developed three applications.

5   Analysis

The metrics that measure **productivity** address a variable change over time [1]. In the software ecosystem of ResearchKit the growth of the software framework is such a variable. The core framework was provided and enhanced in its first year primarily by Apple, but additions afterwards are mostly added by third-party developers. Commit access to the ResearchKit project repository is strictly controlled by the use of pull requests, consistent with findings from Padhye et al. [15]. Contributors have to sign a license agreement first and do not have direct writing access to the source code. The initial framework appears to be finished, as Apple is no longer committing intensively and the number of commits per month over the last year is significantly lower than in earlier stages of development.

The great variation in the number of end users between the applications emphasizes the notion that ResearchKit as a technical framework alone provides little advantage over an application created without the framework, in terms of recruitment. Still, some applications profited from the media attention during the launch of ResearchKit and mention over 16,000 downloads and another development team thinks it is easier to recruit people by having an application. ResearchKit may have been an incentive for them to create such an application.

Knowledge creation can substantially be increased by developing an application with ResearchKit, due to the predesigned surveys, sensory data and digital informed consent. This is true when comparing to traditional medical research methods and when comparing to development of a research application without ResearchKit.

The **robustness** level covers absolute entities in static metrics [1]. A robust ecosystem is able to "survive disruptions and must persist in the face of environmental changes" [8]. Currently, the number of active ResearchKit projects is limited to 15 applications highlighted by Apple in their U.S. App Store. The exact number of ResearchKit applications worldwide is higher and not all applications are officially recognized in the App Store ResearchKit category. Nevertheless, both end user and developer interest declined significantly after the first three months following the launch of the framework. Over half of the created related projects in ResearchKit's 1.5 years appearance on GitHub are forked within the first month after release.

Paschou et al. [16] emphasize an increasing demand for "continuous software updates of mHealth apps on users' smartphones." Developers mostly meet this requirement, as a new version has been released in the last year for 13 out of the 15 applications. End users rate the applications with an average 3.21 score on a scale from one to five, but the number of ratings applications have received varies substantially. More important for the robustness of the ecosystem is the developer satisfaction and their connection to the ecosystem. Iansiti & Levien [8] even state that niche players (the developers) can wield surprising power in the face of keystones (Apple). In the ResearchKit ecosystem, developers are overall satisfied with the technical functioning of the framework. Minor bugs in the framework or irritations of developers have been attributed to the ecosystem still being nascent.

However, serious threats to the health of the ecosystem concerning its robustness have been identified. These threats come from niche players' outbound links to other ecosystems. Almost all of the interviewees raised concerns about the arising sample selection bias due to the fact that ResearchKit applications can be used by iPhone users only. Moreover, medical researchers tend to look for alternative solutions to overcome this problem, clearly harming the ResearchKit ecosystem. ResearchStack, the Android counterpart of the framework, is proposed and used by some researchers as a method to reach more possible subjects. This open source framework is especially designed to easily adapt existing iOS apps for Android.

Another strategy involves the development of a web application, resulting in the iPhone app becoming only little more than a 'wrapper' for the mobile website. These changes can "loosen the bonds that typically tie a niche player to its keystone partner and make it easier for developers to end a relationship with a keystone whose platform doesn't offer sufficient value" [8].

Next to the productivity and robustness, **niche creation**, an ecosystem's capability to "increase meaningful diversity through the creation of valuable new functions or niches" is an important health measurement [8]. In the ResearchKit ecosystem the projects have widely varied goals. There is no overlap among the projects and currently no competition. This is why new players can easily become active in a new domain or niche. The app initiators come from several sources, including universities, hospitals and non-profit organizations. New entrants already have a relation to medical research, indicating that this market can be characterized as one with high entry barriers. Despite these entry barriers, there is much opportunity to start as a new niche player in the ecosystem because of the large variety in projects on the network level.

On the project level, Jansen [1] makes clear that "a project that can be applied in a wide variety of contexts will be more supporting for niche creation." This comprises that the project should be able to support different languages, markets and technologies. In ResearchKit, these possibilities are currently limited. The technology and market are limited to the use of the iOS developer platform and additional countries are only slowly being adopted due to the strict regulations on medical research that vary for each country. From the results of this paper, three different ResearchKit practices became clear. Traditional medical research, aiming to find a relation between people's perceptions or way of living and a disease, is supplemented with community building applications and exploratory research to the usefulness of iPhone's sensory data for future implementations.

Based on the productivity, robustness and niche creation metrics, this analysis shows that the ecosystem is unhealthy. Although the low scores, mainly on robustness, seems to be attributable to the small size of the ecosystem, the interviews show clear indications of an underlying problem that is unrelated to ecosystem size.

The main finding of this analysis is that all of the third-party developers in the ResearchKit ecosystem have outbound links to other SECOs. Especially developers that have created or are intending to create a web-based application are threatening ecosystem health. These developers are leaving the ecosystem because of the sample bias that persists when developing medical research applications for the iPhone. ResearchKit is unsuitable for medical research in which normal sampling is required. A small number of research applications in the ecosystem is related to exploratory research to test the usefulness of the iPhone's sensory data for medical purposes, which is not stymied by sampling bias. However, this exploratory research does not appear to be large enough to create an ecosystem around these applications. The main advantage that ResearchKit has over a web-based application, the access to sensory data, has not been widely adopted by the actors in the ecosystem.

Iansiti and Levien [8], who define value creation as the first part of an effective keystone strategy, emphasize that "value creation of keystones is crucial to the community's survival." The need for standardized technologies (like HTML5), follows logically after the initial industry-specific technology and tailored software solutions [17]. This is underlined through the need for random sampling in medical research. Since the added value of sensory data is not high enough when compared to the need to retrieve a non-biased sample, the ResearchKit framework in its current shape will be unable to establish a healthy software ecosystem around itself.

6   Discussion

This article aimed to create a health measurement that is not dependent on large quantitative data sources by introducing interviews as a new data source. This new technique has been applied to the ResearchKit software ecosystem. In this chapter, the limitations and implications of this research are discussed.

Using both qualitative and quantitative data sources for ecosystem health measurement provides the best of both worlds. Interviews give in-depth data and insights that may not be easily retrievable from quantitative sources. In the ResearchKit case study, the outbound links of third-party developers may not be retrieved from quantitative data sources. Quantitative methods provide objective data that is easier to collect and larger in volume. Furthermore, quantitative data sources can provide information of the ecosystem over time. Qualitative and quantitative sources complement each other in the analysis of software ecosystems. Trends in interviews may be linked to findings in quantitative methods and vice versa, which strengthens the validity of the analysis.

The method of this paper is especially useful for ecosystems where no plethora of data is available. This can be the case for newly started ecosystems, such as ResearchKit. The method may also find use in closed software ecosystems that have just been opened up. The list of metrics is created with the definition of the health criteria as defined by Jansen [1] in mind. The interviews can theoretically provide information on limitless metrics. To ensure the quality, only few predefined metrics should be researched based on the specific case.

7   Conclusion

Open source software ecosystems are a new research domain within information systems. This paper attempts to contribute to the fresh domain by proposing a new method of measuring ecosystem health of data-scarce ecosystems. The research question of this paper is: How can qualitative research methods be used to measure the health of open source software ecosystems?

To answer the research question, a method that combines qualitative and quantitative data collections for an ecosystem health measurement has been proposed. Based on the OSEHO framework and relevant literature, ecosystem health metrics should be selected that measure the three determinants of ecosystem health: productivity, robustness and niche creation.

The method is operationalized in a case study on ResearchKit. The ecosystem health is measured by combining data retrieved from GHTorrent and interviews at developers of applications in the ecosystem of ResearchKit. The case study shows how interviews provide another perspective of ecosystem health than quantitative methods. The robustness of the ResearchKit ecosystem was found to be severely limiting its health, regardless of the size of the ecosystem. This is caused by the outbound links of third-party developers. Using ResearchKit in development for medical research applications implies that the subjects are iPhone users. This is restraining medical research that relies on unbiased random selection. Therefore, third-party developers have created, or are intending to create, a web-based application or adapt their applications for Android to reach a bigger audience with a smaller sampling bias. The interviews shed light on aspects that may not have been found in a traditional health measurement.

Further research could investigate the impact of ecosystem health on commercial success, because a link between these terms will lead to better understanding of ecosystem health. Another research area is to compare ecosystem health to external factors, as current ecosystems that appear healthy may still be quickly overtaken by superior ecosystems.

Acknowledgements. We would like to thank Prof. Dr. João Fernandes and Dr. Andrey Saltan for providing valuable comments that have improved our paper.

References

1. Jansen, S.: Measuring the Health of Open Source Software Ecosystems: Moving Beyond the Scope of Project Health (2013)
2. Jansen, S., Finkelstein, A., Brinkkemper, S.: A sense of community: a research agenda for software ecosystems. In: 31st International Conference on Software Engineering, New and Emerging Research Track, pp. 187–190 (2009)

3. Kaplan, B., Duchon, D.: Combining qualitative and quantitative methods in information systems research: a case study. MIS Q. **12**, 571–586 (1988)
4. Lucassen, G., van Rooij, K., Jansen, S.: Ecosystem health of cloud PaaS providers. In: Herzwurm, G., Margaria, T. (eds.) ICSOB 2013. LNBIP, vol. 150, pp. 183–194. Springer, Heidelberg (2013). doi:10.1007/978-3-642-39336-5_18
5. Dhungana, D., Groher, I., Schludermann, E., Biffl, S.: Software ecosystems vs. natural ecosystems: learning from the ingenious mind of nature. In Proceedings of the Fourth European Conference on Software Architecture: Companion Volume, pp. 96–102. ACM (2010)
6. Wynn, D.: Assessing the health of an open source ecosystem. In: Emerging Free and Open Source Software Practices. Idea Group Publishing (2007)
7. den Hartigh, E., Tol, M., Visscher, W.: The health measurement of a business ecosystem. In: Proceedings of the European Network on Chaos and Complexity Research and Management Practice Meeting, pp. 1–39 (2006)
8. Iansiti, M., Levien, R.: Strategy as ecology. Harv. Bus. Rev. **82**(3), 68–78 (2004)
9. Alami, D., Rodríguez, M., Jansen, S.: Relating health to platform success: exploring three e-commerce ecosystems. In: Proceedings of the 2015 European Conference on Software Architecture Workshops, pp. 43–49. ACM (2015)
10. van Lingen, S., Palomba, A., Lucassen, G.: On the software ecosystem health of open source content management systems. In: 5th International Workshop on Software Ecosystems (IWSECO 2013), pp. 38–51 (2013)
11. Goeminne, M., Mens, T.: A comparison of identity merge algorithms for software repositories. Sci. Comput. Program. **78**(8), 971–986 (2013)
12. Lakhani, K., Wolf, R.: Why Hackers Do What They Do: Understanding Motivation and Effort in Free/Open Source Software Projects. MIT Press, Cambridge (2005)
13. Stoyanov, S.R., Hides, L., Kavanagh, D.J., Zelenko, O., Tjondronegoro, D., Mani, M.: Mobile app rating scale: a new tool for assessing the quality of health mobile apps. JMIR mHealth uHealth **3**(1), e27 (2015)
14. Gousios, G.: The GHTorrent dataset and tool suite. In: MSR 2013, pp. 233–236 (2013)
15. Padhye, R., Mani, S., Sinha, V.S.: A study of external community contribution to open-source projects on GitHub. In: Proceedings of the 11th Working Conference on Mining Software Repositories, pp. 332–335. ACM (2014)
16. Paschou, M., Sakkopoulos, E., Tsakalidis, A.: easyHealthApps: e-Health apps dynamic generation for smartphones & tablets. J. Med. Syst. **37**(3), 9951 (2013)
17. Tyrväinen, P., Warsta, J., Seppänen, V.: Evolution of secondary software businesses: understanding industry dynamics. In: León, G., Bernardos, A.M., Casar, J.R., Kautz, K., De Gross, J.I. (eds.) TDIT 2008. ITIFIP, vol. 287, pp. 381–401. Springer, Boston (2008). doi:10.1007/978-0-387-87503-3_22

Coopetition of Software Firms in Open Source Software Ecosystems

Anh Nguyen Duc[1(✉)], Daniela S. Cruzes[2], Geir K. Hanssen[2],
Terje Snarby[3], and Pekka Abrahamsson[1]

[1] Norwegian University of Science and Technology, Trondheim, Norway
{anhn, pekkaa}@ntnu.no
[2] SINTEF Digital, Trondheim, Norway
{daniela.s.cruzes, geir.k.hanssen}@sintef.no
[3] Genus AS, Lysaker, Norway
terjesnarby@gmail.com

Abstract. Software firms participate in an ecosystem as a part of their innovation strategy to extend value creation beyond the firm's boundary. Participation in an open and independent environment also implies the competition among firms with similar business models and targeted markets. Hence, firms need to consider potential opportunities and challenges upfront. This study explores how software firms interact with others in OSS ecosystems from a coopetition perspective. We performed a quantitative and qualitative analysis of three OSS projects. Finding shows that software firms emphasize the co-creation of common value and partly react to the potential competitiveness on OSS ecosystems. Six themes about coopetition were identified, including spanning gatekeepers, securing communication, open-core sourcing and filtering shared code. Our work contributes to software engineering research with a rich description of coopetition in OSS ecosystems. Moreover, we also come up with several implications for software firms in pursing a harmony participation in OSS ecosystems.

Keywords: Coopetition · Collaboration · Competition · SECO · Software ecosystem · Case study

1 Introduction

Increasingly, software products are no longer developed solely in-house, but in a software ecosystem (SECO), where developers collaborate with *"distributed collaborators"* beyond their firm boundary [1, 12]. This differs from traditional outsourcing techniques in that the initiating actor does not necessarily own the software produced by contributing actors and does not hire the contributing actors. All actors, however, coexist in an interdependent way. Game developers in App Stores, for instance, might share a similar game engine, but independently produce different applications to mobile users. By integrating with SECOs, firms can benefit from developing projects of a size that exceeds their own capabilities, exploring opportunities to enter new markets [14], performing a inside-out process [2], and employment of a recruitment strategy [15].

© Springer International Publishing AG 2017
A. Ojala et al. (Eds.): ICSOB 2017, LNBIP 304, pp. 146–160, 2017.
https://doi.org/10.1007/978-3-319-69191-6_10

Before the full potential advantages of SECOs are leveraged, commercial firms need to consider several concerns. At the organizational level, the firm's benefit and the ecosystem's goal are not always the same [3]. Participation of commercial firms in SECOs with their diverse motivations and business strategies might introduce dynamics, and sometimes conflicts in navigating the project evolution [14]. The body of knowledge in open source software (OSS) projects provide sufficient amount of knowledge on firms' motivation, collaboration patterns, and business models when participating in such an open collaborative firm network [4–7]. However, one often-neglected aspect is the consideration of both competition and collaboration among firms, as two sides of the same coin.

Coopetition, as a concept, relates to the coexistence of competition and collaboration, and conceptualizes the interaction among firms with a partial congruence of interests [8, 9]. In a coopetitive environment, firms cooperate with each other to reach a higher value creation as compared to the value created without interaction and struggle to achieve competitive advantage. A good example of coopetition in a restaurant business is when a large number of restaurants are concentrated in a relatively small area ("*the restaurant district*" or "*the restaurant quarter*"). Coopetition takes place when companies' being in the same market work together in the exploration of knowledge and research of new products. Since coopetition applies to inter-firm relationships, open source SECO offers an ideal context for understanding coopetition among firms that develop and utilize a common software codebase [11].

Our research objective is to explore the state-of-practice on coopetition among commercial firms in open SECOs. To our knowledge, there exist only a few studies that examine the coopetition phenomenon between commercial firms in SECOs [10, 11, 14], making it an interesting research topic. A research question (RQ) was derived from this research objective:

RQ: How do commercial firms maintain both collaboration and competition in an open source software ecosystem?

The study is organized as follows: Sect. 2 presents a background about coopetition and firm participation in open source SECOs. Section 3 describes our research methodology, Sect. 4 presents our findings, and Sect. 5 discusses the findings. Finally, Sect. 6 concludes the paper.

2 Background and Related Work

2.1 Coopetition Among Software Firms

Coopetition, as a business management concept, conceptualizes the interaction among firms in relation to their strategic development [8, 9]. Dagnino et al. is among the first authors that proposed a definition of coopetion as a new way to capture inter-firm dynamic interdependence, which includes both cooperative and competitive perspectives [26]. The authors proposed two forms of coopetition, dyadic coopetition (concerns among two-firm relationships) and network coopetion (involving more than two firms, i.e. value chain) [26]. Our case represents a simple network coopetition, which is described by coopetition among multiple firms at the same level of a value chain.

In general, coopetion is a complex yet important phenomenon that is worth further research [28]. Coopetition is also considered as an important element for linking between R&D and production within the firms. By selecting an OSS project with high innovation that provides technical advantages to a software firm, we investigate a suitable case for building an understanding of coopetition in the software industry.

There exist few empirical studies about coopetion among software firms [10, 11, 14]. Valenca et al. explored the concepts of competition and collaboration in requirement engineering processes [14]. The authors investigated two firms that participated in a collaborative network evolving towards a SECO. The firms faced challenges in requirement negotiation and lack of sufficient coordination with the common project. The authors conclude that even though competition is inevitable among companies, establishing long-term partnership are crucial drivers for innovation and performance. Our study, however, investigates the coopetition at the implementation stage instead of the requirement stage.

The more relevant work to our study is from Bengtsson et al. [9], Teixeira et al. [11, 29] and Linaker et al. [10], by exploring how rival firms collaborate in an OSS project using data mining and social network analysis techniques. Teixeira et al. observed a different result compared with traditional management literature, stating that competition for the same business model does not necessary affect collaboration within the SECO. Bengtsson et al. argued that developers within a firm need to be divided to take charge of either collaboration or competition [9]. Linaker et al. investigated the changing stakeholder influence and collaboration patterns in the Hadoop project [10]. The authors highlighted that independent of business model, all firms work together towards the common goal of advancing the shared platform [10]. Our study complements to these findings, but also bring new understanding about coopetition via a comprehensive research approach.

2.2   Firm Participation in Software Ecosystem

Multiple definitions of a SECO exist [15], while we refer to the one by Jansen et al. [12], as *"a set of actors functioning as a unit and interacting with a shared market for software and services, together with relationships among them. These relationships are frequently underpinned by a common technological platform or market and operates through the exchange of information, resources and artifacts."* Manikas performed a literature review on recent SECO research [15], describing social characteristics of SECO, i.e. geographical distribution and management of engineering practices [11, 17–19]. There are also empirical studies about actors-to-actors dependencies and relationship, such as software supply networks [20, 21], collaboration patterns among SECO actors [22, 23].

The influence of firm participation in OSS communities has been studied from different angles, leading to different observations. Mehra et al. showed that the heterogeneity, which existed between firm-paid developers and voluntary developers shaped the evolution of OSS community and product [24]. Dahlander et al. studied the network of relationships within the GNOME project, discovering that the presence of hired developers often generates an initial diffidence among unpaid programmers [25]. Lamastra et al. found that firm's involvement improved the ranking of OSS projects, but, on the other hand, lowers software quality, probably because of corporate constraints put on the OSS developing practices [13]. These studies provide a basis for understanding firm participation in OSS, as well as possible methodological approaches to explore the topic.

3   Research Approach

3.1   Study Design

We conducted this work by using a multiple-case study design [27]. Exploratory case studies are suitable to explain the presumed causal links in real-life interventions. There are abundant OSS projects available, many of them are abandoned or individual efforts. We are interested in OSS projects which are large enough and impactful. A brainstorm session was conducted among the paper's authors and an external collaborator to decide the case selection criteria:

- Commercial participation: the selected case should have multiple commercial firms participating in the development. In addition, there must be an adequate way to identify them.
- Successful and on-going: the OSS project must be successful and on-going. This implies that the project attracts developers and the development of the software is progressing.
- Active projects with many activities: There must be a high level of communication and code commits in the project.

As a result, we came up with a list of possible projects that satisfy all criteria. Two projects, that we found most relevant to our research were selected, namely Wireshark and Samba. Wireshark[1] is an OSS toolkit developed by a community of networking experts around the world under the GNU General Public License. The project is officially operated under the Wireshark name since May 2006. Out of the 802 developers listed in Wireshark contributor list, 342 were classified as firm-paid developers (43%). The remaining 460 developers (57%) were classified as volunteering developers. The firm contributions come from 228 firms. Samba[2] is an OSS suite that provides file, print and authentication services to all clients using the SMB/CIFS protocol. Samba is licensed under the GNU General Public License, and the Samba project is a member of the Software Freedom Conservancy. In Samba, 316 developers were evaluated, where 182 (57%) of them were classified as firm-paid developers. The contributions come from 45 firms. Communication and collaboration between developers in the Wireshark and Samba community mainly occur in two places; the developer mailing list and the bug tracking system.

Later, a third OSS project was selected following the same criteria, in order to (1) update the project sample, which might be aging and (2) provide complementary

---

[1] https://www.wireshark.org.

[2] https://www.samba.org.

qualitative data. Bootstrap[3] is a frontend Javascript-based framework for developing responsive, mobile first projects on the web. The project was released as an OSS project since 2011. At the time the research is conducted, Bootstrap is the most-starred project on GitHub, with over 90 thousands stars and more than 38 thousands forks. Source code and issue management is done via Github. The communication in Bootstrap was done via many channels, i.e. StackOverflow, Slack, and Github tracker. Besides studying available document and project infrastructure, we were able to interview three developers in the Bootstrap project.

3.2 Data Collection and Analysis

The main data collection process occurred between Sep 2012 and May 2013. During this phase, both quantitative and qualitative data was collected. Complementary data was collected between April 2015 and August 2015. The main source of quantitative data is from mailing lists, code and issue repositories, as they are common data sources when studying OSS [4, 10, 19, 22]. The main qualitative data comes from semi-structured interviews with firm-paid developers in Wireshark and Samba.

Table 1. The most crowded firms participating to Wireshark and Samba

Wireshark			Samba		
Firm	# of devs.	% of devs.	Firm	# of devs.	% of devs.
Cisco	16	2%	IBM	17	5,4%
Ericsson	11	1,4%	RedHat	14	4,4%
Siemens	8	1%	SerNet	8	2,5%
Netapp	6	0,7%	SUSE	8	2,5%
Citrix	5	0,6%	EMC	4	1,3%
Lucent	5	0,6%	SGI	4	1,3%
MXTelecom	5	0,6%	Exanet	3	0,9%
Nokia	5	0,6%	HP	3	0,9%
Axis	4	0,5%	Cisco	3	0,9%
Harman	4	0,5%	Canonical	2	0,6%

We decided to extract data from all available project public infrastructures, such as project wiki pages, developer mailing lists (referred to as mailing lists), bug tracking systems and code repositories. We collected developer profiles from public sources of information, such as project wiki and confluence pages. Basic information, like developer email addresses and the time stamp when changes to a specific file had been made can be extracted from JIRA and GIT. The communication data was collected from two main sources, which are bug tracking systems and mailing lists. We used a name and an email address to identify whether a participant is from a firm. The approach has been successfully used to do similar classifications [4, 24]. The top ten firms participating in the OSS projects with regard to number of developers is presented

---

[3] http://getbootstrap.com.

in Table 1. The percentage represents the portion of developers for the referring firm in the total number of project contributors. In Wireshark, only 8% of the firms have 3 or more developers participating in the community. Whereas, 78% of the firms have only one developer participating.

Regarding to qualitative data, interviews were selected from a convenient sample consisting of the firm-paid developers from Wireshark, Samba and Bootstrap. As we did not know much about the population, we aimed for a non-probabilistic sampling technique using a conjunction of purposive and snowball sampling. In Wireshark, we used an existing connection to one of the core contributors as a starting point, and asked for suggestion of developers that could be interesting to interview next. The core contributor pointed out relevant developers for the research topic, and assisted in contacting them by posting our interview invitation on the core contributor mailing list. In Samba, we selected relevant developers in the OSS project based on the quantitative data and sent interview invitations to these by email. In Bootstrap, we had a developer actively contributing to the project in our personal network. From him, we got two more interviews with firm-paid participants in Bootstrap (Table 2).

Table 2. Summary of interview profiles

Alias	Domain	Firm type	Firm size	SECOs
D1	Telecommunication	Corp.	10 000+	Wireshark
D2	Wireless networking services	SME	11-50	Wireshark
D3	Messaging system	SME	11–50	Wireshark
D4	Telecommunication	Corp.	10 000+	Wireshark
D5	IT security services		51-200	Samba
D6	Server and OS development	Corp.	10 000+	Samba
D7	Telecommunication	Corp.	10 000+	Samba
D8	Social media	Startup	1-10	Bootstrap
D9	Hosting and file sharing	SME	51-200	Bootstrap
D10	Social media	Startup	1-10	Bootstrap

The interview guide consisted of four to five main topics, with both closed and open questions. The closed questions were mainly used in the introduction phase of the interview to solicit background information about the respondent, firm and OSS project context. In addition, closed questions were used to confirm or attribute statements given by other developers. The open questions were used to collect information about: (1) work process/bridge engineer role, (2) firm awareness/organizational boundary and (3) position in the community/contributions. The interviews were conducted in English, except for one. The duration of the interviews ranged from 45 min to 72 min. All the live interviews were recorded to facilitate subsequent analysis and minimize potential data loss due to note-taking. These recordings were thereafter transcribed verbatim. Transcribing audio records resulted in 55 pages of rich text.

The analysis of the qualitative data was undertaken following guidelines and recommended steps for thematic synthesis in SE [16]. This thematic analysis approach allows the main themes in the text to be systematically summarized and is also familiar

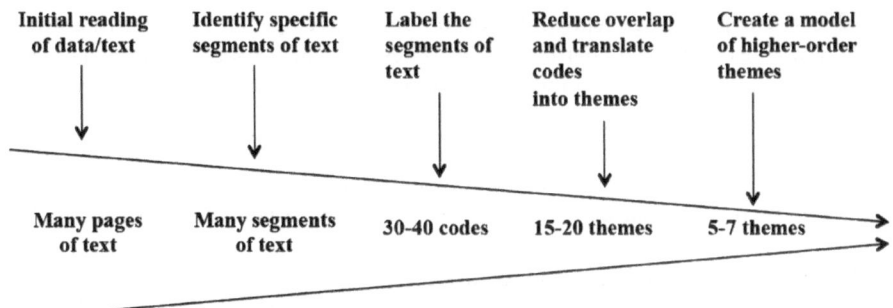

Fig. 1. Thematic analysis [16]

by the first two authors of the paper. A basic outline of the process is illustrated in Fig. 1. Segments of text about firms' interaction, i.e. activities, attitudes about communication, collaboration and competition were identified and labeled. After two rounds of reviews of the data, we ended up with 84 codes.

The following step of the thematic analysis was to translate the codes and the corresponding text segments into themes. A theme in this context is essentially a code in itself, however, a theme is an increased distanciation from the text, and thus an increased level of abstraction. The codes were evaluated and combined to form an overreaching theme, which describes how software firms interact with each other in OSS projects.

4 Results

We found six main themes related to coopetition among firms, which are: Organizational boundary spanning via gatekeepers (Sect. 4.1), Securing communication among actors on firm competitive advantages (Sect. 4.2), Open-core sourcing policy (Sect. 4.3), Business driven filtering of code sharing (Sect. 4.4), Value of social position in OSS community (Sect. 4.5), and Friendly competitiveness (Sect. 4.6).

4.1 Organizational Boundary Spanning via Gatekeepers

The perceptions of a gatekeeper, who **navigates code and information flow** between his/her firm and external actors, were acknowledged by all the interviewees (as shown in Fig. 2). D1 stated that when his coworkers found issues with the third party components, they informed D1, but not project managers. D7 expressed a similar perception: "*Yes, I act as a bridge between [Firm Name] and Samba and forward bugs/errors to the community.*" The gatekeeper is the hub of information and issues that can be reached by different developers across the organizations, as stated by D4: "*Yes, everybody definitely knows that I am the Wireshark guy. All the developers, testers and customer support people know that they can come to me if they have Wireshark issues...*". The gatekeeper is often an active actor in contributing to the ecosystem, as mentioned by D2: "*Many of our core developers are working for smaller companies, and have a responsibility for the internal protocols that their company needs. (...) I think most developers work individually, and have the role of providing Wireshark functionality to the other developers in the firm.*" In firms with multiple developers active in upstream development, i.e. committing to OSS projects, there is often a recognized gate keeper role among them. D5 mentioned: "*In general when it comes to contributing patches upstream each developer in [Company Name] is independent and can directly approach the upstream project... The [Company Name] Samba package maintainer usually has a task of being the **gatekeeper** for those bugs that have been reported against [Company Name] products by the customers or the support teams...*" In this case, while code is contributed independently by individuals in the firm, the bugs is managed by a gatekeeper who submits bug reports on behalf of the firm into the OSS project's bug tracking system.

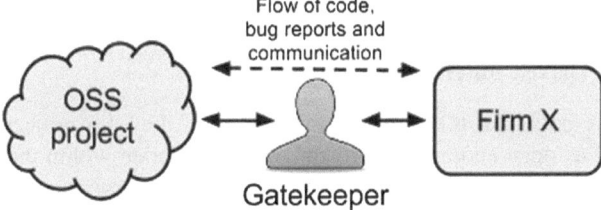

Fig. 2. The role of gatekeeper in a commercial firm

4.2 Securing Communication Among Actors on Firm Competitive Advantages

Among various communication channels in the OSS projects, firms secure communication related to firms' competitive advantages. Communication channels are mainly e-mail and instant messaging, and in some cases Skype and telephone. D3 said: "*I have done it [contacted developers directly] different times in the past. Not just as a general 'I am stuck, can you help', but because it would be an area I knew the other guy was working on.*" D6 mentioned: "*Usually I tend to do R&D tasks myself. I often seek for reviews of my work. When I need assistance, I will go directly to a developer in the community.*" D8 considered private communication as a way to establish **high-quality contact point** and **potential collaboration for further projects**. D9 mentioned: "*We try to address as much as we can of the issues that come to us... Normally if we get a private message about an issue, we will give it higher priority ...*". D5 mentioned that when **discussing legal or security sensitive issues** he used a private communication channel. The nature of such issues invokes the use of private channels as posting it in the public channels may result in security breaches or similarly bad situations. Although none of other developers said anything about the use of direct channels for such issues, we believe that it is a common procedure in most OSS projects.

4.3   Open-Core Sourcing Policy

Despite of risks and issues with competitors, commercial firms are quite open in sharing and collaborating in their source code. In an open-core approach, firms participating in an upstream approach **contributing all the code** they develop to the OSS project's public sources, and collaborate exclusively within the OSS project to develop the software. D5 described the upstream development approach by his firm: *"In general, our philosophy is to develop upstream first and then back-port changes that have been approved by the upstream community into our products. We stay very involved in the communities and try to keep the differences between our packaged software and upstream software to the minimum necessary."* One of the expected benefits was **to avoid maintenance and merging issues** when combining public parts of private parts of source codes. D10 illustrated for this idea: *"... if you are to make a change in the core, and you want to keep it private, you will have to fork the project and maintain it yourself. (...) I believe, in the general case, that you gain more from contributing to the development, that retaining your code from the community"*.

4.4   Business Driven Filtering of Code Sharing

Firms contribute code that is (1) related to the core of the OSS projects and (2) code that is regarded as open and/or standardized, and collaborate within the community to develop the code they contribute. Such firms typically have private repositories where they have code related to the OSS which is proprietary and thus retained from the public sources. **Not all the code** that is written in the firm is contributed back to the OSS project. D4 mentioned: *"The majority of the stuff I have written for Wireshark has been pushed up... But you sort of draw a line in the stuff that is obscure enough to not push. The only people who should be looking at our proprietary protocol should be us..."*. Some of the code is regarded as proprietary and is retained in the firm's private code repository, due to **technical specific**, or **legal and authorization issues.** D2 mentioned: *"Mainly protocol dissectors for protocols used in our equipment, if the protocol is based on open protocol descriptions from 3GPP, ITU or IETF (RFC) it is considered OK to make an individual contribution to OSS..."*.

4.5   Value of Social Position in OSS Community

For a firm, the social position in the ecosystem is perceivably useful and important. It is apparent that a central position in the community is closely related to being a core developer in most cases. Two concrete benefits mentioned by the interviewees are: (1) **easier for code inclusion** and thereby avoid the need of having a private code repository, and (2) **receiving more help** from other community members. D1 elaborated the value of his position within the community: *"Researcher: do you think that it is an important position for firms to have in OSS communities? D1: Yes, because when we are doing changes, we can incorporate them into Wireshark pretty quickly. We don't have to maintain our own code base and synchronize it. We just commit code to the source and have it there."*

D4 highlights the importance of social position in OSS community: *"I think it [having a position] helps a lot. I think there is a difference if, lets say, D2 asks for help, then I'll help him if I can. But if Joe from I have never really heard of, is asking for help then my level of effort is usually lower. And part of that is because I know D2 personally, and part of that is because I know that he does a tremendous amount of work."*

Firms seem not to utilize their social positions to dominate the OSS development. D6 mentioned: *"Before working on Samba I used to think that big companies may have big influence in OSS projects simply by "buying" core developers. Now, that I know most of the people working on Samba, I know that this is not feasible."* Hence, having a position, or *"buying"* one, is neither the way firms relate to nor the tactic firms influence the OSS development.

4.6 Friendly Competitiveness

Firms working within the same business domain are often competitors in the market, and thus it is interesting to see how influential the firm awareness is when firms come together in community based OSS projects to develop software collectively. Surprisingly, the firm-paid developers say that they **perceive** other developers **as partners and/or friends rather than competitors**. D5 pointed out that he had met many of the developers at the developer conferences, and considered many of them as friends. D1 explained that he did not make any distinction between a firm-paid developer and a volunteering developer, and said: *"I think of them as developers, and not about which firms they represent."* D7 say that he perceives others as partners. D6 mentioned: *"I've always thought of others as partners. Even more - I think about them as colleagues."* D4, D8 and D9 shared similar thoughts, and dismissed the perception of other firm-paid developers as competitors: *"I guess as things have evolved we do actually compete in some respects with some of these people at this point. But that hasn't really occurred to me much... I have noticed more people who tend to be customers of ours, rather than true competitors. We might be competitors within some areas, but I have never really thought about it I guess"*, stated by D9.

The issues of competition from a firm from the other side of the world might not be relevant for a startup and a SME who are **pushing efforts on having their product released**. Without a clear vision on how their market or technical advantages are influenced by sharing and using OSS source code, the concern of competition is not much relevant. D8 also mentioned: *"...you think about other firms as your competitors, but I don't think that really comes in to my interactions really. They have their own users somewhere around the world.... I have sometimes seen contributions from their developers, but I think that is good..."*

The firm awareness in the community is perceived as valuable. However, developers remark that it is not the knowledge of what other firms work for that is valuable, rather it is **the knowledge of what business domain** they are working within. D2 replied when was asked about other firm awareness: *"Yes, but I don't know that much about the firms of the other developers. They typically say that they work for Firm X, and that's it. What firm they are working for is not that important to me."* D3 emphasized the potential value of having the firm awareness: *"... I know that D2 may* *have some role as a contact for Firm X... I know that D2 may be someone who is good at getting log files for specific things. In the past when I was working with voice over IP, I thought sometimes he was able to give me some log files from within his company, but I didn't really think of him as the company representative. I think of him as a company person who may be able to get logs for me, like he does."*

Additionally, the interviewees were asked if they considered that their contributions could be used by others firms to gain or recapture competitive advantage. The majority dismissed this perception, for example: *"As Firm X does not directly control Wireshark, I guess we have to be a bit careful when we are in contact with other developers. (...) I believe, in the general case, that you gain more from contributing to the development, that retaining your code from the community"*, stated by D2. A final remark by D5 about the competitiveness: *"Although there may be some competition between companies, as engineers we seek collaboration for mutual benefit. We already know any advancement will be used by everybody, that's not a problem, we get back as much as we give out."*

5   Discussion

Table 3 summarizes the identified themes that describe how firms interact with each other in three popular OSS projects. For each theme, we classified whether they belong to a collaborative relationship or a competitive relationship. While some of the concepts are not surprising compared to what is known in OSS research, i.e. social position in OSS community [10, 11, 19], open-core sourcing [2], they are interesting contributions in exploring how software firms manage both collaboration and competition in OSS ecosystems. We also found novel concepts about coopetition, such as securing communication and friendly competitiveness. Interestingly, some phenomenon that we initially thought as competitive activities, turned out to be collaborative, such as gate keepers and friendly competitiveness.

Table 3. Summary of key findings

Themes	Description	Category
Organizational boundary spanning via gatekeepers	One/few persons who navigates code commits, Q&A	Collaborative
Securing communication among actors on firm competitive advantages	Limited sensitive information to certain partners	Competitive
Open-core sourcing policy	Publish all of their code, complete in sync with upstream development	Collaborative
Business driven filtering of code sharing	Filtering technical specific, legal, strategic modules	Competitive
Value of social position in OSS community	Appreciate the better position in OSS community	Competitive
Friendly competitiveness	Attitude of cooperating rather than competing	Collaborative

Dagnino et al. highlight that coopetition does not simply emerge from joining competition and collaboration, but rather it implies that collaboration and competition merge together to form a new kind of strategic interdependence between firms [26]. Alternatively, our cases show that firms focus on activities that create a common value with an awareness of not sharing their technical and legal sensitive information. Our study reveals the competition mode partly appears at software code level, which is represented by the filtering of code sharing and the open-core sourcing policy. Even when firms are aware of their competitors, the attitude of collaboration is still overwhelming. Valença et al. raise a question whether firms are collaborators or competitors in SECO context? At the requirement engineering level, the authors found several significant challenges among firms within the same collaborative network [14]. OSS projects and firms might have divergent interests but firms can manage to discover areas of convergent interest and be able to adapt their organizing practices to collaborate [3]. In our case, this is clearly shown at the source code level. The finding also matches with observations by Linåker [10].

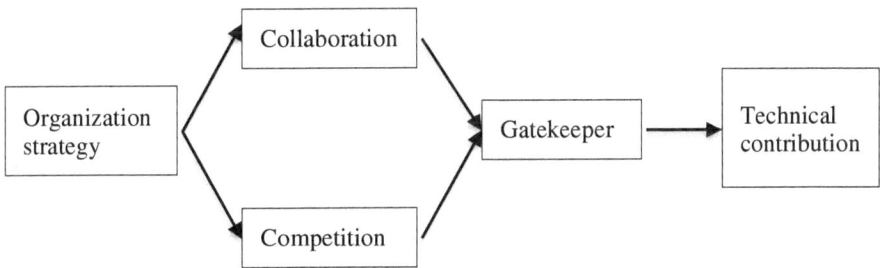

Fig. 3. A model of firm coopetition in open source SECO

Bengtsson et al. argued that individuals within a firm can only act in accordance with one of the two logics of interaction at a time, i.e., either to compete or to collaborate [9]. Our observation on the gatekeeper role gives a possible alternative theory on how firms manage such coopetition scenario. By influencing the gatekeeper, who manages code flows and information flows between the firm and the SECO, the firm can implement competing or collaborating strategies. The firm strategy can be flexible, for example fully open core sourcing at one time, and filtering of shared code at another time. The implementation of such strategies is done via the firm gatekeeper, who does actual technical contribution to the SECO. Therefore, in contrast with Bengtsson's findings, we argued that it is possible to implement a firm-level dynamic interaction via individuals in software projects, as shown in Fig. 3.

We propose a framework of coopetition in open source SECOs, as described in Fig. 3. Derived from the firm's strategy when participating in an open source SECO, the firm involves in both collaborative and competitive relationships with other firms participating in the SECO. Balancing and managing both logics of interaction were done by a gatekeeper role, which can be one or a group of key developers that are active in the SECO. The gatekeepers implement coopetition by carrying out different mechanisms (i.e. described in Sect. 4.1 to Sect. 4.4), which eventually realizes as technical contributions to the SECO.

6 Conclusions

Coopetition is an important foundation for economics and management research [26], but often overlooked or oversimplified in other domains. In SECOs, where inter-firm interactions are crucial for both firms and SECO development, coopetition is a relevant and also a new way of looking at SECOs. Our contributions are two folds (1) we portrayed the situations where both competition and collaboration occurs in OSS projects and (2) we proposed a framework to explain how a gatekeeper could help to manage such coopetition relationship.

For coopetition research, we offer an alternative explanation of how coopetition is performed by software firms in an open source SECO. We observed that software firms emphasized the co-creation of common value and partly react to the potential competitiveness on OSS ecosystems. For Software Engineering research, the work illustrates the adoption of a management theory in understanding and exploring both technical and business aspects of SECOs. Through the lens of coopetition, novel aspects of inter-firm interaction in OSS projects were highlighted. The research contributes to the current body of knowledge on SECO by adding the competition perspective.

For software firms who participate in an open source ecosystem, our findings offer a descriptive insight about different coopetition strategies observed in a community-driven OSS project. Firms can refer to different ways of co-creating via collaboration and awareness of competition when they participate in such an ecosystem. For proprietary SECO steering members, the harmony interaction observing in our open source SECOs can help direct implication on how to design and to influence the SECO policy to support a healthy coopetition.

For future work, the next step would be to refine and to validate the coopetition model (described in Fig. 3) with a larger set of cases. Our research here only uses three community-driven OSS projects, which limits the generalization of findings to other types of SECOs, such as proprietary platforms, firm-driven OSS projects, etc. Future work is needed to explore the concept of coopetition in such contexts. Besides, a longitudinal observation on how coopetition evolve among firms can provide knowledge that goes beyond cross-sectional observations. Furthermore, we also plan to triangulate the observations from manager and developer's viewpoint. Last but not least, further investigation about employing the role of gatekeepers for coopetition is needed to validate our observation.

References

1. Messerschmitt, D.G., Szyperski, C.: Software Ecosystem: Understanding an Indispensible Technology and Industry. MIT Press, Cambridge (2003)
2. Morgann, L., Feller, J., Finnegan, P.: Exploring inner source as a form of intra-organisational open innovation. In: 19th European Conference on Information Systems, Helsinki, Finland (2011)
3. O'Mahony, S., Bechky, B.: Boundary organizations: enabling collaboration between unexpected allies. Adm. Sci. Q. **53**(3), 422–459 (2008)

4. Bonaccorsi, A., Rossi, C.: Comparing motivations of individual programmers and firms to take part in the open source movement: From community to business. Knowl. Technol. Policy **18**(4), 40–64 (2006)
5. Ghapanchi, A.H., Wohlin, C., Aurum, A.: Resources contributing to gaining competitive advantage for open source software projects: an application of resource based theory. Int. J. Proj. Manage. **32**(1), 139–152 (2014)
6. Ghapanchi, A.H.: Rallying competencies in virtual communities: a study of core processes and user interest in open source software projects. Inform. Organ. **23**(2), 129–148 (2013)
7. Riehle, D.: The single vendor commercial open source business model. Inform. Syst. e-Business Manage. **10**(1), 5–17 (2012)
8. Nalebuff, B.J., Brandenburger, A.: Co-opetition. Harper Collins Business, NYC (1996)
9. Bengtsson, M., Kock, S.: Coopetition in Business Networks: To Cooperate and Compete Simultaneously. Ind. Mark. Manage. **29**, 411–426 (2000)
10. Linåker, J., Rempel, P., Regnell, B., Mäder, P.: How firms adapt and interact in open source ecosystems: analyzing stakeholder influence and collaboration patterns. In: Daneva, M., Pastor, O. (eds.) REFSQ 2016. LNCS, vol. 9619, pp. 63–81. Springer, Cham (2016). doi:10.1007/978-3-319-30282-9_5
11. Teixeira, J., Lin, T.: Collaboration in the open-source arena: the webkit case. In: 52nd ACM Conference on Computers and People Research, pp. 121–129 (2014)
12. Jansen, S., Finkelstein, A., Brinkkemper, S.: A sense of community: a research agenda for software ecosystems. In: 31st ICSE, pp. 187–190 (2009)
13. Lamastra, C.R.: Software innovativeness: a comparison between proprietary and Free/Open Source solutions offered by Italian SMEs. R&D Manage. **39**(2), 153–169 (2009)
14. Valença, G., Alves, C., Heimann, V., Jansen, S., Brinkkemper, S.: Competition and collaboration in requirements engineering: a case study of an emerging software ecosystem. In: IEEE 22nd International Requirements Engineering Conference (RE), pp. 384–393 (2014)
15. Konstantinos, M.: Revisiting software ecosystems Research. J. Syst. Softw. **117**, 84–103 (2016)
16. Cruzes, D.S., Dybå, T.: Recommended steps for thematic synthesis in software engineering. In: 2011 International on Empirical Software Engineering and Measurement (ESEM), pp. 275–284 (2011)
17. Santos, R., Werner, C.: Reuseecos: an approach to support global software development through software ecosystems. In: 7th International Conference on Global Software Engineering Workshops (ICGSEW), pp. 60–65 (2012)
18. Goeminne, M.: Understanding the evolution of socio-technical aspects in open source ecosystems. In: Conference on Software Maintenance, Reengineering and Reverse Engineering (CSMR-WCRE), pp. 473–476 (2014)
19. Scacchi, W.: Free/open source software development: recent research results and emerging opportunities. In: 6th ESEC-FSE, pp. 459–468 (2007)
20. Angeren, J.V., Blijleven, V., Jansen, S.: Relationship intimacy in software ecosystems: a survey of the dutch software industry. In: International Conference on Management of Emergent Digital EcoSystems, pp. 68–75 (2011)
21. Handoyo, E.: Software ecosystem modeling. In: Herzwurm, G., Margaria, T. (eds.) ICSOB 2013. LNBIP, vol. 150, pp. 227–228. Springer, Heidelberg (2013). doi:10.1007/978-3-642-39336-5_25
22. Cataldo, M., Herbsleb, J.D.: Architecting in software ecosystems: interface translucence as an enabler for scalable collaboration. In: 4th European Conference on Software Architecture, pp. 65–72 (2010)

23. Knauss, E., Damian, D., Knauss, A., Borici, A.: Openness and requirements: opportunities and tradeoffs in software ecosystems. In: 22nd International Requirements Engineering Conference, pp. 213– 222 (2014)
24. Mehra, A., Dewan, R., Freimer, M.: Firms as incubators of Open Source software. Inform. Syst. Res. **22**(1), 22–38 (2011)
25. Dahlander, L., Wallin, M.W.: A man on the inside: unlocking communities as complementary assets. Res. Policy **35**(8), 1243–1259 (2006)
26. Dagnino, G.B., Padula, G.: Coopetition strategy, a new kind of inter firm dynamics for value creation. In: The European Academy of Management Second Annual Conference (2002)
27. Yin, R.K.: Case Study Research: Design and Methods. Applied Social Research Methods, 5th ed. SAGE Publications, Inc., Thousand Oaks (2014)
28. Annika, T.: Causes of conflict in intercompetitior cooperation. J. Bus. Ind. Mark. **24**(7), 508– 516 (2009)
29. Teixeira, J., Mian, S.Q., Hytti, U.: Cooperation among competitors in the open-source arena: the case of OpenStack. In: ICIS (2016)

Mobile Software Security Threats in the Software Ecosystem, a Call to Arms

Andrey Krupskiy$^{(\boxtimes)}$, Remmelt Blessinga, Jelmer Scholte, and Slinger Jansen

Utrecht University, Utrecht, The Netherlands
{a.krupskiy,r.d.blessinga,j.scholte2}@students.uu.nl,
slinger@slingerjansen.nl

Abstract. This paper studies security policies of the Android and iOS software ecosystems. These platforms have experienced security issues since their public release in 2007. This research creates an overview of the results that security issues cause and the actions available to limit security infractions based on scientific literature. Following the overview, this paper attempts to explain premises of those issues by analyzing the security recommendations of both platforms and comparing them to OWASP security guidelines. This is done by comparing development guidelines set up by both platforms and assessing the importance of each of these guidelines in the ecosystem perspective. The conclusion highlights vulnerabilities in the developer guidelines of mobile platforms and recommends appropriate action to improve the situation.

Keywords: Software ecosystems · Software security · OWASP · Development policies

1 Introduction

As smartphones increased in popularity, so did the research in the field of smartphone security. Smartphones rely on the security architecture of the mobile platform that supports them. These platforms have different architectures, aside from sharing several issues each one is also subjected to security issues specifically harmful for the platform. This paper takes a look at the security issues of the mobile platforms Android and iOS which both have a marketplace called app stores. App stores are typical occurrences of a software ecosystem which is defined by Jansen et al. (2009) [1] as: a set of actors functioning as a unit and interacting with a shared market for software and services, together with the relationships among them [1]. The marketplace opened up smartphones for third-party developers as is also recognizable in personal computer platforms [2]. As personal computer platforms have struggled with security, open marketplaces for mobile platforms resulted in a challenge for smartphone security.

Software created by third-party developers for mobile platforms are called smartphone applications or apps which, as a result of interacting with the platform, cause security issues. The OWASP foundation is a non-profit organization

© Springer International Publishing AG 2017
A. Ojala et al. (Eds.): ICSOB 2017, LNBIP 304, pp. 161–175, 2017.
https://doi.org/10.1007/978-3-319-69191-6_11

which tries to bring visibility and evolution in the safety and security of the worlds software. Most relevant for this paper is the OWASP top ten list of security flaws that applications contain. These flaws adversely affect the actors in the software ecosystem and therefore mobile platforms should support developers in creating secure applications. This paper attempts to gain insight into the main security concerns of open mobile platforms and standard prevention methods. This paper will refer to OWASP as the golden standard of security which means that conclusions are based on how well results fit with the OWASP recommendations. Therefore the main research question is: To what extent do the developer guidelines for mobile platform application development follow OWASP security recommendations? Literature is consulted to create a general overview of the security concerns and some methods of prevention in the Android and iOS platforms. Next, how security issues affect the actors in the mobile platforms. Lastly, the Android and iOS guidelines are analysed in context of the OWASP top ten in order to see if they are an effective prevention method.

The structure of this paper is as follows: Sect. 2 is the research approach which describes what is done in order to research this topic. Section 3 contains literature overviews of the Android and iOS security. OWASP and the Android and iOS developer guidelines are researched in Sect. 4. Sections 5 and 6 contain the discussion and conclusion respectively.

2   Research Approach

To answer the main question, two research questions (RQ) are defined: RQ1: To what extent are ecosystem actors vulnerable to security threats? RQ2: Are there any significant security vulnerabilities in the developer documentation?

A literature overview creates the context for the RQ1 since it delves into the security issues regarding the mobile platforms. It approaches several issues of a mobile platform in an attempt to highlight the most prevalent. The method to collect literature regarding these topics consists of researching common security threats. Papers are consulted afterwards in order to create an detailed explanation and understanding of the threats and their possible solutions. References found in papers that are useful for this research are also researched. This creates a snowball effect resulting in detailed information about a topic.

To adjust from prevalent issues and to place the OWASP recommendations in a refined ecosystem perspective, actors are defined and an assessment is made to estimate to what measure ecosystem actors are vulnerable to security threats. The top ten list created by OWASP is explored and used to see if it addresses the security threats for the ecosystem. This allows to find specifically which issue in OWASP has an impact on which ecosystem actor and together with the literature overview answers RQ1. The issues addressed in the overview and derived from the ecosystem perspective can be compared to the findings of RQ2.

Lastly this research is focused on reviewing development guidelines of Android and iOS platforms in terms of security. Using the top ten list of OWASP mobile security recommendations the security policies of the Android and iOS platforms are analysed. This results in a comparison of the two platforms and an overview of their security guidelines. The comparison results in a table with the complete overview offering an answer to RQ2. It is important to note that some guidelines have different terminology than used by OWASP, this is taken into account by searching for similar keywords and by looking at the underlying security concern instead of just the name of the guideline.

3 Literature Overview

This section contains the overviews derived from the literature studied on Android and iOS security in order to picture the circumstances in said field. The split between users and developers is based on Jansen et al. definition of an app store which has two distinct groups; users and developers [3]. In this section the Android and iOS developers are assumed as not wanting to benefit from deliberately releasing malicious applications or misusing user information. They are instead assumed as wanting to provide secure applications for the users, themselves and the software ecosystem as a whole.

3.1 Literature on Android Ecosystem Security

A literature survey by Rashidi and Fung [4] summarizes security threats caused by applications to a users' privacy and device. This survey consists of Android security threats and solutions collected from literature dating from 2010 till 2015. The three relevant threats are; 1: Information leakage, 2: Privilege escalation, and 3: Repackaging applications. Information leakage occurs since Android uses a permission-based system which applications use to gain access to, possibly sensitive, data on a phone [5]. A newly downloaded application adheres to this system since it has to explicitly request permissions up-front to access personal information and phone features [6]. In 2012 the permissions requested by 44% of the applications exceeded the minimum number of permissions needed to function. This violates the principle of least privilege, a longstanding principle in the world of computer security [7], it defines the importance of software only accessing the minimum information to function. Davi et al. [8] conclude from their research that the permission based system damages security for the user as it allows for privilege escalation attacks. Furthermore, Meng et al. [9] state that some OEM weaken the existing security of the device by customizing Android image that may lead to privilege escalation attacks or information leakage.

Android developers can opt to make earnings from their application by integrating an in-app billing service. Muliner et al. explain this service as follows: The in-app billing service allows users to pay for options, services, subscriptions, and virtual goods from within mobile apps themselves [10]. In their paper they developed an attack against the in-app billing service allowing them to bypass paying for in-app services in 60% of the 85 most popular applications. Another issue, one which can lose developers revenue streams and credibility is repackaging of their application Applications that normally cost money to use or have an in-app billing service can be repackaged and then released for free on the Internet. Repackaged applications, like banking applications, can be distributed on the Android store.

Reverse-engineering of Android applications is impossible to prevent without violating the open policy of Android. There is however a tool provided by Android that defends applications from being simple reverse-engineering targets without violating the open policy. The Android provided tool Proguard changes features, like class and variable names, of a code to random strings. This technique is called code obfuscation, a way to prevent analysis of the code of an application. For the security issues that concern application users, developers have a bigger array of options to the threats mentioned earlier. Following Rashidi and Fung [4] developers can choose for one or two different types of strategies in regards to securing their applications. The first is making use of existing techniques and mechanisms which consists of using options provided in the Android OS. The second is to use software created by others which can detect security threats.

3.2   Literature on iOS Ecosystem Security

Academic literature regarding iOS security issues shows that user privacy can be at risk. Large scale mobile application analysis of iOS apps conducted by Orikogbo et al. shows that a large fraction of apps contain references and make connections to domains using the HTTP scheme [11]. Around 26% of apps studied just use HTTP connection schemes while 72% of apps use both HTTP and HTTPS and 2% use only HTTPS. Since personal information can be sent to a remote service, usage of HTTP is a privacy threat, since this kind of connection is not encrypted in any way and can be read by a third party if intercepted.

When examining the literature regarding security and the iOS system it is shown that there have been cases of security breaches in the iOS built-in security systems. A paper by Heider and El Khayari [12] shows that up to the iOS version 6.0.1 there was a security flaw that allowed to perform an attack on the iOS keychain service, which allowed to get an access to all data stored on the device and perform jailbreaking of the device. Jailbreaking is defined as a process of getting a root access to the device. Root access provides elevated privileges and allows user to avoid most restrictions of iOS enforced by Apple.

Additionally, Renard [13] describes a number of attacks that can be performed on iOS. First, Renard points out attacks that can be performed without jailbreaking a device. Those include getting access to the data of applications and the users credentials, retrieving data from a devices backups, monitoring communications, attacking secure communications to the server. In case of a jailbroken device it is possible to gain access to all data stored on the device, making reverse engineering an issue. For several versions of iOS it was possible to jailbreak a device without having an access to device's keychain and then hide the fact of a jailbreak.

The iOS platform makes apps work in a strictly restrictive environment [14] and it has two important security features: the app vetting process and the app sandbox. Although these two features have proven to be effective for the iOS ecosystem, as shown in the survey conducted by Felt et al. [15] there was no harmful malware present in the iOS appstore, both methods still have some security issues, code signing can be evaded for example as discovered by Miller [16].

Another security issue that iOS developers encountered was an XcodeGhost attack [17]. This attack was designed so that app developers would download an infected copy of Xcode, a development environment for iOS apps, which would infect any apps created within it with malicious code. This is an example of the developers not following security protocols and using software downloaded from the not verified source. The paper by Renard [13] gives several suggestions on how developers can avoid these security threats. These suggestions include code obfuscation, creating kill-switches to delete user credentials in case of a reverse engineering attempt, secure usage of memory and some recommendations on how to prevent hooking. Hooking is as "a mechanism that allows users to alter or augment the behavior of applications".

A study by Teuf et al. [18] confirms, that jailbreaking a device allows to effectively disable the iOS file system encryption, allowing attacker to gain access to all data without knowing the passcode of the use.

4   Results

4.1   OWASP Guidelines and the Ecosystem Perspective

In this section each of the ten points is placed in an ecosystem perspective, enabling to take a closer look at each threat and estimating what actors in the mobile ecosystem are impacted by each vulnerability should they be left unprotected.

In their 2013 literature review Hansen and Manikas [19] identified five of the most common types of actors in software ecosystem literature. Each of these roles (Orchestrator, Component Developer, External Developer, Vendor and Customer) is directly affected by the security vulnerabilities mentioned in the OWASP top 10. In the context of this research we can identify these roles as the following ecosystem elements:

1. **Customer.** Also called end user this is the person. This actor is responsible for bringing monetary value into the ecosystem. If customers feel insecure, for example when their privacy is at risk, they might abandon an ecosystem or it might affect their purchasing behavior, affecting every involved actor.
2. **Orchestrator.** These are the ecosystem platform owners. Affected primarily in loss of reputation or competitive advantage when ecosystem security is threatened.
3. **Component Developer.** Also called the niche player, the app developers contribute directly to the ecosystem by providing its content applications.
4. **External Developer.** These are often passive participants in the ecosystem. They play a non-developing role in the ecosystem. These actors can

for example offer certain supportive services such as ad networks to component developers. They are mostly impacted by loss of clientele or reputation
damage if the ecosystem performs badly.

5. **Vendor.** Also called the reseller or added value reseller. This could be for
example a game publisher that buys game apps from component developers
and sells them under the umbrella of cross-app marketing efforts. They are
vulnerable to security threats due to being the face of the product, thus being
held responsible for the product.

4.2   The OWASP Mobile Security Top 10

OWASP Mobile Security Top 10 in Context of SSN Roles. Looking at
the top 10 mobile security threats defined by OWASP it becomes clear what each
security threat entails and how to defend against such threats. Yet what actors
are affected by such threats is not immediately clear, and neither is how the
ecosystem as a whole is affected. The technical and business threats highlighted
by OWASP do give us sufficient information to extrapolate what each threat
means for the ecosystem entire. This section looks at how the security threats of
the mobile top 10 can affect the software ecosystem, this is followed by a threat
analysis for each ecosystem actor in Sect. 4.3.

1. **Weak Server Side Controls.** In the ecosystem perspective this means
customer data can be lost or affected during an attack. It can also mean
that an app becomes unusable.
2. **Insecure Data Storage.** In the ecosystem perspective this means that customer privacy and security is at risk from attacks. In extreme cases sensitive
data of developers or vendors could also be at risk.
3. **Insufficient Transport Layer Protection.** In the ecosystem perspective
this means that customer data is at risk from interception, this might not
only affect customer privacy but also external developers that rely on the
exclusivity of specific data.
4. **Unintended Data Leakage.** In the ecosystem perspective this means that
customer privacy is at risk from attack, damaging the reputation of and trust
in some ecosystem actors.
5. **Poor Authorization and Authentication.** In the ecosystem perspective
this is primarily a risk for customers, but hacked accounts can be of concern
to component developers or vendors who rely on the proper usage of their
apps, the spread of spam through such accounts could for example damage its profitability. Malicious users might be able to obtain privileges they
should not have.
6. **Broken Cryptography.** In the ecosystem perspective this affects customer
privacy violations. It can also lead to information theft, code theft, intellectual property theft and reputation damage, affecting vendors.
7. **Client Side Injection.** Not only is this a risk to the customer due to
privacy violations but the component developer as well as their security
precautions could be directly affected by injected code. In extreme cases the
orchestrator reputation might be affected.

8. **Security Decisions Via Untrusted Inputs.** In the ecosystem perspective this is a threat primarily for the actors that can be at risk from users with malicious intentions, customer data might be vulnerable to attack.

9. **Improper Session Handling.** Customer privacy and security could be at risk from attack. Component developers might be directly affected by security breaches, vendors might experience an interruption in common business procedures.

10. **Lack of Binary Protections.** In the ecosystem perspective a lack of binary protections is of great concern to all involved actors. A reversed engineered app is a great way for malicious parties to spread malicious content, relying on the trust customers place in certain ecosystem actors. Duplicate apps are a security risk. A hacked app can lead to privacy or confidential data theft. For the orchestrator it will lead to brand damage and revenue loss through pirating.

Table 1 shows an overview of the relations between ecosystem actors and how each actor is affected by the OWASP security top 10 threats.

4.3 Comparing the Effect of Security Threats to Ecosystem Actors

Given the five types of roles and how they are affected by security vulnerabilities, we can compare them to the OWASP mobile top 10. Table 2 shows the security threat identified by OWASP in the first column, followed by a threat assessment for each role of either low (no or little direct impact), moderate (some threats but either case specific or limited impact) or severe (certain to suffer some damage). The following table is primarily intended to give an overview and visualization of security threats to the ecosystem as a coherent set of actors.

The further away from using or directly developing the application with the possible security vulnerability, the less security risks affect the actor. Customers are shown to be most at risk from vulnerabilities in the ecosystem, followed by component developers while the orchestrator is shown to be least vulnerable.

4.4 Android and iOS Developer Guidelines

Both ecosystem orchestrators offer comprehensive guidelines for their developing partners. The Android guidelines are set up in a training and reference format, taking on the role of teaching the developer using any means deemed effective. Apple structures the documentation as a reference guide instead of guiding the developer through a series of trainings, as such this documentation is primarily text based and most effective when searching for specific advice.

In terms of security the iOS guidelines include a section named the Secure Coding Guide while Android offers a section under the header Best Practices for Security & Privacy. The Secure Coding Guide by Apple is the central reference point for their security recommendations, and they always link back to this document. Android is less inclined to discuss security concerns in other parts of the documentation, concentrating most advice in the best practices section.

Table 1. Security threats for the SSN stakeholders

Group	Activity	Needs	Cooperative / Financial Relationship					Security Threat
			Customer	Orchestrator	Component Dev.	External Dev.	Vendor	
Customer	Purchase product	Privacy, trust, exclusivity of data, reliable and valuable marketplace		X	X		X	Breach of confidentiality / privacy, loss or theft of sensitive data, loss of trust in the ecosystem, loss of ecosystem investment
Orchestrator	Support Ecosystem	Brand power, stable market environment, competitive advantage	X		X		X	Brand power damage, loss of ecosystem partners, loss of ecosystem power, loss of competitive advantage, possible decrease of revenue
Component Developer	Develop and deliver ecosystem content	Reliable open platform, brand power, reliable marketplace	X	X	X	X	X	Loss in revenue, brand power damage, loss of trust in ecosystem, loss of competitive advantage, possible decrease in ecosystem participation
External Developer	Develop and deliver supportive services	Stable market environment,			X		X	Loss in revenue, brand power damage
Vendor	Resell products	Brand power, stable market environment, open platform, good component dev. relations	X	X	X	X		Loss in revenue, brand power damage, loss of partnerships, loss of competitive advantage, possible decrease in ecosystem participation

4.5   Guidelines Comparison Table

Comprehensively studying the developer guidelines allows for the creation of a comparison table to see if and how Android and iOS make security recommendations suggested by OWASP in the mobile top 10. There are three levels designed to indicate if each guideline is present:

Insufficient: There is no advice or reference present in the developer guidelines on how to develop for the security vulnerability, developers are not made aware of the security risks. If a developer depends on sole advice offered by the guidelines this will result in an insecure application.

Table 2. Vulnerability effect on ecosystem roles. L is low threat, M is moderate threat, S is severe threat.

OWASP guideline	Customer	Orchestrator	Comp. Dev.	Ext. Dev.	Vendor
Weak server side controls	M	L	S	L	L
Insecure data storage	S	M	S	M	S
Insufficient transport layer protection	S	L	M	M	L
Unintended data leakage	S	M	S	L	M
Poor authorization and authentication	S	M	S	L	M
Broken cryptography	S	M	S	L	S
Client side injection	S	M	S	M	M
Security decisions via untrusted inputs	M	L	M	L	M
Improper sessions handling	S	L	M	M	M
Lack of binary protections	S	M	S	M	S

Partial: Some advice is given or the guideline is mentioned but not comprehensively enough to adequately assist developers to secure an application. Alternatively the security recommendation in the documentation is outdated.

Sufficient: Either coding guidelines, explanation of the security vulnerability with recommended precautions or specific advice on how to prevent the vulnerability is given. If a developer relies solely on the developer guidelines it will not pose a danger to application security.

When the results of the comparison table are transformed to scores (where insufficient is 0%, partial is 5%, and sufficient is 10%) the results show a 55% completeness score for iOS and 60% completeness score for Android. The Android documentation has six points out of ten that could do with improving, the iOS documentation has five points of out ten that could do with improving.

IOS Explained. The following overview explains where and how each OWASP guideline is present in the developer documentation (Table 3).

1. The Apple developer documentation focuses on how to handle authentication when exchanging information with a server. No mention of server configurations, backend services or best practices when setting up a server could be found.
2. Apple refers to storing information in the appropriate directory and setting the right file system permissions. Apples File Protection mechanism is considered to be safe for use for consumer-grade data. The documentation states that the various APIs should be sufficient. This is contrarian to the OWASP recommendation that developers should consider adding an additional layer of encryption.
3. Apple recommends choosing the appropriate transport protocol and highlights some concerns for each option. A set of secure networking pages is available, offering comprehensive guidelines and coding recommendations to create sufficient transport layer protection.

Table 3. Comparison of OWASP, iOS and Android developer guidelines.

OWASP guideline	iOS guidelines	Android guidelines
Weak server side controls	Insufficient	Insufficient
Insecure data storage	Partial	Sufficient
Insufficient transport layer protection	Sufficient	Sufficient
Unintended data leakage	Insufficient	Partial
Poor authorization and authentication	Sufficient	Sufficient
Broken cryptography	Sufficient	Sufficient
Client side injection	Sufficient	Partial
Security decisions via untrusted inputs	Sufficient	Partial
Improper sessions handling	Insufficient	Insufficient
Lack of binary protections	Insufficient	Partial

4. Apple does not refer directly to data leakage, nor to the ways mentioned by OWASP on how data leakage could occur on iOS. They consider the platform to be inherently secure due to apps being restricted in the files and system resources it can access.
5. Apple has a number of pages dedicated to authentication and authorization, they offer various coding recommendations as well as best practices and explanations on why or how something should be build to be considered secure.
6. iOS applications are, in theory, protected from reverse engineering via code encryption. Apple offers comprehensive explanations on cryptography topics, an API to use for cryptographic tasks and coding guidelines on how to securely implement cryptography.
7. Apple has dedicated an entire page to this security vulnerability, offering coding advice, examples of risks and information on injection attacks.
8. Comprehensive advice on how to validate input is present. Coding guidelines are offered, as is information on what kind of vulnerabilities might lead to security breaches and how.
9. The Apple developer guidelines offer no recommendations, coding advice or information on secure sessions handling.
10. Apple does not refer to the risks of not including binary protection and relies solely on its app review and submission process, binary encryption is central to iOS. However, this process is vulnerable to attacks when jailbreaking a device [13]. Apple does not recommend to developers that they take additional action such as jailbreak detection or certificate pinning controls.

Android Explained. In this section two main Android guidelines were used as a source: a training guide for developers and a guide for android source code.

1. The Android documentation does not provide any guidelines for setting up a server.

2. The Android guidelines describe all possible ways of storing app data on the device and secure ways of sharing data between apps. These guidelines also provide information on how to implement app data encryption and handle sensitive data.

3. The Android security guidelines dedicate a section to securely implementing HTTPS and SSL.

4. The Android guidelines mention the problem of data leakage and provide advice for some cases on how to avoid such a risk. There are some recommendations on how to work with log files, regarding them as being potentially vulnerable. The guidelines do not cover URL caching, keyboard press caching, Copy/Paste buffer caching, application backgrounding, HTML5 data storage, browser cookie objects or analytics sent to 3rd parties, which are mentioned in the OWASP guidelines.

5. The Android documentation has a number of sections describing authentication procedures. The documentation has a section dedicated to implementation of OAuth2 Services, which is an open standard for authorization.

6. Android provides a number of recommendations on how to implement cryptography. The guidelines encourage developers to use standard protocols instead of creating their own, this approach is also recommended by the OWASP guidelines.

7. Android guidelines acknowledge the danger and offer security advice of how to prevent XSS and SQL and JavaScript code injection on Android devices. Nevertheless, the list of security issues in Android guidelines does not include some problems mentioned in the OWASP security recommendations.

8. Android guidelines provide basic information on input validation methods, input validation security threats, and also state that Android has a number of countermeasures build in to prevent input related security problems. The guidelines do not provide concrete examples of tools used to reduce this security threat. Furthermore, no coding examples or best practices are described in this section.

9. Android security guidelines provide no information on secure session handling.

10 Android provides some guidelines on binary protection in context of Google Play in app billing. These guidelines suggest signature verification, code obfuscation and modifying sample code for in app billing system to decrease the ease of its detectability. OWASP also mentions a root detection problem. Rooting an Android phone is similar to jailbreaking iPhone, but Android guidelines provide no information about security in context of rooting.

5   Discussion

Security is one of the big issues for developers who have the optimal security for themselves and their users in mind. In this paper the belief is that developers want the most secure software ecosystem as to benefit the actors that participate. Therefore something not touched on is that there are also developers and organizations who intentionally force privacy risks on users.

This research does not include the orchestrator actors perspective on the importance of ecosystem security aspects, interviews with Apple or Google would have been an excellent source of data but setting this up did not fit in the scope of this research. Additional research could be done to investigate why both the studied platforms did not include specific OWASP guidelines and the role of the developer guidelines in the development process. One way to execute such research is to create app security conceptualization similar to mobile application usability conceptualisation performed by Hoehle and Venkatesh [20]. For example, the most recent research on iOS apps, which included an inspection of almost 42.000 apps, showed that almost 26% of apps reference external resources strictly via HTTP, which is considered to be an insecure way of transferring information by OWASP, iOS and Android guidelines. Both iOS and Android guidelines actively encourage developers to use the HTTPS protocol, which is considered to be far more secure, and provide detailed guidelines on how to implement it.

Although attacking a jailbroken iOS system was proven to be a much simpler task for attackers, no literature or reports were found regarding a working mechanism for jailbreaking a device running iOS 10 protected with passcode without knowing a passcode for the device. This leads to conclusion that at this time, passcode of sufficient length and base (number of characters used to create a passcode) serves as a sufficient way of protecting a device against jailbreaking, this does not take into account for the risk of social engineering being used to recover the passcode or user negligence when setting a passcode.

It should be mentioned that the mobile top 10 list dated 2012 was used. It was considered to use mobile top 10 dated 2016, but this list is still in development and incomplete.

This paper was written from the perspective of security in the software ecosystem domain. As such it did not look at the quality of advice and information offered in the developer documentation. This is considered a task more suited for security experts.

6   Conclusions

The literature used for the overview shows that there are several issues apparent for the two groups that participate in app store based mobile platforms. For user issues both ecosystems are lacking in offering full protection. Both ecosystems have different foundational functionalities that cause insecurities for the users. Developers seem to encounter more problems on the Android platform, mainly revenue based, in comparison to iOS developers since the iOS environment is more restricted. Both platforms however also provide integrated and external options for developers to create secure applications for both themselves and the users. These options do not always offer a working solution in regards to one of the issues.

Justified by the results from the actor/OWASP guideline impact evaluation on a software ecosystem level, it is concluded that the biggest impact of security breaches is felt by customers and component developers. This aligns with the literature overview which reveals that there are numeral issues affecting these groups. Vendors are moderately at risk, depending on how close they are to the direct development, management or publishing of the application. External developers and the ecosystem orchestrators have the least risk as they are furthest removed from the security vulnerabilities. This answers RQ1: *To what extend are ecosystem actors vulnerable to security threats?*

From the developer guideline evaluation results, it is concluded that the evaluated guidelines form a solid basis for the development of a secure application but can still be improved. The documentation for iOS offers a comprehensive security guide that helps with many issues not included in the OWASP mobile top 10. However, four out of ten points in the OWASP mobile top 10 are not sufficiently presented in these guidelines and one point offers incomplete advice, leading to the conclusion that the iOS guidelines need improving before they can be considered fully secure. The results of this study confirm that inherent protections can sometimes be circumvented, leading to the conclusion that additional advice should be offered to developers in case this occurs.

It can be concluded that the Android guidelines leave the impression of being a good starting point for the developer. However, the results show that some sections only acknowledge a security issue and let a developer either find a solution himself, or suggestively use a solution built into the Android framework, which has its downsides according to OWASP. The results from the comparison of the OWASP guidelines with Android guidelines allow for the conclusion that the Android guidelines should be further developed, particularly in a sense of improving existing sections with concrete solutions and best practices on how to deal with security threats.

It is difficult to decisively conclude if one of the platforms does a better job offering secure guidelines following the OWASP framework, as both have their individual strengths and weaknesses.

The results show significant security risks are posed by the incompleteness of advice on server side controls, secure data storage, unintended data leakage, client side injection, security decisions via untrusted inputs, improper session handling and lack of binary protections. This answers RQ2: *Are there any significant security vulnerabilities in the developer documentation?* with a yes. The significant risks as a result from incomplete advice correspond with the findings of RQ1 in regards to the issues users, developers and other software ecosystem actors encounter. This correspondence can be derived from the descriptions of the lacking guidelines and their interaction with the issues.

The comparison tables and subsequent evaluation of the results lead to the conclusion that neither platform adequately adheres to the security guidelines set by the OWASP mobile security project. This provides an answer to the main research question posed in this paper.

Final Conclusions and Recommendations. The literature regarding the security issues in both analysed ecosystems show that they are not completely secure for their users and developers. Customers do not always understand how the applications can seriously affect their security. Developers are not always capable of securing their applications as a result of problems like repackaging. Problems like these add to the importance of secure ecosystems especially in the form of well-defined security guidelines that follow security recommendations.

The impact on the entire ecosystem was assesed when the OWASP framework was placed in the context of software ecosystems, it is considered of high importance to the security and health of the mobile software platforms that security guidelines are fully included in the developer documentation. Based on the conclusions presented in this paper, the recommendation can be made that platforms should consider including more comprehensive information on secure development using a framework such as OWASP. Regardless if the operating system has been designed with protections in mind, orchestrators should still include information on secure development in their documentation, as it has been shown that these measures can be circumvented in some cases and the additional measures taken by developers can only benefit the ecosystem. Some platforms already show the value of the OWASP guidelines by referring to them on the introductory page of the security guide, while others do no such thing. It is recommended that the value of these guidelines is more clearly referred to in the developer documentation.

References

1. Jansen, S., Finkelstein, A., Brinkkemper, S.: A sense of community: a research agenda for software ecosystems. In: 31st International Conference on Software Engineering-Companion Volume. ICSE-Companion 2009, pp. 187–190 (2009)
2. Asokan, N., Davi, L., Dmitrienko, A., Heuser, S., Kostiainen, K., Reshetova, E., Sadeghi, A.R.: Mobile Platform Security Synthesis Lectures on Information Security, Privacy, and Trust. Morgan & Claypool Publishers (2013)
3. Jansen, S., Bloemendal, E.: Defining app stores: the role of curated marketplaces in software ecosystems. In: Herzwurm, G., Margaria, T. (eds.) ICSOB 2013. LNBIP, vol. 150, pp. 195–206. Springer, Heidelberg (2013). doi:10.1007/978-3-642-39336-5_19
4. Rashidi, B., Fung, C.: A survey of android security threats and defenses. J. Wirel. Mob. Netw. Ubiquitous Comput. Dependable Appl. (JoWUA) 6(3), 3–35 (2015)
5. Wei, X., Gomez, L., Neamtiu, I., Faloutsos, M.: Permission evolution in the android ecosystem. In: Proceedings of the 28th Annual Computer Security Applications Conference, pp. 31–40. ACM (2012)
6. Grace, M.C., Zhou, Y., Wang, Z., Jiang, X.: Systematic detection of capability leaks in stock android smartphones. In: NDSS, vol. 14, p. 19 (2012)
7. Saltzer, J.H., Schroeder, M.D.: The protection of information in computer systems. Proc. IEEE 63(9), 1278–1308 (1975)
8. Davi, L., Dmitrienko, A., Sadeghi, A.-R., Winandy, M.: Privilege escalation attacks on android. In: Burmester, M., Tsudik, G., Magliveras, S., Ilić, I. (eds.) ISC 2010. LNCS, vol. 6531, pp. 346–360. Springer, Heidelberg (2011). doi:10.1007/978-3-642-18178-8_30
9. Meng, X., Song, C., Ji, Y., Shih, M.-W., Kangjie, L., Zheng, C., Duan, R., Jang, Y., Lee, B., Qian, C., et al.: Toward engineering a secure android ecosystem: a survey of existing techniques. ACM Comput. Surv. (CSUR) 49(2), 38 (2016)

10. Mulliner, C., Robertson, W., Kirda, E.: VirtualSwindle: an automated attack against in-app billing on android. In: Proceedings of the 9th ACM Symposium on Information, Computer and Communications Security, pp. 459–470. ACM (2014)
11. Orikogbo, D., Büchler, M., Egele, M.: CRiOS: toward large-scale iOS application analysis. In: Proceedings of the 6th Workshop on Security and Privacy in Smartphones and Mobile Devices, pp. 33–42. ACM (2016)
12. Heider, J., El Khayari, E.: iOS keychain weakness FAQ. Frauenhofer Institute for Secure Information Technology (SIT) (2012)
13. Renard, M.: Practical iOS apps hacking. GreHack 2012. 14 (2012). https://papers. put.as/papers/ios/2012/GreHack-2012-paper-Mathieu_Renard_-_Practical_iOS_ Apps_hacking.pdf
14. Han, J., Yan, Q., Gao, D., Zhou, J., Deng, R.H.: Comparing mobile privacy protection through cross-platform applications (2013)
15. Felt, A.P., Finifter, M., Chin, E., Hanna, S., Wagner, D.: A survey of mobile malware in the wild. In: Proceedings of the 1st ACM Workshop on Security and Privacy in Smartphones and Mobile Devices, pp. 3–14. ACM (2011)
16. Miller, C.: Inside iOS code signing. In: Symposium on Security for Asia Network (SyScan) (2011)
17. Meng, W., Luo, X., Furnell, S., Zhou, J.: Protecting mobile networks and devices: challenges and solutions (2016)
18. Teufl, P., Zefferer, T., Stromberger, C., Hechenblaikner, C.: iOS encryption systems: Deploying iOS devices in security-critical environments. In: 2013 International Conference on Security and Cryptography (SECRYPT), pp. 1–13. IEEE (2013)
19. Manikas, K., Hansen, K.M.: Software ecosystems-a systematic literature review. J. Syst. Softw. **86**(5), 1294–1306 (2013)
20. Hoehle, H., Venkatesh, V.: Mobile application usability: conceptualization and instrument development. MIS Q. **39**(2), 435–472 (2015)

Short Papers

Experimentation that Matters: A Multi-case Study on the Challenges with A/B Testing

Helena Holmström Olsson[1(✉)], Jan Bosch[2], and Aleksander Fabijan[1]

[1] Faculty of Technology and Society, Malmö University,
Nordenskiöldsgatan 1, 211 19 Malmö, Sweden
{helena.holmstrom.olsson,aleksander.fabijan}@mah.se
[2] Department of Computer Science and Engineering, Chalmers University
of Technology, Hörselgången 11, 412 96 Göteborg, Sweden
jan.bosch@chalmers.se

Abstract. From having been exclusive for companies in the online domain, feature experiments are becoming increasingly important for software-intensive companies also in other domains. Today, companies run experiments, such as e.g. A/B tests, to optimize product performance and to learn about user behaviors, as well as to guide product development and innovation. However, although experimentation with customers has become an effective mechanism to improve products and increase revenue, companies struggle with how to leverage the results of the experiments they run. In this paper, we study the reasons for this and we identify three key challenges that make feature experimentation a difficult task. Our research reveals the following challenges: (1) the impact of experiments doesn't scale, (2) business KPIs and team level metrics are not aligned and (3) it is unclear if the available solutions are applicable across domains.

Keywords: Data-driven development · Feature experimentation · A/B testing

1 Introduction

Over the past years, software-intensive companies in a variety of domains have started adopting feature experimentation practices to evaluate ideas with customers and to accelerate innovation cycles [1–4]. As one common technique, A/B testing refers to the capability to test different variants of functionality with customers in order to learn what variant is the optimal one. While this technique has become mainstream in online companies, it is increasingly gaining momentum also in the embedded systems domain [1, 4]. In prior research, feature experimentation has proven useful for optimization of product performance, for evaluating new product concepts and for improving data-driven development practices [5–8]. As a result, companies that are adept at acquiring, processing and leveraging customer data become more profitable as early validation with customers can have a profound impact on annual revenue [8]. However, although experimentation with customers has become an effective mechanism to improve products and increase revenue, companies fail in leveraging the results of experiments [9].

A. Ojala et al. (Eds.): ICSOB 2017, LNBIP 304, pp. 179–185, 2017.
https://doi.org/10.1007/978-3-319-69191-6_12

In this paper, and based on multi-case research in three online and three embedded systems companies, we explore the reasons for why experimentation is a difficult task and we identify three key challenges with A/B testing. These challenges are: (1) the impact of experiments doesn't scale. Although companies have access to large amounts of valuable data, the impact of the data is poor, (2) business key performance indicators (KPIs) and team level metrics are not aligned. Team level metrics used for experimentation focus on short-term goals, smaller improvements and factors that change fast. On the contrary, business level KPIs focus on long-term goals, bigger innovations and factors that change slowly, and (3) it is unclear if the available solutions are applicable across domains. Although previous research provides guidance for how to optimally run experiments in the online domain, there is little research that translates these learnings and explore to what extent they are applicable also outside of this domain.

The paper is organized as follows. In Sect. 2, we detail the background of our research. In Sect. 3, we describe the research method and the case companies involved in our work. In Sect. 4, we present the empirical findings and we identify the key challenges associated with feature experimentation. In Sect. 5, we discuss our findings and conclude the paper.

2 Background

Data collection and analysis practices are becoming increasingly important as the new mechanisms to learn how a product performs in the field, how it is used by its customers and what usage patterns and behaviors that evolve [3, 7, 10, 11, 12]. With automated practices for data collection and analysis, queries can be processed frequently to provide software developers and managers with rapid feedback. As a result, continuous improvements can be made based on data from the users of the systems. This reflects an interesting shift from a situation where traditional requirements engineering practices inform development of new features [13], towards a situation in which customer and product data is continuously collected and where companies use this data to inform development [2, 5, 14]. Feature experimentation is critical as it allows continuous validation with customers [15]. As the most common technique, controlled experiments (e.g. A/B testing) constitutes a practice of comparing two versions of functionality to determine which one performs better in relation to predefined criteria such as e.g. conversion rate, click rate or time to perform a certain task [6, 8]. In online companies, A/B experiments are the norm with companies such as e.g. Amazon, eBay, Facebook, Google and Microsoft running thousands of parallel experiments to evaluate and improve their sites at any point in time. A growing number of A/B testing tools and solutions are available on the market [6, 10]. During recent years, similar practices are emerging also in the embedded systems domain. As one example, companies in the automotive industry run A/B experiments in their infotainment systems [4]. Recent studies on feature experimentation [2, 6, 8, 15, 16], focuses predominantly on the roles involved (e.g. data analysts, data scientists, product managers, software developers etc.), the task at hand (e.g. development of roadmaps, design and analysis of experiments, development of products, deployment of products etc.) and the technical infrastructure that is the platform for the experiments (e.g. the application programming interfaces, experiment databases, analytic tools, instrumentation, integration and deployment systems etc.). Also, there is prominent research providing detailed examples of how A/B tests are conducted in relation to advanced services such as e.g. the Google and Bing search engines [10].

3   Research Method

This research builds on multi-case study research [17] conducted in close collaboration with companies in the online domain and with companies in the embedded systems domain. Below, we provide a short description of each company.

Online companies:

- *Company A* provides payment services.
- *Company B* is a media streaming company.
- *Company C* is a developer of IT solutions for businesses and individuals.

Embedded systems companies:

- *Company D* is a developer of navigational information systems.
- *Company E* is a developer of connected monitoring and alarm solutions.
- *Company F* is a developer of mobile phones, tablets and smart wear devices.

For the purpose of this research topic, we organized workshops as well as conducted interviews with project managers, product managers, product owners, software developers, software and system architects, data scientists, data analysts and a number of agile team coaches and scrum masters in the case companies. While the collaboration with the embedded systems companies has been an on-going engagement since 2012, and in relation to a number of different topics, the specific work on how to improve feature experimentation practices was initiated in 2015 and is on-going. The collaboration with the online companies was initiated in 2015 and is on-going. In all companies, meetings are typically scheduled for one hour, workshop sessions for two – three hours and interviews for one hour. In both workshops and interviews, the focus is to learn about the data collection and analysis practices in the companies, their use of feature experiments, what metrics they use for A/B testing and what challenges they experience in relation to this. Our empirical data consists of interview transcripts, meeting and workshop notes, notes from informal meetings, e-mails and telephone conversations. During analysis, the transcribed interviews were read with the intention to identify recurring elements and concepts.

4   Case Study Findings

In this section, we present our case study findings by summarizing the experimentation practices in the case companies we studied. We structure our findings according to the two domains in which the case companies operate and we provide examples of (1) the *current practices* and (2) the *current challenges* the companies experience. In Table 1, we summarize the key challenges we identify.

Table 1. Key challenges associated with feature experimentation.

Key challenges	Description
Scaling impact of experiments	Experiments support only smaller improvements of features rather than having an impact on high-level business decisions such as larger re-designs, new product development or innovation initiatives
Aligning business KPIs and team level metrics	Team level metrics that are used for experimentation focus on short-term goals, smaller improvements and factors that change fast. On the contrary, business level KPIs focus on long-term goals, bigger innovations and factors that change slowly
Applicability of solutions across domains	While there is guidance for how to optimally run experiments in the online domain, it remains unclear to what extent this is applicable for companies outside of this domain

4.1   Feature Experimentation: The Online Domain

Current practices: The online companies run frequent, and often parallel, feature experiments with their customers. In these companies, A/B testing is considered the most important technique to learn about customer behaviors and preferences. In company A, A/B tests are run when developing new features and with the main purpose to confirm their value to customers as early as possible. Company B runs dozens of experiments per month in their product in order to optimize existing functionality, to learn about customer behaviors and to evaluate new product functionality. Company C is the most advanced company and uses a large number of metrics for every experiment to track product performance and user behaviors.

Current challenges: The online companies have instrumented their products in order to collect relevant data, they have experimentation platforms available to run frequent and parallel A/B tests and they have software tools that help them analyze the data. Still, to fully leverage the results of the experiments they run is challenging. This is due to a number of problems. First, the companies find it difficult to have impact of individual experiments scale. Experiments tend to support only smaller improvements of features rather than having an impact on high level business decisions such as e.g. larger re-designs, new product development or innovation initiatives. Second, the companies experience difficulties in having business KPIs and team level metrics align. Team level metrics that are used for experimentation focus on short-term goals, smaller improvements and factors that change fast. On the contrary, business level KPIs focus on long-term goals, bigger innovations and factors that change slowly. As a result, there is the risk that teams optimize for certain outcomes using metrics they can influence but without verifying the relationship between the metrics they use and high-level business KPIs.

4.2   Feature Experimentation: The Embedded Systems Domain

Current practices: In similar with the online companies, the embedded systems companies run frequent feature experiments with their customers. However, the embedded systems companies run sequential experiments with selected customers. In company D, A/B testing is gaining momentum as a technique to learn more rapidly from customers. In company E, A/B testing is a well-established technique to explore customer preferences and product performance. Company F runs A/B tests focusing on optimization of product performance and puts a lot of effort on improving user experience.

Current challenges: The embedded systems companies have instrumented their products in order to collect relevant data and they have software tools that help them analyze and access the data. However, and as a common problem in the companies, they fail in fully leveraging the results of the experiments they run. This is due to a number of problems. First, the embedded systems companies find it difficult to have impact of individual experiments scale. Typically, the A/B tests focus on smaller improvements and optimizations of certain features and although the companies have initiated work on defining high-level metrics they are uncertain to what extent these will affect current practices. Second, also the embedded systems companies experience difficulties in having business KPIs and team level metrics align. Often, teams use a number of different metrics to monitor and improve the features they develop and metrics can indicate either positive or negative results depending on what perspective you take and what you strive to optimize. Finally, and as a third challenge experienced in the embedded systems companies, it is unclear to what extent A/B testing solutions for the online domain are applicable also in their domain. This problem is recognized in all three case companies as people feel they are uncertain how to translate insights from the online to their own domain. In the embedded systems domain, the hardware dependence makes things more complex, the requirements engineering process is rigid and often companies are distant from the users.

5   Discussion and Conclusion

In this paper, we explore the challenges that companies in the online and in the embedded systems domain experience with regards to feature experimentation. From having been exclusive for companies in the online domain, feature experiments are becoming increasingly important for software-intensive companies also in other domains and today companies run A/B tests to improve and optimize existing products, to explore new concepts and to learn about customer preferences and behaviors. The increasing importance of feature experimentation is acknowledged in a number of recent studies [3, 6, 8, 9, 10]. However, what most previous studies don't recognize, is that the impact of experiments is poor and that even the most advanced companies struggle with how to leverage the results of the experiments they run. Our research captures three key challenges that cause this situation. *First,* impact of experiments doesn't scale. Instead, they tend to support only smaller improvements of specific features. *Second,* business KPIs and team level metrics are not aligned. Team level metrics used for experimentation focus on short-term goals, smaller improvements and factors that change fast. On the contrary, business level KPIs focus on long-term goals, bigger innovations and factors that change slow. *Third,* it is unclear if the available solutions are applicable across domains.

References

1. Olsson, H.H., Bosch, J.: Towards data-driven product development: a multiple case study on post-deployment data usage in software-intensive embedded systems. In: Fitzgerald, B., Conboy, K., Power, K., Valerdi, R., Morgan, L., Stol, K.-J. (eds.) LESS 2013. LNBIP, vol. 167, pp. 152–164. Springer, Heidelberg (2013). doi:10.1007/978-3-642-44930-7_10
2. Olsson, H.H., Bosch, J.: From opinions to data-driven software R&D: a multi-case study on how to close the 'Open Loop' problem. In: Proceedings of EUROMICRO, Software Engineering and Advanced Applications (SEAA), 27–29 August, Verona, Italy (2014)
3. Olsson, H.H., Bosch, J.: Towards evidence-based development: learnings from embedded systems, online games and internet of things. To appear in IEEE Software (forthcoming)
4. Bosch, J., Eklund, U.: Eternal embedded software: towards innovation experiment systems. In: Margaria, T., Steffen, B. (eds.) ISoLA 2012. LNCS, vol. 7609, pp. 19–31. Springer, Heidelberg (2012). doi:10.1007/978-3-642-34026-0_3
5. Bosch, J.: Building products as innovation experiment systems. In: Cusumano, M.A., Iyer, B., Venkatraman, N. (eds.) ICSOB 2012. LNBIP, vol. 114, pp. 27–39. Springer, Heidelberg (2012). doi:10.1007/978-3-642-30746-1_3
6. Kohavi, R., Longbotham, R.: Online controlled experiments and A/B tests. In: Encyclopedia of Machine Learning and Data Mining, no. Ries 2011, pp. 1–11 (2015)
7. Fagerholm, F., Guinea, A.F., Mäenpää, H., Münch, J.: Building blocks for continuous experimentation. In: Proceedings of the 1st International Workshop on Rapid Continuous Software Engineering (RCoSE), pp. 26–35 (2014)
8. Fabijan, A., Dmitriev, P., Olsson, H.H., Bosch J.: The evolution of continuous experimentation in software product development: from data to a data-driven organization at scale. In: Proceedings of the 39th International Conference on Software Engineering (ICSE), 20–28th May, Buenos Aires, Argentina (2017)
9. Olsson, H.H., Bosch, J.: So Much Data; So Little Value A multi-case study on improving the impact of data-driven development practices. In Proceedings of the Ibero American Conference on Software Engineering (CIbSE), 22nd–23rd May, Buenos Aires, Argentina (2017)
10. Dmitriev, P., Frasca, B., Gupta, S., Kohavi, R., Vaz, G. (forthcoming). Pitfalls of Long-Term Online Controlled Experiments. (To appear in IEEE Big Data)
11. Fagerholm, F., et al.: The RIGHT model for continuous experimentation. J. Syst. Softw. **123**, 292–305 (2016)
12. Bosch, J.: Future trends in software engineering. IEEE Softw. **33**(1), 82–88 (2016)
13. Pohl, K.: Requirements Engineering: Fundamentals, Principles, and Techniques. Springer Publishing Company, Incorporated (2010)
14. Ries, E.: The Lean Startup: How Today's Entrepreneurs Use Continuous Innovation to Create Radically Successful Businesses. Crown Business, New York (2011)

15. Fabijan, A., Olsson, H.H., Bosch, J.: Time to say 'Good Bye': feature lifecycle. In: 42nd Euromicro Conference on Software Engineering and Advanced Applications (SEAA), Limassol, Cyprus. 31 August–2 September, pp. 9–16 (2016)
16. Kim, M., Zimmermann, T., DeLine, R., Begel, A.: The Emerging Role of Data Scientists on Software Development Teams, no. MSR-TR-2015–30, p. 10 2015
17. Runesson, P., Höst, M.: Guidelines for conducting and reporting case study research in software engineering. Empirical Softw. Eng. **14**, 131 (2009)

Why Do Users Install and Delete Apps?
A Survey Study

Selim Ickin$^{(\boxtimes)}$, Kai Petersen, and Javier Gonzalez-Huerta

Blekinge Institute of Technology, Karlskrona, Sweden
selimickin@gmail.com, {kai.petersen,javier.gonzalez.huerta}@bth.se

Abstract. Practitioners on the area of mobile application development usually rely on set of app-related success factors, the majority of which are directly related to their economical/business profit (e.g., number of downloads, or the in-app purchases revenue). However, gathering also the user-related success factors, that explain the reasons why users choose, download, and install apps as well as the user-related failure factors that explain the reasons why users delete apps, might help practitioners understand how to improve the market impact of their apps. The objectives were to: identify (i) the reasons why users choose and installing mobile apps from app stores; (ii) the reasons why users uninstall the apps. A questionnaire-based survey involving 121 users from 26 different countries was conducted.

Keywords: Mobile application development · Success factors · Failure factors · Users survey

1 Introduction

The number of mobile applications available has grown dramatically in the last few years, and the app stores are indeed the main channel for dissemination of such applications [2]. The number of mobile apps available in leading app stores reached the 5.7 billion by the end of 2016[1]. By 2017, the number of app downloads is estimated to increase up to 268 billion[2]. The penetration factor that allows reaching customers with apps is extremely high as there is a large customer base owning smart-phones whereas, at the same time, there is a huge competition in this market.

Mobile application developers and companies usually rely on app-related[3] success factors, the majority of which are directly related to their economical/business profit (e.g., number of downloads, or in-app purchases revenue). However these success factors are limited by how well the application fits user's needs or how well satisfies the user's expectations (among many others). Based on empirical evidence [4]: some studies suggest relations between API quality

---

[1] https://www.statista.com/statistics/276623/.
[2] https://www.statista.com/statistics/266488/.
[3] According to the terminology used in [4].

© Springer International Publishing AG 2017
A. Ojala et al. (Eds.): ICSOB 2017, LNBIP 304, pp. 186–191, 2017.
https://doi.org/10.1007/978-3-319-69191-6_13

and app success [3,9], whereas the study by Guerrouj and Baysal [4] showed that even more significant factors were app-size and category. Similarly, Corral and Fronza [1] found that source code quality only had marginal impact on app success (measured as penetration and satisfaction), while the most important quality attributes were *"responsiveness, easiness, functionality and performance"*. Several studies used data mining to understand the information in app-stores [8,10], e.g. to find issues in applications and thus ways to improve them [8].

App stores include certain user-visible information (e.g., such as description of the app, screenshots, application size, last update, rating, and permission require ments). Some of these information items are under control of the app developers (e.g., the app description, the screenshoots, or the permission requirements), whereas some others are the direct expression of the users opinions (e.g., reviews and rating). These reviews and ratings have become an important factor for app success [6] and its impact has been analyzed in several studies (e.g., [5,7]). However user ratings might also be helpful for developers and application vendors to identify and prioritize missing features [11]. Developers can also improve the information on the app stores aiming at increasing the number of downloads of their apps. In this scenario, it is important to gain understanding on the criteria that make users to choose, download and install mobile apps, but at the same time, it is also important to analyze the rationale behind users removing mobile apps once it has been already installed in their mobile phone.

In this paper, we study the mobile application quality from the user perspective through an online survey. We analyze the set of reasons (i.e., user-related factors (see Footnote 3) that might influence the users while choosing to install mobile applications via app stores and the reasons that cause them to uninstall an app from their smartphones.

2   Survey Definition

Research questions: The two main research questions addressed in this work are:

- *RQ1:* What are the user-visible information items from the app stores that are taken into account by users when choosing, downloading and installing applications?
- *RQ2:* What are the main reasons for deleting an application?

Target population: The survey was executed at the end of 2015 and it includes results obtained from 121 users, some of which were contacted through mobile apps forums such as IPhone Forum, EverythingiCafe, Android forum, and AndroidPit. Hence, a convenience sampling approach was used.

Questionnaire design: The survey questionnaire comprised the following aspects: (i) Demographics (categories of questions: gender, age, occupation, years of experience using smartphones, nationality, and country of residence); (ii) application and network usage (e.g. cellular data plan); (iii) reasons for installing and deleting applications; (iv) important characteristics of mobile applications,; and (v) qualitative feedback on mobile application and smartphone experience.

Data analysis: Descriptive statistics and histograms are used to illustrate the distribution of the data. In addition, we applied pair-wise Fisher's exact test to analyze the differences between the reasons to download or uninstall apps, although the main goal of the study was not to generalize the results for the population based on the results of these tests.

Validity threats: The main threats to validity are: (i) use of convenience sampling, sample size and inclusion of personal contacts, which might limit the ability to generalize the results to a large population; (ii) objectivity in the coding of the open questions, which may introduce bias; (iii) the inclusion of participants from mobile applications forums, which might have also influenced the results.

3   Results

Demographics: The demographics of the subjects that participated in the online survey is given in Fig. 1, including age, gender, smartphone experience, phone type, as well as user nationality and occupation.

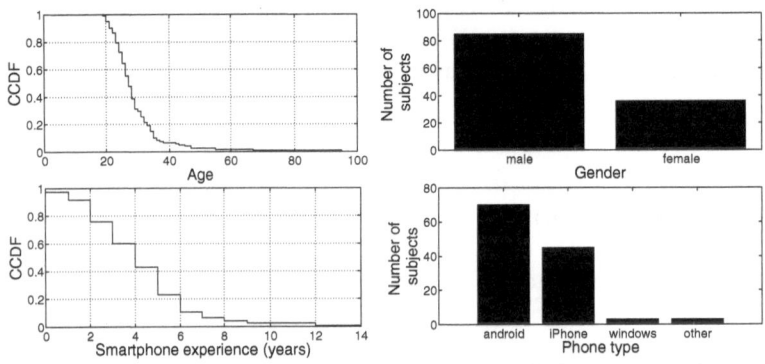

Fig. 1. User demographics and Mobile platforms.

The subjects were from 26 different nationalities, although the majority of them are Turkish (25%) and Swedish (21%) citizens. The participants' occupations spanned through 23 different occupations, with a vast majority of students (57%), engineers (17%), or researchers (11%).

Reasons for installing new apps from the App Store: The participants were asked to prioritize the relative importance of a set of reasons they have into account when deciding to download certain mobile applications via app stores. Figure 2 shows a summary of the participants responses. We have found statistically significant differences ($p < 0.005$) when participants' responses in relation description of tool and user reviews are both compared to the remaining seven reasons. Key observations are: (i) user reviews are significantly more important than application size, content rating, editor's choice, last update, number of downloads, permission requirements, and screenshots; (ii) no significant differences were found between number of reviews and review content, and (iii) no statistically significant differences were found between rating values, frequency of ratings and number of ratings, which indeed goes in the same direction than previous studies (e.g., [7]).

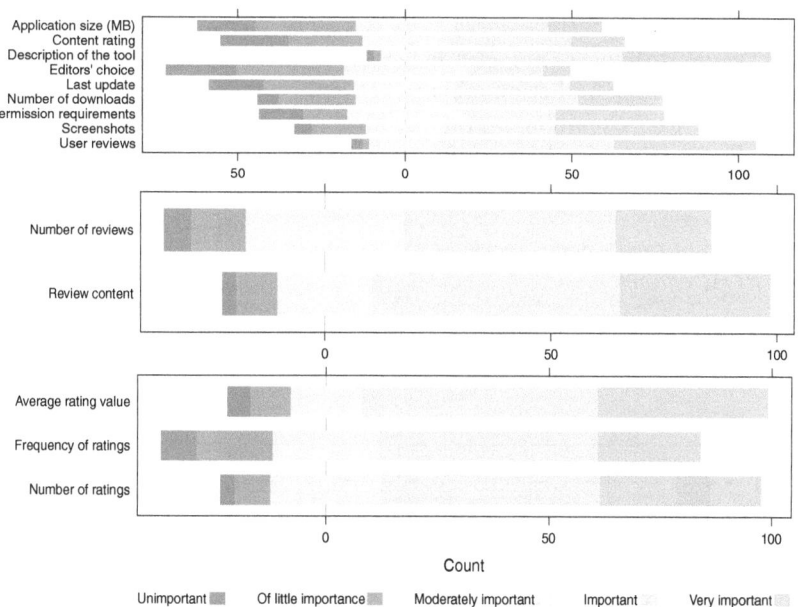

Fig. 2. Reasons from users to install apps.

In addition, the users have provided additional items that they think are important, resulting in the following list: open source, graphics, e.g. videos/screenshots, source company programmer reputation, bad naming of apps for advertising such as "Free version", social popularity (e.g. if a friend is using and recommending it), compatibility with other apps, needs, position in the list, or existence of an external app website.

Reasons for deleting apps: We coded the different reasons for deleting apps, and categorized them in 16 categories. The main reasons for users to uninstall applications from their smartphones is given in Fig. 3.

– *Unstable/Inconsistent:* Involuntary behavior, uncontrolled actions, Inconsistency between description and functionality, unreliable, change in privacy terms, side effects (i.e. together with the main purpose, it does extra unwanted things), permissions, high amount of notifications, expectations not met.

- *Intrusive Advertisements*
- *Lack of Improvement:* outdated, lack of Improvement/others outperform, finding a better one
- *Useless/Not needed:* Usefulness, not using anymore, not needed
- *Frequent application updates:* Frequent application updates, fee for upgrade, too many updates
- *Getting bored:* e.g. Finished game
- *High memory allocation:* Size of the app, too much memory usage (RAM), uninstallations by relying on the backup to use it later
- *Poor User Interface:* Slick animations, complex to use, GUI, user unfriendly
- *High battery usage*
- *Crashes:* Performance, Sluggish behavior, freeze, slow, laggy, force quit
- *Time consuming:* Addiction, abuse
- *No offline use:* No offline use, no caching
- *Poor Popularity:* friends not using, overall reputation
- *Abusing privacy:* login required, required integration via login (i.e. with Facebook, Google)
- *Compatibility with device version*
- *OS/ROM change*

The most important reason was due to the fact that they find that the app has become useless or is not needed any more.

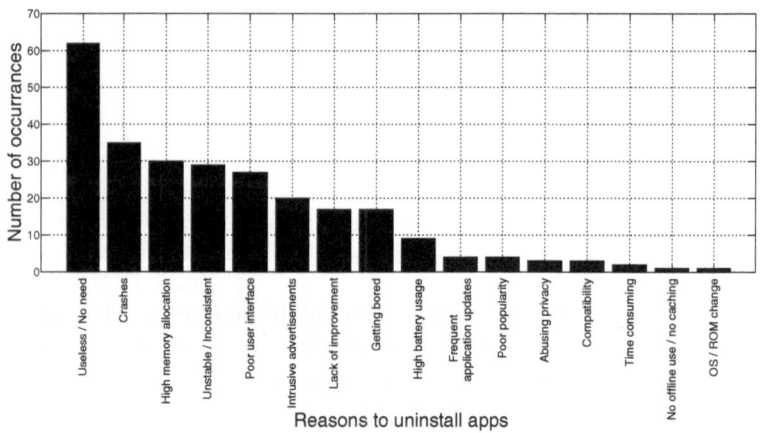

Fig. 3. Reasons from users to uninstall apps.

4   Conclusion

In this paper we have presented the results obtained via user surveys focusing on the user-related success that might lead users to choose and install certain apps, as well as user-related failure factors, that might lead users to uninstall the apps. The description of the tool and user reviews are the most important factors influencing users while choosing and installing application from app stores. The most important reason for a user to uninstall an application from smartphone is users finding some apps as "useless". The other important factors found as relevant are crashes, high memory allocation, instability and inconsistency, poor UI, intrusive advertisements, lack of improvement, boring apps. We are aware that this study only provide preliminary results on the user-related success and failure factors, and that further surveys and user studies need to be conducted, in particular expanding the target groups and covering different locations.

References

1. Corral, L., Fronza, I.: Better code for better apps: a study on source code quality and market success of android applications. In: Proceedings of the Second ACM International Conference on Mobile Software Engineering and Systems, pp. 22–32. IEEE Press (2015)
2. Cortimiglia, M.N., Ghezzi, A., Renga, F.: Mobile applications and their delivery platforms. IT Prof. **13**(5), 51–56 (2011)
3. Guerrouj, L., Azad, S., Rigby, P.C.: The influence of app churn on app success and stackoverflow discussions. In: Proceedings of the 22nd 2015 IEEE International Conference on Software Analysis, Evolution and Reengineering (SANER), pp. 321–330. IEEE (2015)
4. Guerrouj, L., Baysal, O.: Investigating the android apps' success: an empirical study. In: Proceedings of the 24th 2016 IEEE International Conference on Program Comprehension (ICPC), pp. 1–4. IEEE (2016)
5. Hao, L., Li, X., Tan, Y., Xu, J.: The economic role of rating behavior in third-party application market. In: Second International Conference on Information Systems, Shanghai, China, pp. 1–15 (2011)
6. Li, H., Zhang, L., Zhang, L., Shen, J.: A user satisfaction analysis approach for software evolution. In: Proceedings of the 2010 IEEE International Conference on Progress in Informatics and Computing, pp. 1093–1097 (2010)
7. Hyrynsalmi, S., Seppänen, M., Aarikka-Stenroos, L., Suominen, A., Järveläinen, J., Harkke, V.: Busting myths of electronic word of mouth: the relationship between customer ratings and the sales of mobile applications. J. Theor. Appl. Electron. Commer. Res. **10**(2), 1–18 (2015)
8. Khalid, H., Shihab, E., Nagappan, M., Hassan, A.E.: What do mobile app users complain about? IEEE Softw. **32**(3), 70–77 (2015)
9. Linares-Vásquez, M., Bavota, G., Bernal-Cárdenas, C., Di Penta, M., Oliveto, R., Poshyvanyk, D.: Api change and fault proneness: a threat to the success of android apps. In: Proceedings of the 2013 9th Joint Meeting on Foundations of Software Engineering, pages 477–487. ACM (2013)
10. McIlroy, S., Ali, N., Khalid, H., Hassan, A.E.: Analyzing and automatically labelling the types of user issues that are raised in mobile app reviews. Empirical Softw. Eng. **21**(3), 1067–1106 (2016)
11. Pagano, D., Bruegge, B.: User involvement in software evolution practice: a case study. In: Proceedings of the 35th 2013 International Conference on Software Engineering (ICSE), pp. 953–962. IEEE (2013)

Evolving Software Products, the Design of a Water-Related Modeling Software Ecosystem

Konstantinos Manikas[1,2]([⊠])

[1] DHI Group, Hørsholm, Denmark
kman@dhigroup.com
[2] Computer Science Department, IT University of Copenhagen,
Copenhagen, Denmark

Abstract. Software product evolution by means of improving their architecture, tools, or development methodologies are rather common in the lifetime of a software product. Especially if the product is in the domain of engineering where some of the basic calculation principles were established in some cases more than 50 years ago. However, a radical change of software products to evolve both in the software engineering as much as the organizational and business aspects in a disruptive manner are rather rare.

In this paper, we report on the transformation of one of the market leader product series in water-related calculation and modeling from a traditional business-as-usual series of products to an evolutionary software ecosystem. We do so by relying on existing concepts on software ecosystem analysis to analyze the future ecosystem. We report and elaborate on the main focus points necessary for this transition. We argue for the generalization of our focus points to the transition from traditional business-as-usual software products to software ecosystems.

Keywords: Software ecosystems · Ecosystem design · Product modernization

1 Introduction

Software ecosystems have been gaining in popularity in the past decade. We have noticed an increasing number of software systems and products being either converted from an existing system to an ecosystem or designed from the beginning to support the ecosystem approach [1]. The field of software ecosystems arguably appeared around the previous decade. Since then, the field has been shaped by a number of publications such as several literature studies [2–5] as much as a number of influential studies proposing, among other, means of analysis or categorizing software ecosystems [6–9]. Software ecosystems arguably come with several advantages such as increased level of innovation, better quality of software products, accelerated development, or reduced time to market. However not all

© Springer International Publishing AG 2017
A. Ojala et al. (Eds.): ICSOB 2017, LNBIP 304, pp. 192–198, 2017.
https://doi.org/10.1007/978-3-319-69191-6_14

ecosystems have been equally successful or effective in achieving the advantages that are promised with this approach. This the ecosystem design with respect to success has been a focus of both research and academia.

In related work, [10] follow the transition of a software product line to a software ecosystem with the parallel transition from waterfall development processes to agile. [11] follow a similar transition of a proprietary platform but to an open source software ecosystem. In a somewhat different approach [12,13] describe the steps of analyzing and designing a software ecosystem around the telemedical services of the Danish healthcare. As noted form these studies, software ecosystems can mainly emerge from a successful software product (or system, company). However, the telemedicine ecosystem is an example the design of an ecosystem by identifying a need for an ecosystem rather than evolving from an existing platform. The steps towards the design of an ecosystem are elaborated more in [14]. One of the methods for analyzing and designing software ecosystems from a wide perspectives is the concept of "software ecosystem architecture" that we are using in this study [12]. The concept proposes that a software ecosystem can be analyzed by three different perspectives using three structures:

Software structure. That contains the different software elements of an ecosystem as much as their relationships (including software interaction). In some cases it helpful to separate between the common software infrastructure, i.e. the platform of the ecosystem, and the software extensions, i.e. contributions on top of the infrastructure.

Organizational structure. The different organizational elements of the ecosystem, such as the different actors that are involved in the ecosystem, their roles, and relationships.

Business structure. The different business elements of the ecosystem such as the incentives that motivate the actor activity in the ecosystem.

In this paper we focus on the design of a software ecosystem and report on the analysis of one of the market-leader suites of products in water-related modeling and prediction. Our case focuses in designing the evolution of the development and distribution from traditional means to a software ecosystem with utter aim to "solve the worlds toughest challenges in water environments" [15].

2   Approach

The studied systems are a set of software systems that, among other, perform complex calculation and modeling scenarios in a wide variety of water resource problems. These systems have been evolved and improved over the years with the first calculation algorithms dating back to the 1960's. The architecture of the different products includes high level or reuse and conceptual separation. The organization developing the systems is part of a wider non-profit organization of more than 1000 employees world-wide with main business water resources engineering expertise. The organization's products include project development and consultancy, software products, and knowledge distribution.

In the following section we discuss the result of analysis of the ecosystem to-be. We do so, in a generic manner so to be applicable in wider domains. We use the three structures of the software ecosystem architecture.

2.1 Software Structure

The transition to a software ecosystem poses a number of requirements to the software structure. This structure includes both the ecosystem *platform*, i.e. the software infrastructure that forms the core of the ecosystem where extensions are build upon, and the *software extensions*, i.e. plug-inns or apps that provide additional functionality or services to the ecosystem by extending the platform. Bellow we elaborate on the main aspects that the software structure of the ecosystem should cover.

Modularity and Independence. The clear separation of the (software and logical) components of an ecosystem is essential to the well-functioning and prosperity of the ecosystem. The better each logical (and thus software) entity is defined and separated from the rest, the more probable it is for the system to be to keep faithful to the architectural design. This is especially relevant to existing systems transitioning to an ecosystem as the effort of re-designing and refactoring is arguably greater than design from scratch. In such cases apart from re-designing, analysis of architectural evolution and specifically architectural drift and decay is very relevant as much as information on the initial architectural decisions and trade-offs. The proposed architectural smells [16] can be an relevant starting point. Today there is a number of architectural patterns and tactics that can facilitate this transitions, e.g. the use of service oriented architecture and microservices, as much as different tools.

Independent and Continuous Release. One positive effect of an optimal modularity in a system is that this logical structuring allows for releasing modules independently from each other. Independent release of modules is essential for the (rapid) evolution of large and complex systems as (a) it enforces complete control of dependencies - otherwise the system fails at runtime, (b) better supports the actor extension development as it allows the actors to focus only on the module(s) that are relevant, (c) allows for organizational independence, i.e. different organizations (or teams) can limit their scope easier. Apart from the platform, independent release and release roadmapping should also be a requirement for extensions that are reused by other components.

Standardization of Platform and Extension. In order to facilitate the rapid and proper extension development, the aspects of this development should be standardized to the extent possible. In that respect, the ecosystem should provide and enforce standardized means of development, deployment, and testing/quality assurance. Standardization could be included in following ways:

Documentation and Support. The ecosystem orchestrators should facilitate the ecosystem extension by "flattening" the learning curve of ecosystem contributors and establishing and communicating official "ways of doing". Examples here include good guides and documentation on how to create extension or standard functions e.g. user interface, logging, or error-handling. This should already by considered by design time by including relevant system architectural qualities, e.g. buildability.

Enforcement and Control. Some of the standardized procedures, might be imperative to be followed e.g. procedures dealing with authentication, authorization, or privacy. In those cases, apart from communication and support, there should also exist means of enforcement and control of the proper design and implementation. Depending on the governance the ecosystem is following, different ways of enforcement can be applied. Practices can vary from automated controls (e.g. during commit/deployment or binary controls), to manual and resource-demanding controls e.g. it is common approach to establish compliance and certification organizations or auditing procedures for systems with high requirements in quality assurance.

Coordination, Plan Communication, and Roadmapping. Development both internally in the platform and externally in the extensions can be rather distributed and independent. This can cause several issues related to the distributed work, e.g. extensions being build on a platform component/service that changed, or platform releasing similar functionality to what an external actor was building in an extension. This kind of issues can be arguably prevented by setting requirement for communicating changes and roadmaps of system evolution that other actors can align with. In some cases, a special organizational entity or automated system can be responsible for the communication and co-ordination of the software interaction.

2.2 Business Structure

The transition to a software ecosystem arguably has a great impact to the business structure. Below we elaborate on some of the aspects that should be covered:

2.3 Disruption and Business Development

Transitioning to an ecosystem potentially includes a disruption to the "business-as-usual" model that an organization might have established. Identifying the new business models and incentives both for the (orchestrating) organization itself but also for potential external organizations is essential for this transition. Aspects in this work include challenging the existing and identifying new: (i) value propositions, (ii) customer segments, (iii) revenue streams, (iv) strategic alliances.

Business and Software Structure Alignment. Similar to a single organization, the alignment of the business and the software is essential. Naturally, in the ecosystem perspective the complexity is of higher magnitude. The platform should reflect the business and the business should support the operation and evolution of the software structures. A proper set of value propositions and incentives both for the orchestrator - organization opening the platform and the software extension organizations is equally important (if not more) with a proper software structure. Means of designing the business structure moves towards traditional business development. Moreover the alignment of software and business structures can arguably be facilitated by theories and frameworks in the enterprise architecture. Naturally, these frameworks should also be extended to the ecosystem views.

2.4   Organizational Structure

Internal Organization. The transition to an ecosystem implies challenges to the internal organization that would take the role of the ecosystem orchestrator. A radical restructuring of the software and business in an organization should be followed by restructuring in the organization itself. A relevant example is, assuming that "Conway's law" [17] is valid, the platform would reflect the structure of the organization and the pattern of communication. Thus, the structure of the organization should be evaluated in this light. Moreover, the software and business structure aliment should also be reflected here.

External Organization. The structuring of the external to the orchestrator organizations could potentially include implications that need to be addressed.

Actor Involvement Model. How external actors are to be included is an important aspect on an ecosystem. If the ecosystem is very open to external actors/organizations, there might appear issues with high extension competition that might have a negative effect to the ecosystem. Moreover, the more the ecosystem contributions scale, the more challenging it might be to control and maintain quality. On the other hand, if an ecosystem is to limiting to external actor inclusion, the ecosystem might not be able to obtain and maintain a critical mass for the ecosystem to evolve and eventually survive.

Defining Internal and External. Transition to an ecosystem also implies that external organizations might be occupied with aspects of a systems that was previously internal. It might be necessary to define and make explicit the borders of each system and the responsibilities of each actor in a more formal way to avoid organizational and legal frictions. Moreover, in cases of privacy and risk of leak of important information, employees should have guidance on the right level of communication and the privacy level of information. This is something that is implemented in many organizations today. The challenge increases with the increase in complexity, e.g. more actors in different privacy levels.

3   Conclusion and Future Work

In this paper we report on the transition of a software product suite to a software ecosystem. We rely on the concept of software ecosystem architecture and analyze the current systems. Our work results in a set of focus points that are necessary for the transformation to an arguably healthy ecosystem.

Plans for future work include the evaluation of the focus points and the detailed design of the aspects that the focus points identify. We argue that the identified points can be developed further to a generalized method for evolving from traditional software systems to software ecosystems.

References

1. Manikas, K.: Supporting the evolution of research in software ecosystems: reviewing the empirical literature. In: Maglyas, A., Lamprecht, A.-L. (eds.) Software Business. LNBIP, vol. 240, pp. 63–78. Springer, Cham (2016). doi:10.1007/978-3-319-40515-5_5
2. Hanssen, G.K., Dybå, T.: Theoretical foundations of software ecosystems. In: Jansen, S., Bosch, J., Alves, C. (eds.) Proceedings of the Forth International Workshop on Software Ecosystems, Cambridge, vol. 879, pp. 6–17, 18 June 2012. http://CEUR-WS.org
3. Barbosa, O., Santos, R.P., Alves, C., Werner, C., Jansen, S.: In: Software Ecosystems - Analyzing and Managing Business Networks in the Software Industry. Edward Elgar, Cheltenham (2013)
4. Manikas, K., Hansen, K.M.: Software ecosystems - a systematic literature review. J. Syst. Softw. **86**(5), 1294–1306 (2013)
5. Manikas, K.: Revisiting software ecosystems research: a longitudinal literature study. Syst. Softw. **117**, 84–103 (2016)
6. Bosch, J.: From software product lines to software ecosystems. In: Proceedings of the 13th International Software Product Line Conference SPLC 2009. Carnegie Mellon University, Pittsburgh, pp. 111–119 (2009)
7. Jansen, S., Finkelstein, A., Brinkkemper, S.: A sense of community: a research agenda for software ecosystems. In: 31st International Conference on Software Engineering - Companion, vol. 2009, pp. 187–190. ICSE-Companion, May 2009
8. Knodel, J., Manikas, K.: Towards a typification of software ecosystems. In: Fernandes, J.M., Machado, R.J., Wnuk, K. (eds.) ICSOB 2015. LNBIP, vol. 210, pp. 60–65. Springer, Cham (2015). doi:10.1007/978-3-319-19593-3_5
9. Manikas, K., Hansen, K.M.: Reviewing the health of software ecosystems - a conceptual framework proposal. In: Proceedings of the 5th International Workshop on Software Ecosystems, Potsdam, vol. 987, pp. 33–44, 11 June 2013. http://CEUR-WS.org
10. Hanssen, G.K.: A longitudinal case study of an emerging software ecosystem: implications for practice and theory. J. Syst. Softw. **85**(7), 1455–1466 (2011)
11. Kilamo, T., Hammouda, I., Mikkonen, T., Aaltonen, T.: From proprietary to open source-growing an open source ecosystem. J. Syst. Softw. **85**(7), 1467–1478 (2012)
12. Christensen, H.B., Hansen, K.M., Kyng, M., Manikas, K.: Analysis and design of software ecosystem architectures - towards the 4s telemedicine ecosystem. Inf. Softw. Technol. **56**(11), 1476–1492 (2014)

13. Manikas, K.: Analyzing, Modelling, and Designing Software Ecosystems - Towards the Danish Telemedicine Software Ecosystem. PhD thesis, Department of Computer Science, University of Copenhagen, Denmark (2015)
14. Manikas, K., Hämäläinen, M., Tyrväinen, P.: Designing, developing, and implementing software ecosystems: towards a step-wise guide. In: The 8th International Workshop on Software Ecosystems (2016)
15. DHI Group: Our foundamentals. Accessed 23 Feb 2017. https://www.dhigroup.com/about-us/corporate-social-responsibility/our-fundamentals
16. Garcia, J., Popescu, D., Edwards, G., Medvidovic, N.: Identifying architectural bad smells. In: 2009 13th European Conference on Software Maintenance and Reengineering, pp. 255–258, March 2009
17. Conway, M.E.: How do committees invent. Datamation **14**(4), 28–31 (1968)

Towards Understanding Startup Product Development as Effectual Entrepreneurial Behaviors

Anh Nguyen Duc[1(✉)], Yngve Dahle[2], Martin Steinert[2],
and Pekka Abrahamsson[2,3]

[1] University College of Southeast Norway,
Notodden, Norway
angu@usn.no
http://softwarestartups.org
[2] Norwegian University of Science and Technology,
7491 Trondheim, Norway
[3] Software Startups Research Network, Trondheim, Norway

Abstract. Software startups face with multiple technical and business challenges, which could make the startup journey longer, or even become a failure. Little is known about entrepreneurial decision making as a direct force to startup development outcome. In this study, we attempted to apply a behavior theory of entrepreneurial firms to understand the root-cause of some software startup's challenges. Six common challenges related to prototyping and product development in twenty software startups were identified. We found the behavior theory as a useful theoretical lens to explain the technical challenges. Software startups search for local optimal solutions, emphasize on short-run feedback rather than long-run strategies, which results in vague prototype planning, paradox of demonstration and evolving throw-away prototypes. The finding implies that effectual entrepreneurial processes might require a more suitable product development approach than the current state-of-practice.

Keywords: Effectuation · Entrepreneurial behavior theory · Software development · Software startups · Prototyping · Empirical study

1 Introduction

The software industry has witnessed a growing trend, where software products are developed by startup companies with limited resources and little operating history. With the advancement of technology development, it seems that everyone with a business idea, a website and a pitch can launch a new company. However, not so many business ideas are realized as concrete prototypes. Furthermore, even a smaller portion of prototypes is transformed into commercialized products. It is difficult to repeat successes, as startups operate in chaotic situations, where the links between startups' behaviors and their effects are often not detectable [1].

Decisions made by entrepreneurs is the direct force leading to the success or failure of the startup [3]. Startup's unique characteristics, i.e. dynamic, bootstrapping and

© Springer International Publishing AG 2017
A. Ojala et al. (Eds.): ICSOB 2017, LNBIP 304, pp. 199–204, 2017.
https://doi.org/10.1007/978-3-319-69191-6_15

multiple-influenced environments, make the decision-making tasks for entrepreneurs are different for project managers in more established companies [1]. Entrepreneurs often have to make decisions with little information about market, customer and product, and whether they will be accepted [2]. Entrepreneurial literature offers several ways to understand the startup's decisions and behaviors [3, 4, 8]. One approach is the behavior theory of entrepreneurial firms, which assumes the effectuation approach when developing startups' business [4]. Recent ideologists [5–7] encourage the co-development of business and product in startups. The combination of the two line of thoughts inspires us to explore the effectual behavior of startups from product development aspect. We are interested in understanding how the theory of entrepreneurial behaviors could help to explain the challenges faced during startups' prototyping and product development. Our research question is *"How are theories of entrepreneurial behaviors applicable to explain for startup product development process?"*

The paper is organized as follows; firstly, we present related work about a behavior theory of entrepreneur firm (Sect. 2). Then, we describe our research methodology (Sect. 3). After that, findings are presented (Sect. 4). Finally, we will discuss and conclude the paper (Sects. 5 and 6).

2 Behavioral Theory of the Entrepreneurial Firm

Entrepreneurship literature is intensive on understanding the formation, development and influencing factors to startups. There has been an increased attention on the effectuation theory in explaining entrepreneurial behaviors [8]. Effectuation processes take a set of means as given and focus on selecting between possible outcomes that can be realized [8]. Alternatively, entrepreneurial firms are seen as heterogeneous, bounded rational entities [4]. In the face of environmental uncertainty, therefore, these bounded rational firms form expectations based on available means and information. Dew et al. proposed a behavioral theory of the entrepreneurial firm (BTEF) [4]. Assuming entrepreneurs as an effectual unit, Dew et al. [4] propose four constructs related to entrepreneurial decision-making:

- Means-driven transformation: startup companies tend to be effectual, and available resources drive their action. Effectual action involves transforming extant means into new possibilities, including new problems of interest. Transformation processes are actor-centric, as who comes on board determines goals, not vice versa. The transformation is appeared as a search activity, aiming at solving pressing problems rather than developing long-run strategies.
- Docility: conflict and difference among stakeholders is avoided through stakeholder docility, and goals are residual of the process. Simon et al. defined docility as *"the tendency to depend on suggestions, recommendation, persuasion and information obtained through social channels, as a major basic of choice"* [9]. The decisions made by startups, for instance, can be done by in cooperating other's ideas and not necessary by going through conflict resolution.
- Leveraging contingency: avoiding uncertainty by short run feedbacks, but also encouraging surprise. For startups, even *'bad'* surprises can be leveraged to provide

new means and new opportunities. Actions emphasize commitment and contingency, not choice and determinacy.

- Technology of foolishness: insulation from learning sought through allowing exprcrimental actions with regard to affordable lost. The technology of foolishness allows startups to relax the primacy of functional rationality, to temporarily suspend intentionality, and promote the openness to new actions, objectives and understandings.

3   Research Approach

We conducted this study by using a multiple-case study design with software startup as a unit of analysis [10]. Contacts for startups were searched via four channels, (1) startups within professional networks of papers' authors, (2) startups in the same town with the authors, (3) startups listed in the Startup Norway website and (4) the Crunchbase database. Twenty startups were eventually selected for investigation. The startup cases represent different startup phases, from prototyping to commercialization and scaling. Application domains range from marketplace, education, ecommerce, transportation, and Internet-of-Thing. Regards to software development approaches, startups with five or more people mostly adopt Agile and iterative software development. The sample is dominated by Norwegian software startups, with small teams and bootstrap financing models. We do not consider other types of startups, for example, internal cooperate startups, venture capital invested startups, and USA-based startups.

The major data collection instrument is semi-structured interviews. The interviews were focused on exploring startup's decision making and their behaviors related to their business and product development. The interview guideline is published online[1]. We used a thematic analysis to analyze the data, a common technique for identifying, analyzing, and reporting conceptual themes found from qualitative data [17]. To support the data analysis, we used a tool namely NVivo 11[2], to code, and to categorize such codes in higher order levels, representing different technical challenges when going from ideas to commercialized product. Several theoretical frameworks were considered, such as Cynefin model [11], boundary spanning object theory [12] and BTEF [4]. With the focus on exploring the decision making process behind startup's behaviors, we attempted to apply the four principles of BTEF to explain for how do startups face with such technical challenges.

---

[1] www.goo.gl/r9okCu.

[2] www.qsrinternational.com/product.

Table 1. Explanation for startup's technical challenges

Challenges	Description	Interpretation via BTEF
Vague prototype planning	Prototypes were created in an adhoc manner, mostly throw-away, lack of upfront design for learning, sometimes little lesson learnt, lack of early-stage product roadmap	Startups emphasizing short-run reaction rather than anticipation of long-run uncertain events focusing on the search for a suboptimal set of features or functionalities [4]
Feature creeps	Startups implement requirements from many customers with different needs, divergent product roadmap. *"We are adding features all the time. This is not a product that will ever stop evolving. ... We are talking about this being the core of the company's competence"*	Startups tend to perform different experiments with technology, i.e. features, user experience etc. Many startup features are a good representation of technology of foolishness
Paradox of demonstration	Early demonstration needs to be impressive to attract funding. However there is often a limited budget for developing a minimum viable product	Startups operate based on mean-driven transformation [4]. Demonstrated prototypes were limited by the current human and financial resources
Evolving throw-away prototypes	Many throw-away prototypes accidentally become evolutionary ones. Technical debt caused by the lack of proper refactoring threatens the quality of product in later phases of software startups	Startups leverage contingencies [4]. Tolerating surprises during a series of prototypes might lead to utilize the business-fit prototype for long-term development
Sharing visions between Business and Technology	Communication of business or technical details can be difficult between entrepreneurs and developers. *"it always takes a long discussion to explain her [the CEO] about the importance of having flexible product design..."*	Conflicts do not necessarily happen in a startup context, as startup team members are both persuadable and persuasive to different degrees about different matters [4]
Lack of sufficient and relevant user involvement	Balancing learning fast and learning the right things is a challenging task. Startups might have problems with finding feedbacks from relevant users. *"Most of them don't understand the idea ... It probably came ten years before the app developers can recognize its benefit ..."*	Challenges of early user involvement can be tracked to two problems, (1) to find appropriate early innovators and (2) whether there actually is a market for the product

4   How Are Theories of Entrepreneurial Behaviors Applicable to Explain for Startup Product Development Process?

Six identified themes were directly related to startup's decision making. We found that BTEF can be useful to explain for such themes, as shown in Table 1. The challenge name and description were given along with the theoretical explanation in the table.

5   Discussions

The technical challenges were interpreted in a context of a prototype-centric development paradigm [13–15]. Literature reveals that startups adopt rapid releases to build a prototype in an evolutionary fashion and quickly learn from the users' feedback to address the uncertainty of the market. The rapid development approaches were found to improve the effectiveness of the requirement elicitation of any software development [15]. However, in many cases software startups do not throw away quick-and-dirty prototypes and evolve them (or part of them) into the final products.

By using an effectuation theory [4], we can explain different technical challenges that startups face with during their journeys from idea to commercialization. Technical challenges related to prototyping and product development are linked with startup's current capacity, experimental nature of technology development, risk tolerance and favor of short-run feedbacks. Driven by the existing means and resource, startups search for local optimal solutions, emphasize on short-run feedback rather than long-run strategies. This results in technical challenges, such as vague prototype planning, and paradox of demonstration. All in all, the theory suggests the observed product development approaches do not likely support the entrepreneurial processes or vice versa. Alternatively, the effectual decision making might need a better software development paradigm that can fit to the uncertain and dynamic situations of startups.

6   Conclusions

This paper portrayed six technical challenges in early phases of software startups. Entrepreneurs make decisions to search for local optimal solutions, emphasize on short-run feedback rather than long-run strategies, which might require a more proactive, flexible and agile approach than the state-of-practice software startup product development. Our contributions are two folds. Firstly, we illustrate for the application of firm's behavior theory in the relation to technical decisions, which are essential for achieving core values of software-based startups. Secondly, this is among the first attempt to bring a theoretical framework from entrepreneurship literature in Software Engineering. This is encouraging due to the current limited theoretical contribution to software startups research [13, 14].

There are several possibilities for future work on software startups. Our next step is to extend the map of startups challenge to include non-technical challenges that we identify from the cases, such as lock-in to external resources, changing team composition and market uncertainty. Furthermore, we found that entrepreneurial theories are helpful in understanding and explaining the context of technical challenges and decision-making. Future work would investigate more on how other theories can be adopted in software startup research.

References

1. Nguyen-Duc, A., Seppänen, P., Abrahamsson, P.: Hunter-gatherer cycle: a conceptual model of the evolution of startup innovation and engineering. In: 1st Workshop on Open Innovation on Software Engineering, ICSSP (2015)
2. Ucbasaran, D., Westhead, P., Wright, M.: The focus of entrepreneurial research: contextual and process issues. Entrepreneurship Theory Pract. **25**(4), 57–80 (2001)
3. Cyert, R.M., March, J.G.: A Behavioral Theory of the Firm. Prentice-Hall, Englewood Cliffs (1963)
4. Dew, N., Read, S., Sarasvathy, S.D., Wiltbank, R.: Outlines of a behavioral theory of the entrepreneurial firm. J. Econ. Behav. Organ. **66**, 37–59 (2008)
5. Ries, E.: The Lean Startup: How Today's Entrepreneurs Use Continuous Innovation to Create Radically Successful Businesses, p. 103. Crown Publishing, USA (2013)
6. Maurya, A.: Running Lean: Iterate from Plan a to a Plan That Works. O'Reilly, Sebastopol (2012)
7. Blank, S.: Why the lean start-up changes everything. Harvard Bus. Rev. **91**(5), 63–72 (2013)
8. Sarasvathy, S.D.: Causation and effectuation: toward a theoretical shift from economic inevitability o entrepreneurial contingency. Acad. Manage. Rev. **26**(2), 243–263 (2001)
9. Simon, H.A.: Strategy and organizational evolution. Strateg. Manage. J. **14**, 131–142 (1993)
10. Yin, R.K.: Case Study Research: Design and Methods. Applied Social Research Methods, 5th edn. SAGE Publications, Inc., Thousand Oaks (2014)
11. Snowden, D.J., Boone, M.E.: A leader's framework for decision making. Harvard Bus. Rev. **85**, 69–76 (2007)
12. Tushman, M.L., Scanlan, T.J.: Boundary spanning individuals: their role in information transfer and their antecedents. Acad. Manag. J. **24**(2), 289–305 (1981)
13. Fagerholm, F., Guinea, A.S., Mäenpää, H., Münch, J.: Building blocks for continuous experimentation. In: 1st International Workshop on Rapid Continuous Software Engineering (RCoSE 2014), Hyderabad, India (2014)
14. Giardino, C., Paternoster, N., Unterkalmsteiner, M., Gorschek, T., Abrahamsson, P.: Software development in startup companies: the greenfield startup model. IEEE Trans. Softw. Eng. **42**(6), 585–604 (2016)
15. Teixeira, L., Saavedra, V., Ferreira, C., Simões, J., Sousa Santos, B.: Requirements engineering using mockups and prototyping tools: developing a healthcare web-application. In: Yamamoto, S. (ed.) HCI 2014. LNCS, vol. 8521, pp. 652–663. Springer, Cham (2014). doi:10.1007/978-3-319-07731-4_64

Should We Be Thanking Microsoft, Apple and Google for Their Contributions to Open Source Software?
The Case of Multinational Platform Leaders

Dominique Doorhof, Elizabeth A. Schermerhorn$^{(\boxtimes)}$, Slinger Jansen,
and Sjaak Brinkkemper

Utrecht University, Princetonplein 5, 3584 CC Utrecht, Netherlands
{d.j.doorhof,e.a.schermerhorn,slinger.jansen,s.brinkkemper}@uu.nl

Abstract. Software producing organizations are contributing increasingly to open source software, by making their software open source or contributing to existing projects. Platform leaders contribute to open source software in different manners, but for whose interests are these companies contributing to open source software? Are contributions made by software developers as part of a software vendor or do these software producing organizations want to do what is right without benefits? So how do platform leaders contribute to open source software? By analyzing the data from GitHub repositories, the contributions to open source software by three platform leaders is researched in two dimensions, how are the developers connected and to which projects do these developers contribute. By analyzing their connectedness and analyzing the developed projects, the conclusion is drawn that contributions are made for the strategic advantage of the software producing organizations. The majority of the contributions made to open source software is to their own projects and by developers who contribute to these projects full-time.

1 Introduction

There are ever more open source projects created, maintained and used by software developers as well as by software producing organizations (SPOs) [1–3]. Different reasons for SPOs to contribute to open source software (OSS) are to learn about best practices, to motivate software developers and as business model [4]. Thanks to these motivators, commercial vendors are participating increasingly in OSS and seeing more potential in investing in certain projects or launching their own open source projects [5,6]. Since OSS is becoming increasingly interesting to SPOs, this research focuses on how three SPOs contribute to open source software on GitHub. The focus lies on Apple, Microsoft and Google since each organization has a large software ecosystem [7], with similar products and competing for the largest market share. There is little research on the contributions to OSS by SPOs such as which projects do they contribute to? Why do

A. Ojala et al. (Eds.): ICSOB 2017, LNBIP 304, pp. 205–210, 2017.
https://doi.org/10.1007/978-3-319-69191-6_16

they contribute to these OSS projects and how do SPOs handle the development
of OSS projects? Since multiple motivators for contributing to OSS have been
researched previously, this research focuses on the main motivators for platform
leaders with a large software ecosystem. With this research initial steps are made
at understanding the involvement of platform leaders in OSS and their contributions. This research presents a better understanding on how contributions are
made to OSS and how this reflects to the different motivators.

2   Research Method

To answer the research question data from GitHub is acquired through the
GHTorrent mirror[1] and processing is done with Python.

Table 1. Characteristics of the company policies on OSS and how this is handled.

Aspect of policy	Company	Description
How to contribute	Microsoft	There are defined guidelines and best practices on how to contribute to OSS
	Apple	There are guidelines on how to contribute
	Google	Google feels you need to be able to contribute everything in your own way
Types of contributions	Microsoft	There are seven types of contritbutions identified such as bug reports, feature requests, and bug fixes
	Apple	Bugs can be reported and almost all Apple product can be further developed
	Google	Anything can be contributed to Google projects
Licencing agreement	Microsoft	Before you can be a developer of OSS a licencing agreement needs to be signed so that Microsoft and others can use your code.
	Apple	There is an agreement which needs to be signed between developers and Apple
	Google	There is an agreement which needs to be signed between developers and Apple
Developers	Microsoft	You can apply to Microsoft to become a full-time, paid developer
	Apple	Developers need to pay a fee of 99 dollars per year to develop OSS and remain in the program
	Google	N/A

---

[1] http://ghtorrent.org/.

With the help of NetworkX an initial network is created, where the developers are connected to the projects they are a member of or have committed to. This way the nodes of the network are both the users and the projects. To create a network where the developers that worked on the same projects are connected, this network is transformed to a bipartite graph. These graphs are visualized with the help of PyGraphviz, which offers more styling features in comparison to NetworkX. The latter is used to calculate the network characteristics.

3   Company Policies, Developer Networks and Contributions

To understand their attitude towards OSS the policies of Microsoft, Google and Apple are evaluated. These policies describe how to contribute to OSS, what types of contributions can be done, what the licensing agreement is between the company and the developers and who can participate as a developer. An overview of the policies is presented in Table 1.

The collected data from GitHub is analyzed in different ways. Figure 1 shows the resulting network analysis of contributions to OSS by Microsoft, Google and Apple. In Fig. 2 the Venn diagrams show the projects represented in the developer networks of Fig. 1. All the collected commits over the past five years are analyzed and shown in Fig. 3. Table 2 shows the network characteristics of the developed graphs that are shown in Fig. 1.

Table 2. Developer network characteristics

Characteristics	Total based on number of project members	Total based on number of commits
Unique developers	3.615	6.060
Unique projects	15.533	69.890
Unique links	26.505	77.444
Total links	242.778	119.361
Developers without links	2.059	2.760
Developers that contributed to one project	1.096	356

4   Discussion

From the developer networks shown in Fig. 1 a couple of observations are made. First of all, there is barely any overlap between the contributions by the three SPOs. This is supported by the Venn diagrams in Fig. 2. Second, Google and Microsoft developers contribute more to opens source software on GitHub than

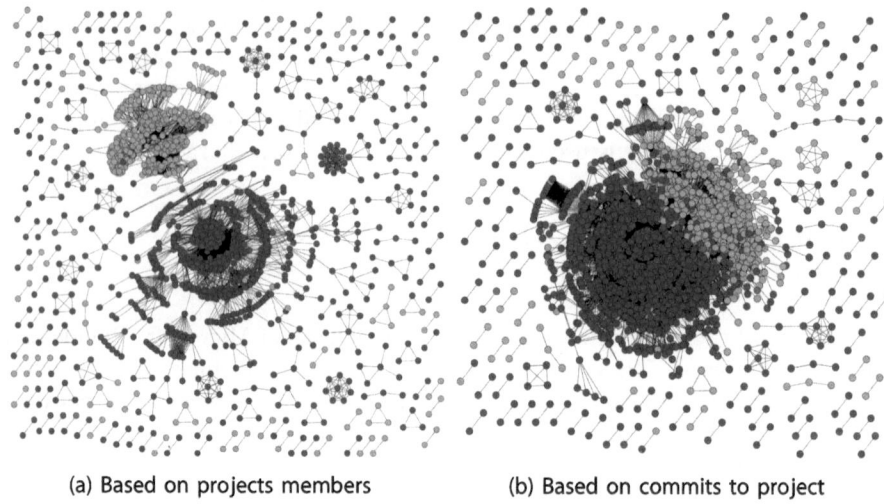

(a) Based on projects members   (b) Based on commits to project

Fig. 1. Networks of overlap in projects. In both networks the nodes represent the developers and the colors represent the different companies: blue for Microsoft, purple for Google and yellow for Apple. The links in the networks are defined differently: in (a) there is a link between two developers if they are member of the same project and in (b) developers are linked if they made a commits to the same project. All nodes with no connections have been omitted from the graphs. (Color figure online)

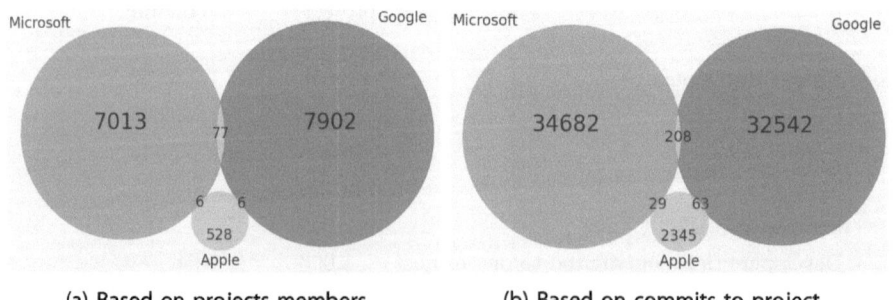

(a) Based on projects members   (b) Based on commits to project

Fig. 2. Venn diagrams of contributions by the three organizations. The size of the circles corresponds with the number of projects and the overlap represents the projects to which multiple organizations have contributed. There are no projects where all three SPOs overlap. Although the absolute number of developers has increased, the percentage of overlap is similar in both cases.

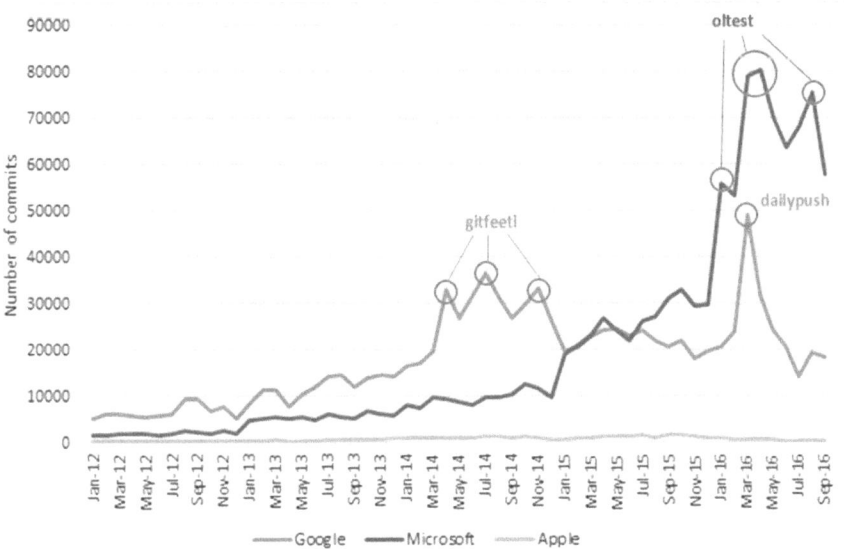

Fig. 3. Evolution of the number of commits per month over the past 5 years (January 2012 to September 2016) for all three organizations. The peak for Google and Microsoft are labeled in the chart. The sources for the peaks are in fact projects owned by the SPO and developed by the SPO.

developers employed by Apple. Google and Microsoft have a similar number of projects they contribute to.

Figure 3 shows that the number of commits by the three SPOs has increased over the last five years. This is in line with research which has already been conducted on the increased contribution to OSS. The following projects correspond to the peaks in the lines of Google and Microsoft:

- Google: Gitfeeti (No description provided)
- Google: Dailypush (Bot that simulates activity on GitHub)
- Microsoft: OpenLocalizationTestOrg (Part of the Azure platform)

These three published projects are all owned by an SPO and developed by the owning SPO. These projects are either private repositories on GitHub (which are only usable by paid accounts) used for backup or personal hidden projects, or in the case of *dailypush*, a bot that simulates activity on GitHub which makes it look like the account is active when in fact it is not. Both kinds of projects do not contribute to open source. This means that the increase in number of commits that is seen in Fig. 3 does not necessarily show the increased participation of the organizations to OSS. Future research could focus on the distribution of the commits made to the own projects of SPOs and to projects which are not owned by the SPOs. Although the research shows that Apple is not as involved in open source as Microsoft and Google, there are a few constraints to this conclusion.

Apple has its own repository for open source project, which was not considered in this research. IBM is not considered in this research since there is less overlap with Microsoft, Apple and Google regarding the software ecosystems.

5   Conclusion

Software producing organizations have increasingly contributed to open source software since 2005. By conducting a developer network analysis on GitHub repositories, the conclusion is drawn that there is minimal overlap between SPOs regarding the projects they contribute to. An analysis on the projects shows that the largest OSS projects contributed to are owned and developed by mainly one SPO. This illustrates that there are few projects on which SPOs collaborate, thus only collaborating on OSS for their own benefit. The contributions to OSS have increased over the past five years, to the extent that it was possible to identify different projects in the streams of commits. This shows that various projects of SPOs have been made open source on GitHub over the past years. So should we be thanking Microsoft, Apple and Google? The results show that SPOs present themselves as contributors to OSS, however when looking closely into their contributions, they contribute to their own projects, within their own teams and on projects which are hidden from the public. This supports the conclusion that SPOs present themselves as OSS collaborators but are in fact developing commercial software which is renamed as OSS.

References

1. Andersen-Gott, G., Ghinea, G., Bygstad, B.: Why do commercial companies contribute to open source software? Elsevier **32**(2), 106–117 (2012)
2. Kalliamvakou, E., Gousios, G., Blincoe, K., Singer, L., German, D., Damian, D.: The promises and perils of mining github. Mining Softw. Repositories Conf. **11**(5), 92–101 (2014)
3. Hecker, F.: Setting up shop: the business of open source softwar. IEEE **16**(1), 45–51 (1999)
4. Brown, A.W., Booch, G.: Reusing open-source software and practices: the impact of open-source on commercial vendors. In: Gacek, C. (ed.) ICSR 2002. LNCS, vol. 2319, pp. 123–136. Springer, Heidelberg (2002). doi:10.1007/3-540-46020-9_9
5. Lerner, J., Tirole, J.: The simple economics of open source. J. Ind. Econ. **50**(2), 197–234 (2002)
6. Lerner, J., Tirole, J.: The economics of technology sharing: open source and beyond. J. Econ. Perspect. **19**(2), 99–120 (2005)
7. Jansen, S., Finkelstein, A., Brinkkemper, S.: A sense of community: a research agenda for software ecosystems. Softw. Eng. **31** (2014)

Author Index